Master Classes with Menahem Pressler

WILLIAM BROWN

Master Classes with Menahem Pressler

INDIANA UNIVERSITY PRESS

This book is a publication of

Indiana University Press
Office of Scholarly Publishing
Herman B Wells Library 350
1320 East 10th Street
Bloomington, Indiana 47405 USA

iupress.indiana.edu

Manufactured in the United States of America

Library of Congress Cataloging-in-Publication Data

Names: Brown, William Paul, [date] author.
Title: Master classes with Menahem Pressler / William Brown.
Description: Bloomington : Indiana University Press, 2019. | Includes
    bibliographical references and index.
Identifiers: LCCN 2018049684 (print) | LCCN 2018051363 (ebook) | ISBN
    9780253042934 (e-book) | ISBN 9780253042927 (cl : alk. paper)
Subjects: LCSH: Piano music—Interpretation (Phrasing, dynamics, etc.) |
    Pressler, Menahem.
Classification: LCC MT235 (ebook) | LCC MT235 B77 2019 (print) | DDC
    786.2/193—dc23
LC record available at https://lccn.loc.gov/2018049684

1 2 3 4 5   24 23 22 21 20 19

To Menahem Pressler, cherished friend and esteemed mentor, whose artistry and humanity have touched countless lives and significantly enriched the international community.

Contents

A Few Words Before

A second book was not in my plans when *Menahem Pressler: Artistry in Piano Playing* was published in 2009. In preparing the manuscript for that book, I had collected materials from 160 former students who had studied with Mr. Pressler over a sixty-plus-year time span with the purpose of preserving his instructions, comments, fingerings, phrasings, and musical images and making them available to interested pianists and other musicians and music lovers. From all these notes, recordings, and musical scores, I had carefully chosen repertoire that illustrated the content of the opening chapters: "The Technical Approach," "Principles of Expressive Performance," and "Guides for Practicing." In these intervening years, I have been enormously gratified that the book has been appreciated by students and teachers throughout the country and around the world, and it was not until I began receiving comments such as "If only more repertoire was included!" that I began to feel a bit guilty that so many of these collected materials remained unpublished and inaccessible for use.

It was when Mr. Pressler asked, "Are there enough pieces for a second book?" and began inquiring, "How's the second book coming?" that I became serious about publishing a second volume. Much like the first book, this volume offers measure-by-measure lessons on thirty-six masterpieces of the piano repertoire. These lessons are composites of Pressler's markings made in students' musical scores as well as transcripts of lessons and master classes. Pressler's Musical Ancestry Chart, included as Appendix A, traces his teachers through many of the great pianists and musicians of history, including Franz Liszt, Frédéric Chopin, Ludwig van Beethoven, and even Johann Sebastian Bach. Appendix B is a collection of tributes from many of his students and fans. The chapter introductions are Mr. Pressler's words, and the interludes between the chapters are anecdotes and stories he has provided for this volume.

In Menahem Pressler's words, "Since the first book surprised me by becoming so well known and so much read, I can only hope that the second book will continue that. Because I have continued looking for whatever it is that makes for a richer life in music, I want that second book to be a partner for all the students who are reading it to find a way into that musical heaven that I'm still looking for and hoping to find."

To receive full benefit from the book, Mr. Pressler's comments should be read with the music score in hand. The measures of each composition are numbered starting with the first full measure of each movement. Where a question might arise about the numbers (e.g., second endings), I've included instructions at that point for clarity.

I would like to thank all those who have encouraged me in this endeavor. Special thanks go to Janice E. Frisch, music editor at Indiana University Press, and to Jane Behnken, the previous music editor, who have both been helpful and encouraging, and also to Edna Pressler, who has been so supportive during the entire process of preparing both books. But of course, all credit for the result is deserved by Menahem Pressler himself, who has done all the work through his exemplary teaching in private lessons and master classes worldwide over a period of more than sixty years.

Acknowledgments

I am grateful to many individuals including Menahem Pressler's students, colleagues, and friends for their help in completing both this text and my previous book, *Menahem Pressler: Artistry in Piano Teaching*. Without their tributes, anecdotes, and other remembrances, and especially their collected comments made by Mr. Pressler during lessons and master classes, these two projects would not exist. Others who have provided invaluable assistance are Tim McCarty, who recorded several of my interviews with Mr. Pressler; Melinda Baird, who made available numerous resources; Dina Kellams and the Indiana University Archives, who provided access to the newly acquired Menahem Pressler Archives; the late Sara Pressler, who shared a wealth of thoughtful insights; Edna Pressler, who has offered unwavering encouragement; and most of all, Menahem Pressler himself, who has willingly devoted the time, energy, and commitment needed to bring these two projects to completion.

The list of former Indiana University students who contributed transcripts and recordings of lessons and other helpful insights includes Jane Abbott-Kirk, John Adams, David Alpher, Fernando Araujo, Konstantine Athanasakos, Mi Jai Auh, Melinda Baird, Margaret Barela, Paul Barnes, Jonathan Bass, Alasdair Beatson, Gayle (Cameron) Blankenburg, Jimmy Brière, William Brown (author of this text), Madeline Bruser, John Burnett, Diana (Haddad) Cangemi, Mark Cappelli, Ted Carnes, Susan Chan, Angela Cheng, Mikyung (Carrie) Choi (Koh), Winston Choi, Alan Chow, Alvin Chow, Jeanne-Minette Cilliers, Lynda Cochrane, Jack Cohan, Jeffrey Cohen, Paula da Matta, Andrew DeGrado, Henry Doskey, Jerry Emmanuel, Paula Ennis, Zoe Erisman, George Fee, John Ferguson, Anne-France Fosseur, William Goldenberg, Frances Gray, Pamela Griffel-King, Charlene Harb, Christopher Harding, Robert Hatten, Valentina Wen-Ting Huang, Mia (Kim) Hynes, Sherri Jones, Manami (Naoe) Kawamura, Peter Kuijken, Julia Lam, Marilyn (White) Lowe, David Lyons, Gordon Macpherson, Steven Mann, Pauline Martin, Robert Mayerovitch, Roger McVey, Fred Moyer, Kevin Murphy, Megumi Nagai, Saori Ohno, Tongsook Han Park, Rebecca Penneys, Mary Rucker, Ann (Heiligman) Saslav, Scott Schillin, Jacqueline Schmitt, Joshua Seedman, Kevin Sharpe, Karen Shaw, George Shirley, Jill (Trudgeon) Sprenger, Mark Sullivan, Rámon Tamaran, William Tucker, Daria van den Bercken, Charles Webb, Sandra Webster, Mei-Huei Wei, and Mary Wong.

Students from Pressler's master classes and those who took private lessons (apart from Indiana University) who graciously shared their remembrances include Jan Deats, Patricia Drew, Elaine Felder, Kevin Fitz-Gerald, Mary Lou Francis, Lily Friedman, Celeste O'Brien Haugen, Janet Hickey, Daniel Paul

Horn, Roger Keyes, Barbara Kudirka, Yvonne Lang, Linda Lienhard, Dina Namer, Jeannete Nettleton, Elaine Newman, Janice Nimetz, Del Parkinson, Edna Pressler, Dmitry Rachmanov, Lynn Raley, Mark Reiss, Tiffany Seybert, Richard Sogg, Joyce Ucci, Ludolph van der Hoeven, and Victoria von Arx.

Research for the book required interviewing many people, including Melinda Baird, Margaret Barela, Jonathan Bass, Angela Cheng, Alan Chow, Alvin Chow, Jeffrey Cohen, Paula Ennis, Robert Hatten, Mia (Kim) Hynes, Steven Mann, Pauline Martin, Robert Mayerovitch, Edna Pressler, Sara Pressler, Ann (Heiligman) Saslav, Joshua Seedman, Karen Shaw, Jill (Trudgeon) Sprenger, and Lady Annabelle Weidenfeld. Those who contributed musical scores with Mr. Pressler's markings were John Adams, Melinda Baird, Jonathan Bass, William Brown, Diana (Haddad) Cangemi, Mark Cappelli, Angela Cheng, Alvin Chow, Jeffrey Cohen, Paula Ennis, Anne-Francis Fosseur, Robert Hatten, Valentina Wen-Ting Huang, Mia (Kim) Hynes, Minami (Naoe) Kawamura, Piet Kuijken, Steven Mann, Megumi Nagai, Tongsook Han Park, Mary Rucker, Joshua Seedman, Kevin Sharpe, Jill (Trudgeon) Sprenger, Mark Sullivan, Joyce Ucci, Daria van der Berchen, and Ludolph van der Hoeven.

Recordings and transcripts of lessons with Pressler were provided by Melinda Baird, William Brown, Andrew DeGrado, Anne-Francis Fosseur, Frances Gray, Valentina Wen-Ting Huang, Mia (Kim) Hynes, Linda Lienhard, Steven Mann, and Joshua Seedman.

Recordings and transcripts of master classes with Pressler were also provided by Adamant Music School (Vermont), Harvard University, Indiana University, Music Teachers National Association, Northwestern University, Shelburne Farms (Vermont), Steinway Hall (New York City), Mark Sullivan Studio Classes (Long Beach, California), University of Missouri (Columbia, Missouri), Vanderbilt University, and Wayne State University.

A Brief Biography

Menahem Pressler, born December 16, 1923, fled to Palestine with his family during the Nazi takeover of Germany. He continued his dedication to piano during these years of turmoil, and while still a student building his repertoire, in 1946 he flew to San Francisco where he won the First Prize at the San Francisco International Debussy Piano Competition and began his solo career, which included an unprecedented four-year contract as soloist with the Philadelphia Orchestra under the direction of Maestro Eugene Ormandy. Since then, his extensive tours of North America and Europe have included performances with the orchestras of New York, Chicago, Cleveland, Pittsburgh, Indianapolis, Mobile, Dallas, San Francisco, Boston, London, Brussels, Dresden, Amsterdam, Oslo, Paris, Helsinki, Berlin, and many more.

While pursuing a highly acclaimed solo career of recitals and performances with orchestra, Pressler joined the faculty of the Indiana University School of Music in 1955, the same year he cofounded the celebrated Beaux Arts Trio, whose long career established it as the world's foremost piano trio, regularly appearing in major international music centers and festivals. The Trio played throughout North America, Europe, Japan, South America, and the Middle East; performed at the Olympics in Korea and Australia; and presented annual concert series at the Metropolitan Museum of Art, the Celebrity Series of Boston, and the Library of Congress. Awards for the Trio include six Grammy nominations, England's Record of the Year Award, Chamber Music America's Distinguished Service Award (1994), the German Critics' "Ehrenurkunde" award in recognition of forty years of being the standard by which chamber music is measured (1995), *Musical America*'s Ensemble of the Year (1997), the Toscanini Award, the German Recording Award, Prix Mondial du Disque, three Grand Prix du Disques, the Union de la Presse Musicale Belge Award, and "Record of the Year" awards from both *Gramophone* and *Stereo Review*. A fiftieth-year anniversary concert was celebrated at the Tanglewood Festival on July 14, 2005, fifty years and one day after the debut concert. The Trio's final concert was on August 23, 2009, in Leipzig, Germany. With the Beaux Arts Trio, Pressler has recorded fifty albums (almost the entire chamber literature with piano), and as a soloist, he has recorded more than thirty albums. In 2015, Decca released a sixty-CD set of the complete Beaux Arts Trio Philips Recordings comprising some 122 works. In addition to performing thousands of concerts with the Beaux Arts Trio, he has collaborated with the Juilliard, Emerson, Guarneri, American, Pacifica, Èbène, Cleveland, and Israel Quartets and the Pasquier String Trio.

Awards for Pressler's phenomenal performing and teaching career are numerous. In 1998, Indiana University named Pressler to the Dean Charles H. Webb Chair of Music, and in the same year, he received one of only five Lifetime Achievement Awards granted in the last fifty years by *Gramophone* magazine, placing him in the distinguished company of Joan Sutherland, Sir Georg Solti, Dietrich Fischer-Dieskau, and Yehudi Menuhin. He has received a Lifetime Achievement Award from the International Chamber Music Association as well as Chamber Music America's Distinguished Service Award. He has been elected to the American Academy of Arts and Sciences, was invited to dinner at the Reagan White House in 1986, and has received honorary doctorates from the University of Nebraska-Lincoln, North Carolina School of the Arts, San Francisco Conservatory of Music, Manhattan School of Music, and Ben-Gurion University of the Negev and an honorary professorship from China's Beijing Central Conservatory of Music. In 2002, he was awarded the Gold Medal of Merit from the National Society of Arts and Letters, which recognized him for "a long and distinguished career not only as an internationally recognized concert artist but also a teacher and mentor of young artists." In 2005, he was named a commander in France's Order of Arts and Letters, France's highest cultural honor, followed soon thereafter by being named the recipient of the German President's *Deutsche Bundesverdienstkreuz* (Cross of Merit), Germany's highest cultural honor. In 2006, he was awarded the Concertgebouw Prize, and in 2007, he was named an Honorary Fellow of the Jerusalem Academy of Music and Dance as well as receiving the Indiana Governor's Arts Award. In 2009, he received a Lifetime Achievement Award from the Edison Foundation and was also awarded Honorary Citizenship in his hometown of Magdeburg, Germany.

His more recent honors and awards include the prestigious Wigmore Medal (2011), the International Classical Music Awards Lifetime Achievement Award (2011), the Menuhin Prize given by the Queen of Spain (2012), inductions into the American Classical Music and *Gramophone* Halls of Fame (2012), the Music Teachers National Association Achievement Award (2012), the Indiana University Medal (2013), the ECHO Klassik 2015 Lifetime Achievement Award in Germany, and the Victoire d'honneur 2016 Lifetime Achievement Award from the French Victoires de la Musique Classique. The documentary *The Life I Love: The Pianist Menahem Pressler* won the Grand Prize at the Golden Prague International Television festival in 2015 and was shown over public television worldwide. He has been the subject of books written to honor his life and legacy, including *Menahem Pressler: Artistry in Piano Teaching* and *Always Something New to Discover: Menahem Pressler and the Beaux Arts Trio*. In 2016, a book of conversations with Holger Nolze, *Dieses Verlangen Nach Schönheit*, was published in Germany by Koerber Stifftung.

Pressler continues to be highly active as soloist and chamber musician and presenter of master classes worldwide. Immediately following Pressler's performance with the Berlin Philharmonic Orchestra and Sir Simon Rattle for their New Year concert in 2015, he underwent life-saving surgery for aortic aneurysm repair, and since then he has resumed his teaching and performance schedule.

In 2018, he celebrated his sixty-third anniversary as a faculty member at the Indiana University Jacobs School of Music, where he holds the rank of Distinguished Professor. He is also in demand as a juror for competitions including the Van Cliburn, Queen Elisabeth of Belgium, Arthur Rubinstein, Paloma O'Shea, and International Piano-e-Competition. His DVDs include a live recital, concertos with Paavo Järvi and the Orchestre de Paris, Sir Simon Rattle and the Berlin Philharmonic's New Year Concert, and his own ninetieth Birthday Concert Live from the Salle Pleyel in Paris. His most recent CD is *Menahem Pressler: Clair de lune* (Debussy, Fauré, Ravel), released in March 2018 by Deutsche Grammophone.

Equally as illustrious as his performing career, Professor Pressler has been hailed as a "Master Pedagogue" and has had prizewinning students in all the major international piano competitions, including the Queen Elisabeth of Belgium, Busoni, Rubinstein, Naumburg, Leeds, and Van Cliburn competitions among many others. His former students grace the faculties of prestigious schools of music across the world and have become some of the most prominent and influential artist-teachers today.

Pressler's cherished wife Sara passed away in Bloomington in December of 2014. His and Sara's children are son Ami, an x-ray technician in Bloomington, and daughter Edna, a clinical psychologist and instructional designer in Boston. In recent years Pressler has resided in Bloomington and in London with his beloved companion, Lady Annabelle Weidenfeld.

The *New York Times* has called Pressler "a prodigious talent" with "exceptional gifts." The *Washington Evening Star* termed him "a poet of the piano," and *La Figaro* in Paris hailed him as "one of the greatest living pianists." The *Los Angeles Times* asserts, "Pressler's contributions . . . cannot be overstated. His joyous pianism, technically faultless, stylistically impeccable, emotionally irrepressible, are from another age and are a virtually forgotten sensibility. . . . [He] is a national treasure."

Master Classes with Menahem Pressler

Master Classes and Lessons

Interlude I
Master Classes

I used to go to master classes and think, "This really doesn't make much difference. You hear the piece one time and you don't feel that it makes a difference." Then I went to a master class by a teacher from Juilliard whose specialty was French music, and he in this master class was teaching the Thirteenth Nocturne of Fauré. He saw what I saw—that no matter what he said to that student, it made no impact whatsoever. So he sat down, and he played that Thirteenth Nocturne and spoke about that beauty, and it made an immense impact on me. I felt, my God, how much this man enriches my life through his insights! It meant that much to me, and from that day on, I took the master classes very seriously. And in the master class, I try to bring the students to the point where the meaning that I got out of playing, they will get out of me. Now that I have difficulty with walking, I don't play in the classes that much, so I have to do it verbally, and that's difficult; but I am willing, and I am happy to. I have seen that I have really a way of getting into the psyche, the soul, the hands of the student in the master class. So a master class has become very, very important and meaningful to me personally, and to my life in general, transmitting that which gives my life a reason to be in music: love.

At the university, I used to be present in the weekly class, and I would ask the students to critique each other, and they were sometimes scared to say anything because I was there. So I began having my assistant supervise the class, and now they speak their minds to each other, and there is no holding back, because they don't have to impress anyone. They learn to look for what they can find in the music, and that is one of the important aspects for having master classes—helping my students on the road to discovery, to discover what this particular piece of music means to them, and the explanation that they find through a master class situation is meaningful because the road to discovery starts inside you. It does not start outside; it starts inside of you. You must want to find it, no matter which composer you play. You must look to find, yes?

1   Johann Sebastian Bach

To play Bach well is to interpret it well—to hear where each voice is going and how it interacts with all the other. He was a great master of all the instrumental forms of his time, and in his *Partitas* we get to appreciate his love for the dance. Certainly, there are stylistic standards to follow, but within these guidelines, you must make the music be very personal. It must sing, it must dance, and it must show us the beauty of the conversation happening between the lines.

Partita No. 6 in E Minor, BWV 830

Toccata

M. 1. The time signature is two, yes? So it should not feel like it's in four. It can start slower but get to a feeling of two. And what does *toccata* mean? It means "play."

Example 1.1. *Partita* No. 6 in E Minor, *Toccata*, mm. 1–2.

Mm. 3–4. Play each of these as if you're improvising.

Example 1.2. *Partita* No. 6 in E Minor, *Toccata*, mm. 3–4.

Mm. 5–6. Do you hear the difference between these? And it's different from the opening, yes?

Mm. 9–10. The left hand goes down from E to B and also from G to D. Your left-hand articulation is good [slurring the first three eighths], but always separate the pickup note [E, D, A#]; that note always leads you to the next note—not so short that it sounds funny!

Example 1.3. *Partita* No. 6 in E Minor, *Toccata*, mm. 9–10.

Mm. 11–12. Hear the left hand ascending. Have a slight *crescendo*. Then it comes down.

M. 15. Improvise from nothing [start less].

M. 16. Resolve that last D# to the E of measure 17.

Mm. 17–18. Play measures 1 and 2 again. Now how is this different?

M. 20. No. Go to the D# [the third quarter note] and then resolve.

M. 25. Why does he ask for an ornament here? Make it beautiful.

Mm. 27–29. This entrance must have a certain presence about it.

Example 1.4. *Partita* No. 6 in E Minor, *Toccata*, mm. 27–29.

Mm. 37–40. Follow all these sequences.

Mm. 40–41. Play the left hand deep into the keys.

M. 46. That sixteenth [alto E] doesn't stand alone; it leads to the second E.

M. 51. Go to the dissonance [third quarter].

M. 60. Separate these eighths [right hand] to lead to the cadence [third quarter note]. But the left hand surprises us and has an F#.

M. 67. Bring out the alto entrance [the F#].

M. 71. Close the phrase [to the third quarter]—a little more on the F# [the fourth eighth].

M. 74. If you pronounce the right hand so clearly [with *staccato*], then the left
   hand must do the same.

Mm. 75–77. I would lift each one [*staccato* each pick-up note, E, D, C, G♯, A].

M. 77. They've all come down but now rise up [last two quarters], so the theme
   can come out.

M. 79. Finish [on the third quarter].

Mm. 85–86. Always separate the top line's sixteenth notes [G, F♯, E]. Not mushy.
   Clarity in the right-hand parts.

Mm. 87–88. Now separate the alto sixteenth notes in the same way [G, F♯, E].

Example 1.5. *Partita* No. 6 in E Minor, *Toccata*, mm. 85–88.

M. 88. A little *ritard* to close the phrase.

M. 91. Start again from nowhere.

M. 94. This one is different.

Example 1.6. *Partita* No. 6 in E Minor, *Toccata*, mm. 93–94.

M. 101. Put an ornament on the F♮.

Mm. 105–107. Use the *chromaticism* to *crescendo* the line so you reach a *forte*.

M. 108. Lean into the last D♯. It's not an accent, and you can have a little *ritard*.

Allemande

M. 1. Remember that this is a dance. When you have a line [he sings the first measure], you have to play it so that we see the outline. In the left hand you have an F♯ resolving to a G, and a G♯ to an A, and a B to a C. You can slur each of these two-note groups. Although these notes could have been chords, he gives us all the functions of a chord.

M. 2. Yes. Add the grace note E to the D♯.

Example 1.7. *Partita* No. 6 in E Minor, *Allemande*, mm. 1–2.

M. 3. When he has the melody in the left hand, there must be a kind of energy to it.

M. 4. That's the maximum [beat 1]. I would place the ornament on the first E [fourth quarter], not on the sixteenth.

Mm. 5–6. You know this is a dance, so you have the dance step in the right hand [thirty-second-note pickups]. Let these short notes dance—not lazy.

Mm. 6–7. In the left hand, be careful that you go to the E, to the G, and to the A♯ leading to the climax.

M. 8. The *arpeggio* is a flourish.

Example 1.8. *Partita* No. 6 in E Minor, *Allemande*, m. 8.

M. 9. The right hand goes down [to beat 3] and now it goes up [beat 4]. Give plenty of A-F♯ [the last eighth].

M. 10. The thirty-seconds are the secondary line. Feel the movement of the G as it continues to beat 2. And have a longer trill on the G♯ [beat 4].

M. 11. The line finishes on the A [beat 1].

M. 14. Not lazy in the left hand [two thirty-seconds leading to the sixteenths]. Keep dancing. Yours gets too weighted down [beats 3 and 4].

Mm. 15–16. Hear the soprano's G [beat 3], then the F♯ [beat 1], then the E [beat 3].

Mm. 17–18. Now the line leads up from F♯ to B. That high B [beat 4] is the climax.

M. 19. A long trill on the left-hand D♯.

M. 20. Yes. It's a flourish—but not faster.

Courante

When you practice something like this, it must take on a quality. We practice not just to learn the notes but so that it makes sense—first to us, and then to the audience. This is a dance, so it must have phrasing, and you must understand what he is doing with the harmony. It would be beneficial to play the left hand alone, just the single notes, until they make some sense to you, until it's like a picture for you. It must be clear; it must say something.

M. 1. It's too fast, and it's ungracious to play "da-DAH da." Of course, there are stresses but not accents. Dance! Your left hand has no reason to be alive there. It's just noise levels, but they represent chords.

M. 2. Don't accent the A. It's coming down; follow the line. And don't play the right hand *staccato*. Only the left hand.

M. 4. Finish [on the D♯].

Example 1.9. *Partita* No. 6 in E Minor, *Courante*, mm. 1–4.

M. 9. No. It goes down. The left-hand D♯ is less than the E [of m. 8].

M. 11. The G is more than the F♮ [m. 10].

M. 12. The C♮ is more than the G [m. 11].

M. 15. But the F♯ is not part of that key, so when you hear this, give meaning to it. Now you hear it, but you're not doing anything. It's a surprise.

M. 18. Finish [the E]. That second E is new; begin it *piano*. You have to have contrast in your life!

Example 1.10. *Partita* No. 6 in E Minor, *Courante*, mm. 17–19.

M. 20. Finish [on E-F#].
M. 21. Go up [to the A]; then go down.
M. 22. Finish [on A-B].
M. 24 The E is less than the F# [of m. 23].
M. 25. Now less again on the D.
M. 26. And less to the C.
M. 28. That's an ending.
M. 30. Come down.
Mm. 31–32. This can be an echo.
M. 38. Finish. Then *piano*.
M. 42. Finish.
Mm. 49–50. The right hand hangs in the air waiting for the left hand.
Mm. 52–54. Go all the way over the top and do a bow [the cadence]. It's a dance, yes? And out. Not accented on the final chord.

Example 1.11. *Partita* No. 6 in E Minor, *Courante*, mm. 52–54.

Mm. 55–57. The left hand has a chord all the way up, and the line finishes on the E [of m. 58].
M. 59. Go up again.
M. 66. That's the climax [beat 1]. Then less, starting with the B♭.
M. 74. That's a finish [beat 1].
Mm. 113–115. No stopping—all the way to the top.
Mm. 115–116. Yes, a bow again—but with finality.

Air

M. 1. It's a dance. But also think *aria*. It must always sing.

Mm. 1–2. Hear how the left-hand chords relate. They all have the same length.

M. 4. Use the ornament to end the phrase with charm.

Example 1.12. *Partita* No. 6 in E Minor, *Air*, mm. 1–4.

M. 6. There's a beautiful duet between the hands.

Mm. 11–12. Feel the cadence settle.

M. 17. It goes over the top with joy.

Mm. 21–22. Climb.

Mm. 24–27. Don't stab these high notes; there's a charm about it.

Example 1.13. *Partita* No. 6 in E Minor, *Air*, mm. 24–28.

M. 29b. [The second ending.] What a surprise that second ending is! Start the left-hand sixteenths a little less to blend with the right hand.

Sarabande

M. 1. Enter a new world here. It's still E minor, but it feels darker, more mysterious. The sense of the meter should always be there. I should always be able to count it out, but with great freedom. Do you think anyone should really be dancing to this movement? It's practically a textbook of improvisation and ornamentation. This is Bach showing us what he expects from a *Sarabande*.

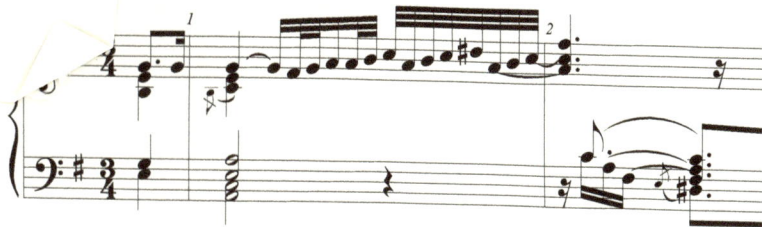

Example 1.14. *Partita* No. 6 in E Minor, *Sarabande*, mm. 1–2.

M. 4. Your rolled chords are too predictable. They shouldn't all be the same. Everything should be like an improvised dance. It should be very personal.

There has to be a reason to repeat. You have much more freedom to change things when you go back—different ornaments, different timings, different inflections.

Tempo di Gavotta

M. 1. Not heavy. Let it dance! It's very much in a two, not a four. The tune is angular, but let it be subtle. It's like a two-part invention with both hands equal. The tune switches back and forth.

Example 1.15. *Partita* No. 6 in E Minor, *Tempo di Gavotta*, mm. 1–2.

M. 3. Start less here. Begin a longer phrase all the way to measure 6.
M. 6. These sixteenths should "rip." Very close fingers. Drill these notes for clarity. Now the theme is in the left hand beginning on the G.

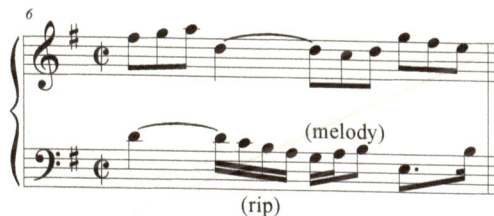

Example 1.16. *Partita* No. 6 in E Minor, *Tempo di Gavotta*, m. 6.

Mm. 8–10. You've brought the line all the way down to the G, so stay quiet and build slowly toward the cadence.

Mm. 11–12. Plan how you want your cadence to sound. You have the D in each hand leading to the Gs. [The second ending is measure 12b.]

M. 13. The high A is a surprise. Let us hear the difference.

M. 14. The left-hand sixteenths should rip again.

Mm. 15–16. Build the line so that it goes over the top to the B.

M. 18. Start the long phrase from here.

M. 26. Cadence on the Bs [beat 2]. The left-hand sixteenths signal the new entrance.

Mm. 29–30. Follow the line up from F♯ to B.

M. 31. Have a hairpin swell toward this B [beat 2].

Gigue

M. 1. This entrance must set the character for the entire movement. There has to be a strength there—not just loudness.

Example 1.17. *Partita* No. 6 in E Minor, *Gigue*, mm. 1–4.

Mm. 5–6. There's no theme again till measure 7. Let it unwind and settle.

M. 7. It builds again from here. Let me hear one time only the bottom two parts.

Mm. 10–11. Follow the line down [F♯, E, D, B].

M. 12. It begins from the lower level. Follow the contour of the line he gives you. I don't hear the relationship of the chords and how the melody fits with the chords.

Mm. 20–21. The texture is thicker now with the thirds and sixths. Use that new color to build the line.

Example 1.18. *Partita* No. 6 in E Minor, *Gigue*, mm. 20–21.

Mm. 22–23. Hear it winding down both in the right hand [G-F♯-F♮-E-D♯] and the left hand [D-C♯-C♮-B-A-G].
M. 24. It ends with a flourish.

Example 1.19. *Partita* No. 6 in E Minor, *Gigue*, m. 24.

M. 33. There's still a strength in these sixteenth notes; it shouldn't sound cute.
Mm. 35–36. It comes down again.
M. 37. It doesn't have to be louder at the high C but be aware of the line.
Mm. 47–48. The left hand answers the right hand; it grows thicker.
Mm. 51–52. It cadences on the downbeat [of m. 51]; all the remaining is almost an extension that grows in texture and sonority.

Example 1.20. *Partita* No. 6 in E Minor, *Gigue*, mm. 51–52.

2 Samuel Barber

The Barber Sonata has withstood the test of time. You always used to hear it in a competition, especially the Fugue, but there is really much depth in the slow movement and also in the first movement—the build is consistent, strong; there is a marvelous sense of drama. I'm sure his example was the big Prokofiev sonatas, although the theme is like a fugue by Max Reger. I'm very fond of the [Barber] Sonata, and I think it's a big vehicle for a pianist to show how formidable he is as a piano player. At the same time, it's a very important part of American music that one can be proud of and should play.

Sonata, Op. 26

Mvt. 1. *Allegro energico*

You must plan your biggest places; and when you take your *ritardando*, you must be sure that the rhythmic values are in relation.

Mm. 1–3. A bigger opening. An aggressive, somber march.

Example 2.1. Sonata, Op. 26, mvt. 1, mm. 1–3.

- M. 4. Don't *crescendo* there; the line comes down. And then phrase. The right hand can help by playing the G♭.
- M. 5. Have a new attack on that C♭. Start less, and then grow in the other lines.
- M. 9. Keep the left-hand rhythm. Don't let it become rhythmically mushy. That line grows [C♭-D♭-C♮-D♮-F♭-E♭].
- M. 15. Take time before the *fortissimo*; let it grow.

M. 16. The right hand is the same as measure 12 but without the jagged rhythm, yes?

Mm. 17–18. Can you actually throw it to the last note? Start the Bb [last note of m. 16] with a 2. Now play thumbs alone [Eb, D♮, Db, C], letting the thumb bounce along. You get stuck on the Bb; save the weight till the Db. Or you could let the left hand help here on the D♮-D-C [m. 17] and the A♮-Ab-G [m. 18].

Mm. 18–19. Use those notes [C-Db-C-B] to change the mood.

M. 19. Come down, but in principle you don't have a *ritardando*. Play those B♮s [mm. 19–20] with the left hand.

Example 2.2. Sonata, Op. 26, mvt. 1, mm. 17–20.

M. 22. Let it run out—but without pause. He shows us what the accompaniment will be. This B answers the previous Bs all the way back to measure 19.

M. 24. Close that phrase [E♮-G♮-Ab] without a *crescendo*.

M. 25. More of the right-hand broken A⁷ chord.

M. 26. Less than measure 25.

M. 28. Play the last note [Eb] with the right hand.

Mm. 32–33. The left hand of measure 32 corresponds to the right hand of measure 33. The right hand of measure 32 corresponds to the left hand of measure 33.

M. 34. The *chromaticism* [last beat] takes you to measure 35.

M. 35. Let these repeated chords bounce. They set up the rhythm.

Mm. 35–36. You must count for me eight eighth notes followed by five. We must find the common connector.

Mm. 35–38. What is the relationship of the repeated notes to the two-note slur? [They practice each occurrence.] The repeated notes bounce each time.

M. 39. The left-hand repeated notes [Dbs] answer the right hand—so a little less.

Example 2.3. Sonata, Op. 26, mvt. 1, mm. 39–40.

Mm. 43–44. The left hand can help each time on these lower notes.

M. 45. The motive sways, goes to the A♭, then away. Now it goes to the B♭ [left hand].

M. 46. He changes from lyric to *marcato*.

Mm. 49–50. It's no longer bouncing but blended. It's as if he writes in a *ritard* with his note values.

Example 2.4. Sonata, Op. 26, mvt. 1, mm. 49–50.

Mm. 51–52. Quiet and steady.

M. 62. Take time to roll the chord and place the D.

M. 63. Hear the two lines. Take the lower notes with the left hand.

Example 2.5. Sonata, Op. 26, mvt. 1, m. 63.

16 *Master Classes with Menahem Pressler*

M. 65. The left hand can help again.

Mm. 68–69. Take a little time here to close the phrase [D♮-C♯-C♮-B].

M. 71. The right hand is a light flicker.

M. 72. Use the last G♭ to ease into measure 73.

M. 74. These last few notes must trail off. And somehow, this last B and the repeated Cs [m. 75] must have some way of connection; and because you are in triplets, you have some freedom.

M. 75. Immediately establish the new tempo. Not fast.

M. 78. Come down with the line.

M. 83. Let us hear that this F [the downbeat] is an arrival, an ending.

M. 88. To sustain the right-hand chord, play the B♭ and C octaves [the sixth and seventh sixteenths] with the left hand.

M. 89. The same as measure 88. You could play the first octave [the Cs] with the right hand.

M. 90. Feel an arm rotation in these notes.

Example 2.6. Sonata, Op. 26, mvt. 1, mm. 88–90.

M. 102. The left-hand octaves change the color.

Mm. 104–106. Bring it down, less, so it can start the *crescendo* in measure 106.

M. 109. Broaden.

Mm. 110–111. A big loose feeling—not fast.

M. 113. Keep the wrist and elbow high in the sextuplets.

M. 116. Take time on the chords.

M. 118. Divide the chord between the hands. The right hand can take the F and B♭.

M. 119. Climb.

Mm. 121–122. In tempo—not pushed.

M. 123. Why is it marked loud? It is an indication of emotion.

M. 127. Dream-like, floating.

M. 140. Less on the inner sixteenth notes.

Mm. 141–143. Practice just the repeated notes [B♭s and Es]; then practice the other part. Shape the repeated notes; come out of them.

M. 148. Really calm and quiet. Bring it down.

M. 149. A little hazy.

M. 152. Don't make the right hand sound difficult; it's *cantabile*.

M. 159. Feel the tension and resolution in the left hand.

Mm. 162–163. Each right-hand flourish has three points; the first flourish has C, then D, then F♭. Thin out the pedal.

M. 164. This is the bottom, so play less. It's a start.

M. 165. Hear the canon.

M. 166. Hear them coming together. We have a resolution; it's like an explosion.

Example 2.7. Sonata, Op. 26, mvt. 1, mm. 165–166.

Mvt. 2. *Allegro vivace e leggero*

It's too heavy at the beginning. There's no difference between your *piano* and a *pianissimo*. It should be very light, and you should use your pedal very judiciously.

M. 1. I can't hear the B to the A♯. Lean into the B.

Example 2.8. Sonata, Op. 26, mvt. 2, mm. 1–2.

M. 4. That's an echo, yes? [starting D-C].

M. 8. Enjoy that second B.

M. 9. Clear the foot so that the D♯ leaves us.

M. 10. Can I have the *mordent* on the beat?

M. 15. Don't let the return surprise you; you have to be ready for it.

Mm. 21–26. I wouldn't play it *staccato*.

Mm. 22–23. No *crescendo*.

Mm. 25–26. I would play a *diminuendo* so that you end up in *piano* so that the *mf* is a surprise, a new texture.

Example 2.9. Sonata, Op. 26, mvt. 2, mm. 21–26.

Mm. 30–31. Hear the bass step down from C♭ to B♭.

Mm. 31–36. Go down from the A to the A♭ [m. 33] to the G [m. 36], and then do his *crescendo* [mm. 37–38].

Mm. 43–46. Go all the way to the note that is the climax [the G of m. 46], but don't push the tempo.

M. 46. No *ritardando*. Take the D with the left hand.

M. 47. It's a waltz, a crazy waltz.

M. 48. I don't hear your left-hand slur; play less on the C.

M. 49. Can you play that E♭ [beat 3] as if a shade comes down, as if you put a veil on top of it?

Example 2.10. Sonata, Op. 26, mvt. 2, mm. 47–49.

Mm. 54–55. A little *rubato* here and less on the echo. Less pedal when you have the ornament; close the phrase.

M. 57. Lean on the one that is the top of the slur [the A].

M. 64. Less sound; answer the previous measure.

Mm. 65–66. Lots of pedal.

Mm. 71–74. Keep a long pedal through this *forte*.

M. 75. We need that accent that puts it back into 6/8. Actually, if you think in terms of four beats and then in terms of two beats it will be easier. Gradually clear the pedal as it descends.

Mm. 79–80. Less and less—like you have a spool of thread and you unwind it till it runs out.

M. 80. And lift the foot so that the upbeat is clear.

M. 116. The F♯-A♮ is less than the F♯-A♯ [m. 115].

M. 119. The F-A♭ is less.

Mm. 130–131. It's an echo this time.

M. 132. Relax over the top. Color it differently than before.

M. 139. Ease into the return.

Mm. 149–150. No false accents.

Mm. 154–155. You can actually feel the *decrescendo* in the left-hand's chromatic scale [D♭-C-B-B♭-A-A♭].

M. 156. Relax.

M. 164–165. Can you make a *diminuendo* going up? The hand must be light. One shouldn't play six or nine or five; it's three beats.

Example 2.11. Sonata, Op. 26, mvt. 2, mm. 164–165.

Mvt. 3. *Adagio mesto*

It's very slow. But when it's 6/8, you must have a feeling of two, not six; then a feeling of three when it's 3/4, not separate beats.

M. 1. It's too dry. You can use one pedal for the three chords, even though there are passing notes. Take the D and D♭ with the right hand.

Example 2.12. Sonata, Op. 26, mvt. 3, mm. 1–2.

M. 2. A little less than the first measure.

M. 5. The *crescendo* is too much; you should use the *espressivo*. Barber was a man who loved the singing voice, who loved singing. He loved melodies.

M. 6. Don't hurry the grace notes.

M. 7. Don't lose the B in the bass; change the pedal and keep the B.

M. 10. Do you hear it closing?

M. 12. Voice the right-hand G. It's doubling the left hand.

M. 13. Why not take the G with the right hand?

M. 17. Beat one is the most.

M. 18. Close the measure.

M. 20. Play it so that the *appoggiatura* leads you to the chord. Don't compete; the right hand is the leading voice. And catch all the *appoggiaturas* in the pedal. The third eighth is pure E minor. Clear the pedal, then change again on the F♯ chord.

M. 22. Change the pedal so that you catch the *appoggiatura*.

M. 24. Use one pedal for the measure.

M. 25. It shouldn't be less; the intensity should be kept.

M. 26. Declamatory.

Mm. 28–29. Each voice unhurried; it's a conversation between the two voices.

Example 2.13. Sonata, Op. 26, mvt. 3, mm. 28–29.

M. 32. There's a feeling of doom in that A♯. And close that measure.

M. 33. Prepare for the *mezzo forte*. Lead us to it.

Mm. 34–39. Use the *sostenuto* pedal; hold the B till the end.

M. 38. Slower to the G.

M. 39. Just float in with the weight of the hand.

Mvt. 4. *Fuga*

M. 1. It's a *non-legato* touch. The way you play that G♭ [the sixth note] has to let us know that it is off the beat.

M. 2. If you are keen on the downbeat, as he was, then you shouldn't have an accent on the G♭. You confuse the meter.

Example 2.14. Sonata, Op. 26, *Fuga*, mm. 1–3.

M. 3. Both accents are too big. The B♭ [beat 4] is a finish. In principle, one would *decrescendo* [D♭-C♭-B♭].

M. 6. It's not a long note [the C♭], so don't overlap with the F. Finish it [G♭-F-E♭]. And then less on the new entrance.

M. 7. Wrist rotation can help the left hand stay relaxed on the slurs—and not heavy.

M. 9. Since you made us aware of those inner notes, you have to keep bringing them out; but don't sit on them.

M. 12. That closes it off [B♭-C-D-E♭]; every voice has had its say, yes? The new theme [at the last three sixteenths] shouldn't have so much urgency.

M. 14. Let those notes in the left hand [F-G♭-F-A♭-F] take us forward.

M. 18. Lean on that A♭, then on the G [beat 3].

M. 19. I need the ending C. We must hear E♭-D♭-C, but you play like a blind man. I shouldn't say that. A blind man could hear it.

M. 26. Play the left hand with that same intensity as the right hand. It's a *stretto*.

M. 30. It should be brilliant over the top, almost brittle on those first three notes [C♭-A♭-E♭].

M. 31. The left hand should not be so short; let it be heard.

M. 33. Let us hear the bass line A-E♮-D♭-B♭ to the A♮ [of m. 34].

M. 36. Catch that F in the *sostenuto* pedal, then the E [m. 40].

M. 46. A splash of color. Feel the wrist moving in and out.

M. 48. Not hurried, broader here. Practice the left-hand thumbs alone for security.

M. 51. This calls for steel fingers!

M. 54. Why such a *ritardando*?

Mm. 55–58. The top line is *scherzando* above the sustained bottom lines. Quick finger releases on these little figures.

Example 2.15. Sonata, Op. 26, *Fuga*, mm. 55–58.

M. 64. Now we have a C; the organ point changes.

M. 65. You really must practice these cadences that immediately start a new theme [beat 4 into beat 5]. It's like a signature of this piece.

M. 66. Graceful swings.

Mm. 81–82. These top entrances become brighter and brighter. The right hand drops into place.

Mm. 88–89. Not just hand slaps; use full body on these chords.

M. 96. It's like a lion roaring.

M. 98. Full sonority on the chord; let it ring. Start the *cadenza* slower, then *acce-lerando.*

M. 99. Start less; you have a long way to go.

M. 120. These are hand slaps with lots of wrist and arm rotation.

M. 131. Here too, you have to clarify what you are doing. He asks for *marcatis-simo*, but it's very difficult to do that without backing off a little.

Mm. 140–143. Accent the downbeats, but keep track of the sequences. [Pressler sings E♭-G♭-B♭-D, F-G♭-B♭-D, E♭-G♭-B♭-D, E♭-G♭-B♭]. Also, practice these octaves starting from the end for security.

M. 143. Up and out.

M. 144. Down and in.

M. 146. Throw your body into that last chord.

Example 2.16. Sonata, Op. 26, *Fuga*, mm. 143–146.

Interlude II
Page Turners

The Trio was playing in Wellfleet, Massachusetts, where Bernie Greenhouse had his house, and he asked a woman that he knew to turn my pages. So we play, and after a while, she turns the page. But there's still a lot to play on that page, so I turn back. She turns again; I turn back. Then we come to the end of a page, and she doesn't turn. I mean, I've been through that first piece and I'm exasperated. I was nearly dying, and we walk out and I say to her, "You play an instrument?" and she says, "No."

I said, "Do you read music?"

She says, "No."

I said, "Why did you decide to turn pages?"

She says, "Oh, Mr. Greenhouse says it's easy; just turn when you nod." But of course, I nod all the time.

Then I got even with him afterward.

Then there was a time in Spain when we played in Madrid, and there came a music teacher to turn the pages. She was really quite heavy, quite large, and she wore a kind of tent. I start to play, and she gets up to turn the pages, and I had to play in the bass, and my hand gets lost in her dress, and there I am, and I don't know where the notes are, and she's hovering over me. Four days later we play in Bilbao, and I see that I had forgotten the music of the Schumann Trio. So we went to the store and bought it. I asked the Music Society to provide a page turner, and there comes to the concert a mother with a thirteen-year-old boy who only speaks Spanish. There are some places where I repeat and some places where I don't repeat, and I had to explain everything to her, and she explains it to him. After the horror in Madrid, I was ready for a real disaster. But this boy was perfect. He remembered everything. And as the concert ended and the public came in to congratulate, I was turning around to find him to thank him, and he had already gone; they had already taken him to bed. That was just the opposite. So you never know.

Another time in Berlin, for instance, I had a page turner, and each time he gets up to turn the page, he goes, "Tch, tch." After a while, you sought to kill him because he's always a critic. Every page, he goes, "Tch, tch."

Another time, which was equally bad, each time the man had to turn the page, he would look at his watch. I asked him afterward, "Did you have to catch a train?" I mean, how is it that every time somebody starts to get up, he looks at his watch? Or there is the one who is more enthusiastic than you, who acts like he's the one playing, who moves all around. That's also bad.

Another terrible one was at Ravinia. She comes to the end of the Rachmaninoff Trio, which was being broadcast, and she stops turning! I'm going 120 miles an hour with both hands very busy, of course, and she doesn't turn! You are not ready; you don't expect that. The ending of the Rachmaninoff is the end of the concert, the last movement, millions of notes, and everybody playing intensely—and she doesn't turn!

3   Ludwig van Beethoven

Beethoven's music is the most varied, and the scale of emotions is absolutely the widest. In Beethoven you mirror, actually, the universe. It is true that Beethoven addresses you less than Schumann does; he always addresses the world. He always speaks for us, to us. And I find playing his music is the most challenging that I can imagine. It is enormously difficult physically, it is difficult emotionally, it's difficult intellectually, and it is difficult stamina-wise. There's not an elitism to this music; it could approach the peasant or it could approach the nobility, because he was as vulgar as he was spiritual. His high spirituality is metaphysical. It is what religions are all about; it speaks to the Holy Ghost, whatever Holy Ghost is in your mind. And the exact strength—the physical strength, the emotional strength—that holds it together, that made him write what he wrote, that made him write that enormous *Hammerklavier* that even today is one of the most modern pieces that you can find. I mean, in that fugue he out-fugues everybody, even the great-grandfather of all fugues, Bach. A fugue like that defies physical difficulties and at the same time is an outreach far into whatever our future may be. I think he is truly whatever everything else is being measured by.

Thirty-Two Variations in C Minor, WoO 80

M. 1. Theme. Always "out" of beat 1 and "down" to beat 2, because it's a Chaconne.
M. 2. "Up and out" on the D; the G is "down and in."

Example 3.1. Thirty-Two Variations in C Minor, mm. 1–6.

M. 8. Close it.
M. 9. Variation 1. There's no excuse for every note not repeating. The last four notes lead to the downbeat of measure 10.

M. 14. The first chord is short. [They practice the last chord of measure 13 and the two chords of measure 14.]

M. 16. Take the second E♭ in the left hand. Pull back the motion a little.

Mm. 17–18. Variation 2. Play the right hand short, no pedal. A little *diminuendo* between the two chords each time.

M. 24. Cadence to the C.

M. 25. Variation 3. Only *mezzo forte*. [Pressler has the student play the right hand of measure 25 followed by the left hand of measure 26 to get the full sweep of the line.] Use touches of pedal on each downbeat.

M. 32. Don't rush; stay *forte* to the end.

M. 33. Variation 4. Touch the pedal on the bass notes.

M. 40. Close it.

M. 41. Variation 5. The same tempo as the previous. Two-measure phrases.

M. 46. A slight agogic delay before the *sforzandi*.

Mm. 46–48. Voice each entrance.

Example 3.2. Thirty-Two Variations in C Minor, mm. 45–48.

M. 49. Variation 6. All are *forte*, more power, but go to the last chord.

M. 54. *Crescendo* to the top.

M. 55. You get stuck at the top. Start with an accent on the second eighth note.

Mm. 55–56. *Fortissimo* all the way to the bottom.

M. 57. Variation 7. Think the line, always *legato*. [Pressler demonstrates a sliding motion and use of the fourth finger on the black keys.]

M. 65. Variation 8. Over the top.

M. 73. Variation 9. A neutral trill, *mezzo piano* in the melody. Lean on the E♭ and out on the eighth. Observe the eighth rests.

M. 81. Variation 10. *Con fuoco*. Wrist rotation to the Cs each time. No pedal.

M. 89. Variation 11. *Crescendo* to the G [right hand of m. 90].

Mm. 94–96. The octaves should *crescendo* all the way to the C. Hear the final cadence [G–C].

M. 97. Variation 12. Rich sound, like a chorale.

M. 103. *Decrescendo*.

Example 3.3. Thirty-Two Variations in C Minor, mm. 97–104.

M. 105. Variation 13. The right hand is like a single flute.
M. 113. Variation 14. Not fast. Graceful.
M. 120. And close the phrase.
Mm. 121–122. Variation 15. Relate the two measures with a little swell.
M. 128. And cadence to the C [of m. 129].
M. 129. Variation 16. The same consistent pulse as variation 15. Let the left hand guide the pulse. Not so *staccato*. Like the previous variation—a little swell.
M. 136. Finish—but without a *ritardando*.
Mm. 137–140. Variation 17. Let us hear each entrance.

Example 3.4. Thirty-Two Variations in C Minor, mm. 137–140.

M. 144. Continue to decrease.
Mm. 145–146. Variation 18. Not too dry. Snap those top notes.
M. 153. Variation 19. Much contrast between the *forte* and the *piano*.
M. 158. Accent the A♭s in both hands.
M. 160. Articulate the right hand. Not mushy.
M. 167. Variation 20. Feel the direction of that chord [G⁷] to the C minor chord [m. 168].
M. 168. The C minor chord is the goal.
M. 169. Variation 21. The last left-hand note is too detached for a difference between the quarters and the eighth.
Mm. 177–178. Variation 22. Create tension between the two lines with the *sforzando* of each hand.

M. 185. Variation 23. *Mysterioso*. Relate each two-measure group.

M. 200. Variation 24. No *ritardando* going into variation 25.

M. 208. Variation 25. In beat 2, take one or two notes with the left hand; it's right there.

Example 3.5. Thirty-Two Variations in C Minor, m. 208.

M. 215. Variation 26. On beat 2, start a *crescendo* to the end.

M. 222. Variation 27. A new start after the *sforzando*.

M. 224. Close *forte* and with an accent.

M. 225. Variation 28. *Legato* line.

M. 232. Close the phrase.

M. 240. Variation 29. *Fortissimo* to the end. Have barely a break; stay in tempo to the next variation.

M. 241. Variation 30. Contrast; almost a murmur.

M. 245. Hear the duet of the inner lines.

M. 248. Softer on the last chord; the arms are weightless.

M. 249. Variation 31. From afar.

M. 263. Variation 32. A big *crescendo* to measure 264 with clear fingers.

Mm. 268–270. The *sforzando* goes with the left hand A♭s, not the right hand. Hear the two-note slurs [A♭–G]. A series of *sforzandi* always *crescendos*.

M. 270. Start your *crescendo* from beat 2.

M. 274. Follow the line [G-A♭-A♮-B♭-B♮-G] and take some time [on the B♮-G]. Continue the *decrescendo*.

M. 275. No *crescendo*; it remains *pianissimo*.

Example 3.6. Thirty-Two Variations in C Minor, mm. 273–275.

M. 288. *Decrescendo* [F#-G].

M. 289. Start *pianissimo*.

M. 299. How do you guarantee getting the bass G? You guarantee it by looking at it.

M. 300. Honor the *sforzando*.

M. 303. Wait just a little longer, then start the octaves and have movement all the way down.

Mm. 305–306. And "out." The chords are *pizzacato*, but with a touch of pedal. Have a *decrescendo* between the two chords.

Example 3.7. Thirty-Two Variations in C Minor, mm. 303–306.

Piano Sonata in A-flat Major, Op. 26

Mvt. 1. *Andante con Variazioni*

Each variation must have its own character, and the sound should never be loud or harsh. It shouldn't be overemotional; it must have a sophistication.

M. 4. That *sforzando* isn't a hit; it's a stress within the *piano*. Plan the third beat in such a way that the B♭ is no louder than the previous one. Play it graciously, with no motion of the arm. It doesn't have to be extreme. [Pressler sings measures 3 and 4 as if there are no expression markings, then sings it with the *crescendo* and *sforzando* added.]

Example 3.8. Sonata in A-flat Major, Op. 26, mvt. 1, mm. 1–4.

M. 5. Actually, when you reach that D♭, it shouldn't be louder than a *piano*.

Mm. 5–6. It only now goes out of the frame a little bit, but still in the same mood and character.

M. 8. [Pressler demonstrates a lifting of the wrist on beat 2 to release the phrase.]

M. 14. There is no accent on that downbeat.

Mm. 120. Finish each phrase.

M. 30. He's written out the ornament for you; it's a turn.

M. 32. The F shouldn't stick out too much. The octaves must be as *legato* as a single line would be.

Mm. 35–38. The character is "freeing." There's a lift between each little phrase, and with that lift he gives you room to breathe.

M. 36. Use the arm to help you get to the next position. As you play the first G, your thumb is already on its way to the D♭.

M. 40. The E♭ is less; your wrist can help you with that.

M. 50. Finish. There's no *sforzando* on that F.

Mm. 51–52. Finger the thirds like an organist would, releasing that A♮ as you cross over. Then be graceful in the left hand. [Pressler gives a left-hand fingering.] Keep the left-hand thumb very close to the third finger [m. 52, beat 2] so the hand doesn't have to pivot very far for the octave. It's already there.

Example 3.9. Sonata in A-flat Major, Op. 26, mvt. 1, mm. 51–52.

M. 52. The right hand would close, and then the left hand closes.

M. 60. The downbeat is *piano*, then you start the *crescendo*.

M. 69. Variation II. And what would be the character of this one? Playful, because the next one is solemn. Stay in tempo with the theme.

M. 72. Phrase it [come down in volume and release the hand]—then the graceful turn again.

M. 75. The D♭ is gentle; don't let it stick out.

M. 76. It closes on beat 2.

Example 3.10. Sonata in A-flat Major, Op. 26, mvt. 1, mm. 75–76.

Mm. 85–86. Again, don't become heavy-handed; it's never violent.

M. 103. Variation 3. Solemn, almost painful. When you play that first chord, you must feel something because you just came from A♭ major. Change fingers, 3 and 2, on the repeated notes. It gives you a fresh stroke for each note and less space between the notes. If you later decide to keep the same finger each time, you'll keep the feeling as if there was a fresh finger for each note.

M. 104. The right hand goes down from the A♭ to the G, but the left hand begins going up. Not an outright *crescendo*, just an inner intensity.

M. 109. Here you can practice changing the fingers again, sometimes 5, sometimes 4, for a fresh sound. But in performance you will probably keep 5 for all of them.

M. 111. But can you feel that note in the bass, or is it just a muscle action? You have to hear the note and understand what it means.

M. 118. The *sforzando* must have a relationship to everything around it. Go in with feeling, lean in with your hand—not harsh. That's too hard. Imagine the sound that you want to make.

Mm. 121–122. Relate; it's different from measures 119–120. It's not just your muscles that play it. [They practice the separate hands.]

M. 137. Variation IV. This variation is humorous, yes? It jumps all over the place, with different registers and also with syncopations. All of a sudden that upbeat seems like a downbeat.

Example 3.11. Sonata in A-flat Major, Op. 26, mvt. 1, mm. 137–140.

Ludwig van Beethoven 33

Mm. 142–144. It's like a four-part choir. [They practice each separate part, then put them together in different combinations.]

M. 149. Don't hit that F. Let the arm help you.

Mm. 158–161. You have this twice [F-E♭]; which one do you think would be more? Yes, the second one.

M. 162. When you hold your hand tight like that on the scale, you can't pivot. You should practice to the note that pivots, to the thumb [stopping and turning on the thumb each time] so that your hand becomes fluid.

M. 171. Variation V. The theme is back, but it's like it has a frame around it. The wrist plays the top of each group.

M. 179. This is like the Opus 111, the melody with the trill. The wrist helps the fingers, in and out, a slight drop with the thumb each time.

Mm. 179–182. You have to hear the duet in that left-hand passage between the bass notes and all the rest.

M. 185. The left arm must remain relaxed so it can move without accents.

M. 187. How loud is that supposed to be? It's still in *piano*.

M. 188. It floats back down from the sky.

M. 205. Sing that fifth finger, but still with a light arm.

M. 215. Let the phrase run out.

M. 217. Come up a little—then it settles again.

Mvt. 2. *Scherzo*

M. 1. It's only *piano.*

M. 4. The E♭ is less; the phrase closes. Then there's a rest.

M. 17. There should be a slight wrist drop on the first third [the pickup] and on the downbeat. But the downbeat is more. The wrist helps shape the melody.

Mm. 26–29. One motion for each group, the two eighths and quarter, then four eighths and quarter, then again four eighths and quarter. Go to the end of each one with the wrist going in on each *sforzando*. You should enjoy that. [Pressler provides a fingering for the thirds.]

Example 3.12. Sonata in A-flat Major, Op. 26, mvt. 2, mm. 26–29.

Mm. 32–33. Go up to the D♭ [m. 33] so you have room to *decrescendo*.

M. 44. Take a breath before the left-hand melody begins on the A♭.

Mm. 44–67. [Pressler has the student play the right hand while singing the left hand and then play the left hand while singing the right hand.]

Mm. 58, 60, 62. Relate these entrances.

M. 62. Don't start the *crescendo* so early that you run out of dynamic room.

M. 68. Think long lines, and that *crescendo* [m. 72] is subtle.

Mvt. 3. *Marcia Funebre*

M. 1. Those first E♭ octaves are played down into the key, not up; it gives more seriousness. The *piano* needs to be more rich. It is a funeral march for a hero. [They work on exact rhythm, inflections, and articulations.]

M. 2. The bass with some pedal—it's too dry.

M. 4. Hear a slight *decrescendo* in those three chords.

Example 3.13. Sonata in A-flat Major, Op. 26, mvt. 3, mm. 1–4.

M. 9. Hear the new key.

M. 14. The left-hand sixteenths lead to the longer note, not accented.

M. 16. That's too soft for a Beethoven *piano*.

M. 21. I would retake the left-hand thumb with a second pedal to achieve the *fp*.

Mm. 27–29. Strengthen these chords with the body, not just the arm.

M. 29. Not three chords just alike; the next chord that gets that much weight is the A♭ [m. 30].

Example 3.14. Sonata in A-flat Major, Op. 26, mvt. 3, mm. 27–30.

M. 38b. [The second ending is measure 38b.]

M. 44. The left hand continues to *crescendo*.

M. 54. Not too soft on the D♮; a *pianissimo* is following.

M. 69. Let me hear in the left hand the G♮.

Mm. 70–72. Voice the left hand. It came up [mm. 68–70]; now it goes back down.

Mvt. 4. *Allegro*

This comes after such a grand piece, and it's definitely more playful and joyous. It's a release, yes?

M. 1. At the beginning I hear your melody, E♭-F, D♭-E♭, et cetera, but then the left hand has it [m. 6] and we must hear it the same way, but you don't play it that way. Block the notes [in groups of two] so you hear what he's doing.

Example 3.15. Sonata in A-flat Major, Op. 26, mvt. 4, mm. 1–6.

Mm. 11–12. Be ready for this left-hand A♭. Sometimes he finishes with the leap going down, or sometimes going up. The hand must be balanced on the E♭ leading to the A♭.

M. 16. You should go "in-out" on the E♭-G.

Mm. 19–20. Hear the cadence.

M. 20. Start the octaves with 4-5 so it can be *legato*. The arm and fingers work together to create the *legato*.

M. 24. That *crescendo* should start *piano*.

Mm. 25–26. Not so much motion with the right arm; let the hand stay in the key.

M. 28. Play that line less loud, like a *fugato*. It interrupts.

M. 30. The *sforzandi* can have more bite.

M. 44. He twice ends on a deceptive cadence [mm. 44 and 46], and then he finishes [m. 48]. And what's beautiful is how he energizes and accentuates and increases the intensity each time, yes?

Mm. 48–49. And when you play that, it's like the right hand is suspended in air.

M. 52. Change the color and the touch with the *piano*. Make it enough of a *crescendo* [mm. 51–52] so that a feeling of tension is created.

M. 72. Use 4 to 5 again so it can be *legato*.

M. 81. Same tempo as before.

M. 88b. [The second ending is measure 88b.]

Mm. 89–90. Both chords have the same length.

M. 96. Yes, it drops down to a *piano*, but don't give away the tension. I would not mind if you inflected down.

M. 130. Each *sforzando* propels you to the next position.

Mm. 136–138. When Beethoven has one *sforzando* after the other, it of course means *crescendo*.

Example 3.16. Sonata in A-flat Major, Op. 26, mvt. 4, mm. 136–138.

M. 155. That's new; he uses the *sforzando* to make you listen to the phrase in a different way.

Piano Sonata in E-flat Major, Op. 31, No. 3

Mvt. 1. *Allegro*

M. 1. Play it as if you stretch to the first note, then come down. On the repeated Fs, I would suggest that you play 3-4; you can play anything you want, but these two notes are "in and out." You must practice in such a way that it is always clear. You can put some words there like, "Do come here." Not hurried.

M. 2. Make this statement different from the first.

M. 3. Then he uses the same notes, but you have no relationship to what you have just started. Start less.

M. 6. The *fermata* is more than three beats. [Pressler counts it slowly and allows 4 beats.]

Example 3.17. Sonata, in E-flat Major, Op. 31, No. 3, mvt. 1, mm. 1–6.

M. 8. Finish the phrase before the run up.

M. 11. The grace note not so labored.

M. 17. Close it with the repeated notes coming in right in time.

M. 18. Quick grace note; it should sound fresh.

Mm. 18–21. Hear where the left-hand chords are going. It must be organic—much more tension, more controlled, more emotion.

M. 22. The ornament begins on the note, not from above. The A♭ is an eighth, not a quarter note.

M. 29. Don't accent the downbeat.

M. 32. No *diminuendo*; the last one is suddenly *piano*.

M. 33. Can that C♭ have a special kind of feeling? Don't hit it. Go deep with the wrist and release the arm.

M. 43. Shape the two notes of the slur.

M. 44. The left hand interrupts. Take that first F in the right hand so you have the others ready in your left hand. And with strength. It's Beethoven!

M. 46. The same tempo! And it doesn't scream!

Mm. 48–49. Play the slurs with charm.

M. 53. Finish on the B♭. You should finish with color, but not with extra time.

Mm. 53–56. Can you play the passage so that it's music, not just a scale?

M. 56. There's no *crescendo* there. Instead go down; you have to end in *piano*.

M. 57. To play it really well, you must play the two-note slurs.

M. 64. Finish.

M. 71. Even if he had not written a *crescendo*, you would have had to make one because it's one *sforzando* after another. It's a *crescendo*, yes? And then you have a *subito piano*.

M. 74. I don't see a *crescendo* marked.

M. 78. The trill is *on* the note. You are already above the note, and with Beethoven at that time, ornaments were always on the note.

M. 81. The maximum is on the Fs, so that you come down to the B♭ [m. 82].

Mm. 96–98. Always take the foot off on the second beat.

M. 99. Let me hear a G in the chord; it's going to C.

M. 108. Play the first third with the left hand but only the first one.

Example 3.18. Sonata in E-flat Major, Op. 31, No. 3, mvt. 1, m. 108.

M. 114. The left hand is a quarter note.

M. 116. The right hand is an eighth note. Play the first third with the left hand.

M. 124. You can play the first F with the left hand.

M. 126. Again, play the first G with the left hand.

M. 138. Keep the rhythmic energy there.

M. 161. It may help to play the E♭ in the left hand.

M. 169. Take the second B♭ with the right hand. The A♭ is still in *forte*.

M. 176. Think three melody notes, not six. Follow the line of E♭-C-D-E♭.

M. 184. Keep the arm light, so the slurs don't get clumsy.

M. 185. Try alternating 1-3, 2-4 on the slurs.

Mm. 191–202. End all the trills with 1-3-2.

Mm. 214–215. The slur has a *decrescendo*.

M. 224. There's no *crescendo* for the repeated chords.

Mm. 225–226. Go down to the second chord of the slur—not up.

Mm. 234–235. You have to finish [on the E♭] before you can start the scale. It's artistic what he's asking you to do.

Mm. 237–239. Can you let us hear three different registers?

M. 246. I would advise you to take that first G in the left hand.

M. 250. No false accents.

Mm. 252–253. The cadence is in your tempo—not slower.

Mvt. 2. *Scherzo*

M. 4. Use 1-3-2-1 on the repeated notes.

Example 3.19. Sonata in E-flat Major, Op. 31, No. 3, mvt. 2, mm. 1–4.

M. 8. The repeated notes are 3-2.

M. 9. Come back to *pianissimo* after the swell.

Mm. 13–17. Use 3-2 in each hand on the repeated notes, and the second note is not so short.

M. 18. The B♭ ends the slur; it is less.

M. 23. Accompany yourself.

Mm. 34–35. To the second chord. Ta-da! We talk a lot about gestures in music. Nothing could be more imperious than this.

Mm. 41–42. The left hand plays 2-3 on the repeated notes; the right hand plays 2-1.

Example 3.20. Sonata in E-flat Major, Op. 31, No. 3, mvt. 2, mm. 41–42.

M. 44. Come down in the left hand between the C♭ and the B♭.

M. 50. The left hand is not an action of the arm; it's an action of the fingers. Use 2-5 and 1-3.

M. 62b. [The second ending begins with measure 62b.]

M. 64. What is the F major chord saying?

Mm. 79–81. Take the downbeats with the left hand.

Example 3.21. Sonata in E-flat Major, Op. 31, No. 3, mvt. 2, mm. 79–81.

Mm. 125–126, 129. Play the repeated notes with 2-1-2-1.

Mm. 129–130. Play these repeated notes with 2-1-1-1.

Mm. 139–140. Touch the pedal with the second chord.

M. 144. This chord needs a touch of pedal.

Mm. 154–155. Close it to the A♭.

Mm. 169–171. It's all the way down from the top.

Mvt. 3. *Menuetto*

M. 1. The left hand has to help the phrase move.

Mm. 1–2. Change the fingers for the repeated E♭s.

Example 3.22. Sonata in E-flat Major, Op. 31, No. 3, mvt. 3, mm. 1–2.

M. 3. Of course, you can't change fingers on these repeated notes, but keep the finger close to the key—"within the escapement."

M. 7. *Subito piano.*

M. 8. The B♭ has two functions. It is melody and it is the lower line.

M. 8b. [The second ending begins with measure 8b.]

M. 10. Lean into the C♭ but not loudly. It could have been to a C♮, but this is special, and it resolves to the B♭. You only play a mordent; don't you have a trill?

M. 11. Close the phrase.

M. 14. Start, but you're hitting the B♭ and the A♭.

M. 17b. [The second ending is measure 17b.]

M. 19. You need more *crescendo*, so you have room to come down.

M. 25. The B♭ octave is still *forte* to close the phrase.

M. 46. It's *subito piano.*

M. 49. Again, lean into the C♭ but not loudly.

M. 50. Close the phrase.

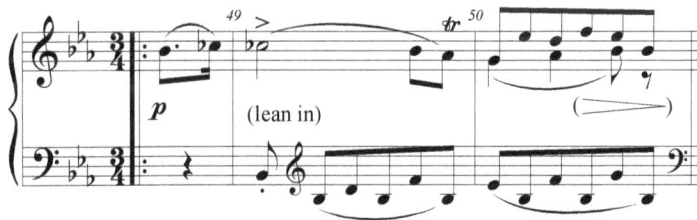

Example 3.23. Sonata in E-flat Major, Op. 31, No. 3, mvt. 3, mm. 49–50.

M. 53. This should not be faster.

M. 56b. [the second ending] Start the Coda *mezzo piano,* so you can come down.

Mvt. 4. *Presto con fuoco*

Mm. 2–3. Change fingers on the B♭s; use 3-4.

Example 3.24. Sonata in E-flat Major, Op. 31, No. 3, mvt. 4, mm. 1–6.

Mm. 23–24. It skips lightly over the top.
M. 29. But change the color with the C♭.
M. 34. Don't hit that high F.
Mm. 39–42. The octaves have a direction.
M. 61. No accent on the B♭; it's a long line.
M. 78b. [The second ending is measures 78b–79b.]
M. 96. It's full body—not just arm. Don't slap the keys.
Mm. 96, 104, 108, 112, 116. Play all these chords. How do they relate?
Mm. 127–130. The B♭s are 3-2.

Example 3.25. Sonata in E-flat Major, Op. 31, No. 3, mvt. 4, mm. 128–130.

Mm. 148, 156, 164. You play all these alike. Color them; they have different functions.
Mm. 238–239. Hear the bass D♭ leading us to the G♭.
M. 264. He's developing it.
M. 309. Tell a story with all these surprises.
Mm. 329–333. *Crescendo* all the way.

Piano Sonata in C Major, Op. 53, *Waldstein*

Mvt. 1. *Allegro con brio*

Mm. 1–2. Use a little pedal and have a slight *crescendo*.

M. 3. "In" on the downbeat—then "out."

M. 4. Use the wrist to create "in, out."

Example 3.26. Sonata in C Major, Op. 53, *Waldstein*, mvt. 1, mm. 1–4.

M. 7. "In, out" again.

M. 9. *Pianissimo.*

M. 12. The E♭ is *mezzo forte*, then *mezzo piano*, then *piano* [m. 13].

M. 17. Use the wrist.

M. 23. Sustain the B.

Mm. 31–34. There must be an energy here even in a *piano*.

M. 34. *Decrescendo.*

M. 36. *Decrescendo* to close the phrase.

M. 38. Hear the A going to the G♯ [m. 39].

M. 42. A *subito piano* which is the close of the phrase.

M. 49. Hear the B-B-C♯-D♯.

M. 50. The left hand syncopation is a "push" but still in tempo.

Example 3.27. Sonata in C Major, Op. 53, *Waldstein*, mvt. 1, mm. 49–51.

M. 56. It reaches a *forte*.

M. 61. *Crescendo* the descending scale.

M. 66. More power. Don't rush.

M. 67. Still more power.

Mm. 71–72. The C to the C♯ is almost a slide. Begin the C♯ *pianissimo*.

Mm. 80–85. Don't stop every phrase.

M. 86b. [The second ending is measure 86b.]

M. 96. Same tempo—not slower.

M. 104. Color the F minor.

M. 111. The F-B♮ is the climax. Pull back a bit.

M. 112. Hear the bass line ascending.

M. 116. Follow the contour of the line.

M. 140. The left hand is not *staccato*.

M. 155. End measure 299 in time and *fortissimo*.

M. 156. It's the same tempo.

M. 170. Don't wait for the B♭.

M. 203. It's a *subito piano*.

Mm. 204–205. It's like a music box.

Example 3.28. Sonata in C Major, Op. 53, *Waldstein*, mvt. 1, mm. 204–205.

M. 223. The scale is not faster.

M. 232. *Decrescendo* to *pianississimo*.

M. 237. Sneak in with those sixteenths.

Mm. 270–274. The left hand doesn't jump. It reaches.

Mm. 284–287. *Legato*, peaceful.

Mvt. 2. *Introduzione: Adagio molto*

M. 4. *Decrescendo* to measure 5.

M. 10. A little accent on the grace note.

M. 11. Be subtle with these entrances.

Example 3.29. Sonata in C Major, Op. 53, *Waldstein*, mvt. 2, m. 11.

M. 21. There's more brooding here. He's searching for the answer.
Mm. 26–28. He creates suspense.

Mvt. 3. *Rondo: Allegretto moderato*

M. 1. We have to hear the top notes of the left hand.
Mm. 20–22. A swell across these measures.
Mm. 32–34. *Legato* octaves. Keep the thumb very close to the keys.
M. 51. The trill is a start.
M. 55. Not slower.
M. 80. No *sforzando* on beat 2.
Mm. 96–97. Gradually less distinct, less articulate.
Mm. 112–113. *Decrescendo.*
M. 168. More powerful. A *sforzando* on beat two and also on the downbeat of measure 169.
M. 175. Energy.
M. 185. The C ends the phrase.
M. 191. The downbeat ends the phrase, still *fortissimo.*
Mm. 233–235. Not faster.
M. 238. *Decrescendo.*
M. 251. *Sempre pianissimo* and no *crescendo.*
M. 264. *Decrescendo.*
M. 319. Still *crescendo.*
Mm. 360 and following. Check where the *sforzandi* are.
Mm. 378–386. You're in *fortissimo,* but the *sforzando* is more.

Example 3.30. Sonata in C Major, Op. 53, *Waldstein*, mvt. 3, mm. 378–386.

Mm. 437–440. Have a *decrescendo.*

M. 441. The right hand takes the second chord.

M. 452. *Decrescendo.*

M. 453. Each phrase is less than the one before.

M. 464. The F-E-C pulls back to resolve to C major [m. 465].

M. 529. Be careful that there are no false accents.

M. 534. Play about *forte* at this point.

Piano Sonata in A-flat Major, Op. 110

The late Beethoven sonatas are spiritual, religious. They reach up to touch heaven. I love to play them for what they can do for myself and the audience, and I love to teach them because of what they can open up in students. I can't get enough of this sonata. The first movement is Beethoven the idealist; the second is Beethoven the hedonist; the third is Beethoven full of grief and regret; and the fugue is a fulfillment of all of this.

Mvt. 1. *Moderato cantabile, molto espressivo*

M. 1. When he says "con amabilita" what do you think he means? Yes, with great tenderness and love but still with arm weight. It's Beethoven, not Chopin; there's more core to the sound. You must phrase it so that the first two notes hang together. Gently ease into the keys; let the fingers and arm sink into the keyboard. A little more melody on the first two chords. Then there's movement from the sixteenth to the next chord.

M. 4. You can't seem to find a proper tempo here, so I would like you to play that measure with an accompaniment [Pressler plays measure 4 with a steady sixteenth-note accompaniment] so that you find the tempo. There is a *fermata* and there is freedom, but there must a tempo. You must treat the *fermata* psychologically. First you count it; then you feel it.

M. 4. The trill is more like a vibrato than a trill. He shows you in the Reprise [m. 59] what he may have had in mind with regard to the *fermata*, because there he fills it out and writes it out. And on the trill you have a little swell, so that at the end of the trill you are back at the level of the beginning. The F-E♭-D♭ goes down naturally to the C.

M. 5. An open sound with the accompaniment clear like woodwinds. It's the same tempo as the beginning.

Example 3.31. Sonata in A-flat Major, Op. 110, mvt. 1, mm. 1–5.

M. 9. Sing the melody; project.

M. 12. Lightly. Think of keeping the weight of the arm back by the elbow. Use the soft pedal. Be aware of the direction and movement of your arm. Allow the arm to move gently with the direction of the notes. Hear each A♭, then each G [m. 13], then each A♭ [m. 14], et cetera.

M. 13. The arm follows the pattern.

M. 17. But there's a *crescendo*. That F [in the bass] would be the low point, a "start," wouldn't it?

Mm. 19–20. I don't like that *ritardando*. He doesn't ask for one. Now, I want you to take a tiny break, a breath, a split second of time at the *subito piano*. [Pressler sings it.] Minimize that break. It is a dynamic break in which you learn how to create a *crescendo* that goes nearly to a *forte*, and all of a sudden it goes to a *piano*. And can the foot be clear so that it doesn't swim? And now can you do the last four notes [m. 19] so that you don't give me a feeling of *ritardando*?

M. 20. The right hand is pristine, exactly in tempo, not slow, and the melodic shape goes down.

M. 22. Gentle; this is a variation.

M. 24. You see that is *crescendo*, and what is interesting is that usually you would go down from the G to the F, but this time you don't because you don't want to give away the *subito piano* in the next bar.

Mm. 25–26. First, it's *subito piano*, then the left hand gives us the beat with the start of the trills, and the right hand plays off of the trills. Don't have false accents.

M. 27. Play those right-hand notes with the arm.

M. 28. Be aware of the distance from the B♭ to the G. Express it.

Example 3.32. Sonata in A-flat Major, Op. 110, mvt. 1, mm. 25–28.

Mm. 28–31. Play the left hand so that it seems natural. Notice that he goes up three times in the right hand, each time higher [E♭, B♭, C]. You can see that the intention is that he *crescendos* within each line. Go toward the *sforzando*. Don't *ritardando* into it.

M. 32. That high E♭ is the softest point.

M. 33. The chromatic line *crescendos* and then diminishes. I don't hear you increasing in the same proportion to your *diminuendo*. And let us hear from the B♭ [last four notes of the scale] as a preparation for beat 3. Now, the up-beat [last sixteenth of the measure] to the *dolce*. There is a difference in color between the upbeat and the downbeat.

M. 34. Although it doesn't say that, go up on the F-G to the A♭, because you'll need to come down to the G [m. 35].

M. 35. It's a duet. In beat 2 he creates a *crescendo* within you without having to say it.

M. 36. Pace it like you're climbing up steps. The right hand rises to the top.

M. 37. Rise all the way to the top, then *diminuendo* [m. 38].

M. 38. A "bell-like" sound on the E♭.

Mm. 39–40. Feel the D♭ to the C. Have a slight hesitation between the D♭ and the C, because that can easily become a *piano*. But the *crescendo* actually begins between the two of them, so the F minor chord is not a fallback in dynamics.

M. 40. In tempo immediately.

M. 44. There is no *crescendo* in the first measure of each phrase, only in the second. Practice the left hand alone.

M. 45. Not slower.

M. 48. Color the new key [D♭ major].

M. 49. Project the top voice [G♭-E♭].

M. 51. Tension [on beat one].

M. 52. Find a new sound [on the downbeat].

M. 54. No *crescendo*.

M. 55. Lift the foot a few times after that G. Let the B♭ trill hang in the air a moment before it slides into the B, and diminish a little bit going into the B♮. [Pressler says he uses 3-1 and then 3-2 on the B♭, then 3-1 on the B♮.]

M. 56. It's the Recap, but don't land on the downbeat. It's not a downbeat that says, "ONE!"

M. 57. You should retract your left thumb each time so that you don't stretch your hand so much. Don't try to hold onto all the notes.

Example 3.33. Sonata in A-flat Major, Op. 110, mvt. 1, mm. 56–57.

M. 59. Be clear about the D♯ going to the D♭. It's a natural flow going into measure 60 [C-B♭-A♭]. It's a continuation, not a *ritardando*.

M. 60. The right hand begin *pianissimo* again.

M. 61. Why do you make a *diminuendo*? That is a *crescendo*, so it takes you into a higher sphere of consciousness.

M. 62. It's an emotional high. I don't hear a relationship between the sixteenths and the thirty-seconds; you have three tempi in the same measure. I obviously want you to be sensitive, but to be sensitive you don't have to distort the piece. It leads into measure 63, but I want it rounded out with the dynamics, not with a *ritardando*.

M. 65. Don't let the accompaniment sound like an accordion: "ooh-pah-pah-pah."

Mm. 66–67. Change the color going from D♭ to C♯.

M. 68. With greater sensitivity—that's down to the B♮.

M. 75. No *ritardando*.

M. 76. A natural breath between the ideas to begin this measure. Delicate, and in the same tempo. We must hear the sixteenths. And you know that C♯-B-A goes a little down, and then A♯-B goes back up again.

M. 77. Come down from G♯ to G, and then settle into E♭ major [m. 78].

M. 78. Intensify the sixteenth-note octaves.

M. 79. This is a release from the tension. Absolutely no slurring—pure and pristine.

M. 81. With even rhythm.

M. 85. Not too loud too soon.

M. 86. You're going to the E♭.

M. 87. Be careful with your pedal, so we hear the left hand A♭-A♭, G-G, F-F, yes?

M. 90. "Out" after the *sforzando* chord.

M. 91. The *crescendo* is just beginning.

M. 92. It doesn't get slower; it just comes down.

M. 94. Follow the line toward the long note—and not slower.

M. 95. "Taste" each note.

M. 100. I feel that it is the chord on the second beat that he is reaching for, so I would move the *diminuendo* to that chord so that we can come down from there. But don't hit; lean into it.

M. 101. Not hard; don't fall into that second beat.

M. 104. Now release the body completely on the E♭ chord. That is like a benediction and it is the open fifth in the left hand that says that to us. Then feel how you have a cadence in the left hand to the A♭ chord? Make a resolution.

Example 3.34. Sonata in A-flat Major, Op. 110, mvt. 1, mm. 101–104.

M. 105. Not such a long pedal at the end of the bar. No more than four notes per pedal. Then resolve to the E♭ chord [m. 106].

M. 110. No *accelerando* and no *ritardando*!

M. 111. A warm chord. Listen to how the melody is enriched by the new lines.

M. 112. Can the left hand come in without hitting? And use that like an opening so that we have a little more of the E♭-C.

M. 113. Is it possible to have a *subito piano*? *Legato* A♮-B♭-C-D♭. At the end, go to the lower A♭ [m. 114].

M. 114. No, not an accent; it is an ending; then you build. Be careful that there is beautiful balance between the hands where it is so widely spaced. Feel the balance between your arms.

M. 115. This is the arrival. Then the A♭ chords are "out," "out."

Mvt. 2. *Allegro molto*

M. 1. This C relates exactly to what came before, but otherwise we have a complete contrast in mood with this movement's extreme contrasts. It's *molto legato*.

M. 8. The *sforzando* isn't harsh, but it pokes at us. He doesn't just end the phrase graciously.

Mm. 11–16. Here he has these harsh, stubborn accents which are against the beat.

Mm. 17–24. Here's where Beethoven introduces the popular song, "Ich bin liderlich, du bist liderlich, wir sind liderliche Leute," meaning, "I'm a bum. You're a bum. We all are bums." Capture the rolicking, bawdy flavor of that tune.

Mm. 37–38. He makes us wait for the ending.

Mm. 39–40. Then he closes it and immediately interrupts.

M. 43. At the Trio, you must play with perfect control, but the effect is wild and crazy. It's almost like Webern or another contemporary composer.

Example 3.35. Sonata in A-flat Major, Op. 110, mvt. 2, mm. 41–72.

Example 3.35. (*continued*)

M. 148. He uses this Coda to slow us down, calm us, to put everything back into place.

M. 162. That F hangs in the air. We hear it even after you've released the pedal, and it connects us to the third movement.

Mvt. 3. *Adagio, ma non troppo*

M. 1. The difficulty with this sonata starts when you play well. At that point, it becomes difficult, because it's not sufficient to play well. Right off the bat, you played wrong rhythm in the first two notes [m. 1]. Can you play the accompaniment *pianissimo*—really *pianissimo*? The chords must be very light so that you are accompanying the melody. The B♭ going to the C♭ [m. 2] would *decrescendo*.

M. 2. Not so fast on the big stretch [to beat 3]. Think of the difficulty of singing that line or playing it on any instrument other than a keyboard.

M. 3. And the E♭ chord is the finish.

M. 4. It's *più adagio*; it's slower than you've been playing. Yes, you keep the pedal, but also, I'd like you to keep your left hand there holding that chord. Why do you make a *crescendo* on the B♭-D♭-F♭? You have to be able to play that phrase very touchingly. Now, at the *Andante*, how big is that *crescendo*? It doesn't go to a *forte*. What it does is that it emphasizes the tension that is in there. And the release is the downbeat of measure 5. When he starts there it is a release.

M. 5. Then that would be less, but you play this as part of the *crescendo*. Play the upper note less and without a hit. This note is for him what you used to have on the clavichord; the note has a *bebung*. It is "*da* da, *da* da, *da* da," not "da, da, da, da, da." So the second one is always less. Even in the *crescendo*, it is always less. Why don't you keep that chord [B major] in the left hand?

M. 7. Those two notes [A♭-E♭] are the end; it is a *recitativo*. In an opera, and here too, he is writing out a *recitativo*. And now the repeated E♭s are a new start. Can you do it in such a way that it is like the accompanist who is waiting for the singer to come in? It's not so pronounced.

M. 9. Now the singer joins in.

M. 12. Can you hear the C♭ [beat 1] going to the B♭ [beat 3] without the other notes? You're making those notes too important. The last two notes [C♭-D♭] are part of the *decrescendo*.

M. 20. You can do the D♮ easier in the right hand.

M. 21. Can we hear the right hand as two voices? Shape the alto voice.

M. 24. Finish on the A♭. This is where Beethoven says, "You're going to be okay, everything's going to be all right."

M. 25. Here I would advise you to take that second octave in the right hand so that you can control it. And then feel the cadence coming down.

M. 26. Now, if you play as softly as you played it that time, then you have to live with that, and your fugue starts on that level. Of all the fugues that Beethoven wrote, one can even take Bach's included, this is the most positive one, the most triumphant. It is one in which he says, "I really had a good life. I did what I was put on earth to do." Imagine, this fugue that is unbelievably positive. But it starts from nowhere into that great moment, yes?

M. 34. This B♭ would actually be coming down from the previous C. The B♭ would be less than the theme in inflection.

M. 37. No *crescendo*; there are no swells. In this music, where he's thought about everything, the swell that you did right now is something that is outside your jurisdiction. His words have to be announced the way he does it. He's building; he's waiting. The only thing is now you have three voices, so naturally it's a little bit more because the top voice has to be projected. But you can't do your swell; you must be more religious, yes?

M. 42. Now less [beat 2].

M. 44. Now it builds, but not faster just because it's loud.

M. 53. Can you enhance that middle voice?

Mm. 57–58. Come down and down.

Mm. 66–70. Go up, and more, and more to the top [A♭].

M. 71. And now it comes down.

M. 73. The thing that I miss that you should have is that you must feel you are imperious. The emperor of Japan comes in, yes? That entrance is grandiose, and when you play it you must feel grandiose. [Pressler sings the theme, measures 73–75]. He is talking here; it's direct to humanity. With you, the piece is there; but it's a Xerox copy. It doesn't have blood. And that's what we need— that it has blood.

Mm. 81–86. Now here, what I would like you to feel is like on an organ. You pull out the stops and it's loud; you push in the stops and it's soft. That's what he does here. It's like on an organ.

M. 87. Now, what I would like is that when you go up, you have a *diminuendo*, so that the middle voice can comes out.

Mm. 95–97. Less and less. Follow it down.

M. 98. It starts again, and you must feel the tension that the syncopation creates.

M. 110. Start the trill from the note—not above.

M. 116. He says, "*Ermattet,*" exhausted, completely. He has no more strength. And "*klagend*" is complaining, not like our word complaining, but when you cry that something has died. "*Dolente,*" with pain, and with the last strength that he has. This line comes down. [Pressler plays D-C-B♭-A-G-F♯

up to the Eb.] This is very painful, yes? It is sighing, with a great deal of inner pain. And feel the pulsing of the left hand.

Example 3.36. Sonata in A-flat Major, Op. 110, mvt. 3, mm. 116–117.

M. 122. More. Now, what I would like is that you play less after he reaches so far out, then he comes down [F-D]. It is a very great change of direction. It's like a catch in the voice.

Mm. 125–126. The second note is less each time.

M. 131. Finish on the G.

M. 132. Now suddenly you can see the sky. It's dark, and all of a sudden you can see it opening up.

M. 135. The same tempo, and the first notes are quite loud.

M. 136. I would use the soft pedal.

M. 160. Not loud. The maximum would be *piano* when you start that entrance.

Mm. 152–160. Practice those two lower lines without the fugue on top.

Example 3.37. Sonata in A-flat Major, Op. 110, mvt. 3, mm. 152–160.

Mm. 159–160. The two lines follow each other down.

M. 161. Save.

Mm. 171–174. Not suddenly faster.

Mm. 179–182. Sing the line. You play them all alike. And can you bring out the *sforzandi* above the regular *fortes*?

M. 194. More. Use your arm.

Mm. 201–209. Plan your dynamics. Each *sforzando* is more until the maximum at measure 209.

M. 210. Take those first six notes with the left hand.

4   Johannes Brahms

Brahms created magnificent pieces with tremendous character and variety. He created a new technique, and many people said it was written against the piano, not for the piano. He was really a master at that time, like Mendelssohn, a craftsman—when you see how carefully the pieces are written, how he refined them, what a perfectionist he was in his attitude to these pieces. And he uses his language, which is so similar to today's language in music. I mean, with Brahms we feel completely at home, speaking in his language, using his vocabulary. What was once said was written against the piano seems so absolutely normal and natural now.

Variations on a Theme of Paganini, Op. 35, Bk. 1

Mm. 1–2. Theme. Not as big as Brahms yet lighter. The As and Es should be like "vibrato" with longer pedal. React to the As, and lead to the Es.

M. 4. Relate the Es. Either *crescendo* or *decrescendo* or take time.

Example 4.1. Variations on a Theme of Paganini, Op. 35, Bk. 1, mm. 1–4.

Mm. 5–8. Say it differently; say, "This has already been said once."

Mm. 9–16. Give room for new possibilities.

M. 17. *Piano.*

M. 24. Hear the first A relating to the top A.

M. 25. Variation 1. It's Brahms now—therefore fuller, immediately different. Give yourself room at end of phrases, as in measures 28 and 32. No holes. Much more pedal.

M. 26. Phrase from the last G# into measure 27.

M. 39. Touches of pedal on beats 1 and 3.

M. 40. Come down.

M. 48. End positive [*crescendo*] leading to variation 2.

M. 49. Variation 2. The *sforzando* is more in the right hand than in the left hand. The right hand is one impulse. The left hand fills in at end of bars leading to the right-hand *sforzando*. Use the last sixteenth to lead to measure 50.

M. 52. Keep the left-hand thumb close to the key.

M. 53. Contrast; start from nowhere, *con pedal*. Use the last sixteenth to lead to the next measure.

M. 56. Pull back in tempo.

Mm. 63–64. Relate D-E-D, E-D, E-D and resolve B to C.

M. 69. Stay light.

M. 72. Close the phrase.

M. 73. Variation 3. The right hand comes out of the key fast, and hard, and up. The left hand catches the bounce of key.

M. 77. Lean on first note of the octave in both hands. *Con pedal.*

Example 4.2. Variations on a Theme of Paganini, Op. 35, Bk. 1, mm. 77–78.

M. 89. *Con pedal.* Lean into the first right-hand note.

M. 97. Variation 4. Two-measure phrases; start less and *crescendo*. Try 5-1-4-1 in the left hand. Drill the right-hand [m. 97] and left-hand [m. 101] trills together.

M. 99. A new start.

M. 121. Variation 5. Rich "Intermezzo" sound of the right hand. Tympani detached notes in the left hand. Hear the left-hand chromatic scale, and "touch" the top notes of the left hand [E, F, F#, G, etc.].

Mm. 145–146. Variation 6. Relate the two measures.

M. 147. Take time.

M. 148. *A tempo.*

M. 149. Variation 7. Not so fast. Use the last three eighths to lead to a *sforzando*.

M. 151. No *sforzando* this time. Lead from the octaves—therefore, two-measure phrases, not segmented.

Mm. 161–163. *Legato* left-hand octaves.

M. 165. Variation 8. Drill the left hand "blind." Touch the pedal to each left-hand octave.

M. 181. Variation 9. Same tempo as variation 8. A dramatic *forte/pianissimo*. Repeated octaves. Not *tremolo*. Practice repeated octaves alone for continuity, and keep them "in the key."

M. 182. Dramatic.

M. 194. Variation 10. Left-hand finger *staccato*.

M. 217. Pull back.

M. 218. Variation 11. Not sudden. Like a music box. The hands are like two different instruments. The right hand plays harmonies. The left hand has a rich sound. Full of continuous pedal, especially covering up the returns [ends of mm. 2, 4, 6, 8]. Follow the threads of melody. Use right-hand fingers only—no arm. Rhythmic flow with the sixteenths.

M. 222. Now both hands playing the same quiet instrument.

M. 233. Use 3-5 for the trill. Let go of the lower notes [B and E].

M. 234. Variation 12. The left hand is always the leader. Use rich sound in the left hand so as to hear the canon. Shape to the F♯.

Mm. 238–245. Express these right-hand stretches.

M. 246. Variation 13. Have a bite on the graced octaves. Get out of key at the end of the measure to get to next position.

Mm. 249, 254, 256. Don't stop the *glissandi*. The thumb leads. Stay light and don't get stuck.

Mm. 250–251. Bind the two measures.

M. 257b. [the second ending] The last octave has charm—a smile, not a grimace.

M. 258. Variation 14. Continuous thirty-seconds with upbeats from group to group. The right-hand thirty-seconds and eighths are trumpets. *Crescendo* to the octave, and bite with an accent.

M. 261. A big *crescendo* on the last four thirty-seconds.

Mm. 266–267. You can *diminuendo* if you want, but the A♭ of measure 27 must have the accent as marked.

M. 272. Take time before the jumps in both hands.

M. 279. Pull back as the octaves begin. He says "*poco sostenuto*."

M. 281. Pull back as the octaves near the top. Then *a tempo* after the *fermata*.

Mm. 282, 284. Inflect down.

Mm. 286–287. Slur each beat.

M. 288. Pull back before the *sforzando* of measure 289.

Mm. 296–299. Like *campanella*. It must sound different from the rest.

M. 307. *Decrescendo*.

Mm. 309, 311. Use the last eighth to lead to the next measure.

M. 332. Accented.

M. 335. Start.

M. 338. Take time at the end.

M. 339. The last chord is a *sforzando*.

Klavierstücke, Op. 76

No. 1. *Capriccio* in F-sharp Minor

M. 1. He says "*due corde*," so begin with the soft pedal. Play the fifth, sixth, and seventh notes with the right hand. What you do wrong is that you don't treat that F♯-A leap as if it's a climb; you treat it as if it's on the same level. There is a rise—not even dynamically so much as emotionally. He goes from a dark A to a higher F♯, and it's the same in every measure no matter what the notes are. We do it with an easier fingering, which means we use the right hand instead of the left. But try it once with the left hand; see how you have to stretch? So now do it with the right hand and still feel that stretch. It's not one hand and the other hand; it's one line. You must lay out the melody for the people who have not heard it before.

M. 2. That little swell brings you back down.

Example 4.3. *Capriccio* in F-sharp Minor, Op. 76, No. 1, mm. 1–3.

M. 6. I would say you should only reach a *mezzo piano* by this point.

M. 8. *Poco sostenuto* on the *rinforzando*. He sits on that note.

Mm. 9–11. It climbs. From the second C♯ in the right hand, hold the pedal all the way. No accents within the *fortissimo*. Go all the way to the bottom of the line.

M. 12. Don't you have dots on these notes, dots under slurs? It's a special touch.

M. 13. End about *mezzo forte*.

M. 14. The accompaniment doesn't get a swell.

M. 16. Rich thirds.

M. 21. Still with volume—and no *ritard*. But the C♯ is sticking out.

M. 24. Don't stop on the A.

Mm. 29–30. You have the F♯-F♮-E in the bass.

M. 36. The A comes down from the B.

Mm. 38–39. Come down to the F♯.

Mm. 39–40. Have a slight hairpin swell to the C♯ within the *diminuendo*.

M. 40. The C♯ is not a new start; it's continuous.

M. 41. End about *mezzo forte*.

M. 47. Don't accent the G♯. It's a new start.

M. 48. Relax the arms, relax the body, and come in with all the weight on the A⁷ chord.

M. 50. Play the second C♯ with strength.

M. 51. I would use the left hand to play that B.

Mm. 54–55. Treat the left-hand sixteenth lines as melody.

Mm. 60–63. It's still in a 6/8. It's churning, churning.

M. 63. Release the pedal for the rests.

M. 64. Still in tempo, not slower. Let's hear where the heartbeat is. It's in the left hand, not the right hand. [Pressler snaps his finger to maintain the tempo.]

M. 65. No accent on the E♯; it comes down.

Example 4.4. *Capriccio* in F-sharp Minor, Op. 76, No. 1, mm. 64–67.

Mm. 72–73. The left hand must be very expressive, and the right hand should be more natural so you don't hang on it and tear it to pieces. Don't climb. Relax your shoulders.

Mm. 74–75. Not faster.

Mm. 80–81. Have the slightest *ritard*.

Mm. 81–82. Hear the octaves between the hands [D-C♯-D-C♯].

Mm. 84–85. Make a *diminuendo* between the two last chords. Play the bass A♯ with the right hand.

No. 2. *Capriccio* in B Minor

M. 2. Sustain the Bs.

M. 4. Sustain the Es.

Mm. 7–8. Let us hear the inner line.

Example 4.5. *Capriccio* in B Minor, Op. 76, No. 2, mm. 7–10.

M. 13 [The second ending is measure 13.]
M. 15. *Mezzo piano.*
M. 19. Hear both lower parts.
Mm. 27–28. *Diminuendo* to the *piano.*

Example 4.6. *Capriccio* in B Minor, Op. 76, No. 2, mm. 27–29.

M. 31. Still *piano.*
Mm. 45–46. Resolve to the B major.
Mm. 59–60. Don't rush.
Mm. 67–68. Use a full pedal on each measure.
M. 69. A clear left hand.
M. 84. *Decrescendo.*
M. 85. Still *allegretto non troppo.*
Mm. 95–96. All notes are short in both hands.
M. 103. The alto is always sustained.
M. 116. "*Due corde*" but use only halfway down.
M. 121. The last note [F♯] is an important note.

No. 3. *Intermezzo* in A-flat Major

M. 1. The left hand is like plucked strings; the right hand is sustained woodwinds. The right hand, although it is syncopated, is played with a great deal of expression, so you have to play it with more *legato*. And since he tells us to play "*espressivo*," I would play the right hand at least in *mezzo forte*. In the broken A♭-E♭ [left hand], the E♭ is lighter.

Example 4.7. *Intermezzo* in A-flat Major, Op. 76, No. 3, mm. 1–2.

Mm. 4–5. There are four sequences, and an E♭ is different from an F.

M. 5. A different color than measure 5.

M. 10. Play the lower two notes of the last chord with the left hand. And finish.

M. 11. Let me hear the high D♭, and I don't think you need the left foot down. He returns twice to the D♭ before going to the E♭, so it's a kind of climb.

Mm. 13–14. Now it's F, then A♭, and finally the C.

Mm. 13–15. Pedal by the measure.

M. 20. Close the phrase.

M. 30. Play the last two chords within the same pedal.

No. 4. *Intermezzo* in B-flat Major

M. 1. It a singing *piano*. It isn't Haydn, but you don't have to hit. The left hand should sound natural; use 2-1-5.

M. 4. The left hand G is sustained and becomes a solo.

M. 5. The F finishes, and the bass melody continues.

Example 4.8. *Intermezzo* in B-flat Major, Op. 76, No. 4, mm. 1–6.

M. 8. An echo.

M. 13. You begin too "real," too present. This should be more like a breeze.

M. 17. Why do you sit there [on the A]? It ends here [m. 19].

M. 20. The new melody sings.

M. 25. He uses head voice. Surprise us. A violinist would do a slide there.

M. 26. Don't hit the B♭. It's continuing.

Mm. 27–31. Practice the right hand omitting the sixteenths. And now omitting the octave line.

M. 32. Coming down.

M. 36. Don't hit that G. Fold it into the line.

M. 41. You're already *pianissimo* here, but it should be at least *piano*. You can be sensitive to that D, but don't take away from the beautiful ending; you'll have nothing left there.

M. 44. How can we have a beautiful phrase if you always stop before the downbeat?

M. 45. Not early on that pickup. And we must have the *pianissimo*.
M. 50. In principle, it should *decrescendo*.

Example 4.9. *Intermezzo* in B-flat Major, Op. 76, No. 4, mm. 49–51.

No. 5. *Capriccio* in C-sharp Minor

M. 1. *Agitato, ma non troppo presto*, yes? He gives you everything you need to
know. It's in 6/8, but it's divided into three beats, so you're excited even before you begin to play.

Mm. 1–8. It's a beautiful long line, a melody. [Pressler plays the single line
melody—first harsh and unmusical, then beautifully shaped.]

M. 4. Less on that C♯ than the one in measure 3.

Example 4.10. *Capriccio* in C-sharp Minor, Op. 76, No. 5, mm. 1–4.

Mm. 13–14. Let me hear the inner voices [C♯-B].

Mm. 31–32. Hear the melody [C♯-G♯-A♯, B-F♯-G♯, A♯-E♯-F♯♯]. More classic in
rhythm.

Mm. 33–35. It starts again from here. Not faster. And hear the changes in these
three measures. When you make a *crescendo* you always seem to run, but you
don't have to.

Example 4.11. *Capriccio* in C-sharp Minor, Op. 76, No. 5, mm. 33–35.

M. 37. There's more sound this time.

Mm. 41–44. Now we have more of these inner notes. Play the two melodies without the bass.

M. 43. Brahms doesn't give you a swell in those notes—just the opposite.

M. 52. It says *piano, tranquillo*, but yours is noisy, excited. It should be sensitive.

M. 59. Now finish.

M. 76. Not holding back. Always more.

Mm. 80–81. Hear C♯-B-A♯ coming down.

M. 82. This would be again a start. The series of *sforzandi* means to *crescendo*.

Mm. 90–91. A loose arm for the resolution to E.

M. 93. Close it.

M. 95. *Espressivo*.

Mm. 97–99. Each one is a different level.

Mm. 107–108. Gradually slower.

M. 110. Begin slower. You should hear C♯-D♯-E-E♯, et cetera.

M. 117. Keep your hands on the keys, then release hands and foot at the same time.

No. 6. *Intermezzo* in A Major

Mm. 1–2. It's too loud; it's too heavy. Look at the orchestration. The first time he has the left-hand octave, then he has the fifth or third. But you play them the same way. *Sanft bewegt* is "gently animated." It's always *piano* with a *decrescendo*. [Pressler sings the phrase.] First it's E to D, then B down to A.

M. 2. Now a different color for the repeated phrase—*più piano*.

Example 4.12. *Intermezzo* in A Major, Op. 76, No. 6, mm. 1–3.

M. 5. The left-hand octaves are *legato*.

M. 6. Not fast.

M. 16. *Dolce* is tender, sweetly, gently.

Mm. 19–20. That's too heavy; I would say he's going for a maximum of *mezzo forte*.

M. 32. In time.

M. 33. Hear how F♯ minor relates to the A major. It's within the A major, yes?

Mm. 33–36. Now, anytime in music, unless the composer asks for something else, when he comes down, you go down. If he falls, you fall with him.

M. 36. The F♯ is the finishing note for one voice, and the C♯ is the beginning note for the upper voice.

Example 4.13. *Intermezzo* in A Major, Op. 76, No. 6, mm. 33–36.

M. 37. The E is a new note in the bass.

M. 40. Beat 2 is the resolution of beat 1, then the thirds bring you home again [to F♯ minor in m. 42].

M. 42. A new start.

M. 53. No swell here because of the big *crescendo* that's coming.

Mm. 57–58. Your right hand has two voices.

M. 67. Very sensitively.

Mm. 98–99. Have enough D so that it goes to the C♯, and the G♯ goes to the A and resolves.

M. 100. He couldn't be clearer. He wants a rest, not a sustained chord.

No. 7. *Intermezzo* in A Minor

Mm. 1–4. So let's have a difference between the two phrases; it's a little more when you start.

Moderato semplice

Example 4.14. *Intermezzo* in A Minor, Op. 76, No. 7, mm. 1–4.

M. 8. The motion must be within the framework. You can go a little bit faster but not so much faster that there's no connection.

M. 10. It's a finish and a start. Play the lower note in such a way that it ends.

Mm. 13–15. I want you to notice that you are going to a G♯ with an F, then a G♯ with an F♯, then an A♭ with a G.

Example 4.15. *Intermezzo* in A Minor, Op. 76, No. 7, mm. 13–16.

M. 24. In that chord, the G is beginning a phrase, but the E is ending one.

M. 25. We have to hear you breathe.

M. 26. Hear the melody beginning on that G.

Mm. 29–30. Not faster.

M. 31. Now Brahms always gives us this *crescendo* on a note after we've already played it; that's very difficult to do! In reality, it's impossible, but it's not impossible to feel. So when you play that, you feel it.

M. 32. The F♯ has to go to the E.

M. 43. You hear the left hand coming up with a D, D♯, E.

Mm. 47–48. Now, it runs out—all the way to the rest.

Mm. 53–54. The left hand octaves must be *legato*.

M. 55. A color change. And again do that swell which Brahms asks; it's in your attitude, in your relationship.

No. 8. *Capriccio* in C Major

Mm. 1–3. The notes swirl and form an arabesque. We hear the line leading up, F-F#-G-G#-A, and this is before his *crescendo* begins.

Example 4.16. *Capriccio* in C Major, Op. 76, No. 8, mm. 1–3.

M. 5. That C begins another phrase.
M. 16. [The second ending is measure 16.]
Mm. 20–21. He asks for the thirds and sixths to be *dolce*. We would expect that.
M. 33. Color that chord.
M. 38. Use the full arm to support those notes.
Mm. 47–48. It begins to grow as you reach for the As. Each A is a different color.
Mm. 60–61. Very gentle between the hands.
Mm. 62–63. This is the first time the eighth-note motion is missing.
Mm. 64–66. Look how he writes in an *accelerando*.

Example 4.17. *Capriccio* in C Major, Op. 76, No. 8, mm. 64–66.

Mm. 66–68. You can keep these three chords in one pedal. And it's an "up," "down."

Intermezzo in A Major, Op. 118, No. 2

M. 1. In principle, an *Andante* should not be hurried. The opening thirds are played toward the downbeat. Hear the bass A going down to the lower A. There is an inner dynamic to those four eighths, and they *decrescendo* so beat 3 can enter.

Mm. 1–4. He waits, then there's measure 2. He waits, then in measures 3 and 4 there is motion. Take the sentence to completion.

Example 4.18. *Intermezzo*, Op. 118, No. 2, mm. 1–4.

M. 2. The top and bottom As should come together, and there should more arm weight in the top A. Don't take so much time on the F♯. [They practice omitting the F♯ to hear how the timing must be.] The four eighths go down [*decrescendo*], so the new line can begin.

M. 4. Now he has a *decrescendo*. But have a little emphasis on the downbeat so the G♯ can be less. Hear the left-hand slurs taking you down dynamically to the G♮.

M. 6. Lean in; love that chord! Beat 3 must match the decay from beat 1.

M. 8. Don't throw beat 3 away; start the phrase again.

M. 15. No accent on the downbeat; it flows to beat 2.

M. 20. The E is a melody note.

M. 23. Sink into the F♯ with your arm.

M. 24. The G♯ decays; that determines the volume of the F♯.

M. 25. Start with the G♯; rise to the A♯ [m. 26], then the B [m. 27], then the C♯ [m. 28].

Mm. 29–30. Stretch the B to the A to create the climax.

M. 30. The right-hand A and the left-hand D must come together.

M. 33. Color the G♮.

M. 34. In breaking the chord, feel the stretch.

Mm. 42–44. Hear the bass line: G♯-F♯, E-D, C♯-B.

M. 45. A free arm over the top.

M. 48. Play the C♯ in the same pedal. Then lift. The C♯ is the link; it is part of the A chord, then it becomes part of the F♯ chord.

Mm. 49–52. [They practice the shaping of the tenor canon line, especially the sighs in measures 50–52.]

Example 4.19. *Intermezzo*, Op. 118, No. 2, mm. 49–52.

M. 55. The C♯ is less than the E [m. 54].

M. 56. Pedal the C♯ the same way as in measure 48.

M. 57. Hear the canon between the top of the right hand and the top of the left hand.

M. 59. Lean into that chord on beat 3 so it can resolve.

M. 64. The C♯ is the link again.

M. 65. Which is the principal voice? Don't you think it's the inner part that takes the melody to completion?

M. 69. When you spread your wings [C♯-C♯-B-A], take a little time, and the sixths are *legato*.

M. 72. There's no *ritardando* here. Come down in dynamics, but come down rich, and only come down to *mezzo forte*.

M. 74. This first *piano* I would say is *mezzo piano*—a rich *piano*.

M. 76. The *pianissimo* is a whisper.

M. 88. The F major chord is a start again.

Interlude III
Poor Pianos

Once when we went to a little town for a community concert and they picked us up at the rail station, the lady who was at the hotel waiting for us said, "Here's the address of the high school where you're playing. We've brought in a piano. I wish you well, but listen: in case something is not in order, we've got the best tuner. Just call him." So I go to practice, and I see there's this one key doesn't play. That happens sometimes. So I call the tuner, and he arrives and says, "Don't worry; I will fix it. You go rest and come back later." So I went to rest, and I came back to the concert and I found a little note on the piano in which he said, "I tried to fix it. I couldn't. Please don't use that note too much."

Another time I was playing on tour with the Royal Philharmonic with Dorati conducting. We played one night the Schumann Concerto, one night Grieg, one night Schumann, one night Grieg, and we were playing in a big outdoor venue in New Jersey, right next to New York. This venue uses the Baldwin piano, but I was a Steinway artist. So I get a telephone call from Steinway: "Menahem, Byron Janis is going to play down there. He will select a piano, he will use it, and then you can use it." Perfect, because I like his selection. I liked his sonority; I liked his sound. So Dorati says to me, "Menahem, we're playing Schumann again this afternoon, and we don't need a rehearsal. I will pick you up, we'll drive down there, play the concert, and we'll come back and have a nice dinner in New York." So we get there, and the orchestra plays the *Russlan and Ludmila* Overture; they push out the piano, and it's time for the Schumann (he sings the opening), and we come to the second theme, and it's "C, A, tock, tock." The middle A is not playing. The entire orchestra including Dorati started laughing. And he leans over to me and he says, "Do you want to stop and we'll get the other piano?" I said, "No, let's keep going." Today I would of course say, "Yes." I would stop myself whether or not he stopped me. I don't know what drove me to say that. And it was just like you read sometimes of someone in the war who has his arm shot off; he still feels the arm. I started hearing that A as if it was right there. And it's interesting that later I ran into Mr. [William H.] Scheide, who was the man who directed the Bach Aria Group. He was at the concert, and he said after a while he started to hear the A too. That is a true story.

Another time, early in the Trio's existence, was at the University of Illinois, which is where the cellist Raya Garbousova taught. She was Paul Biss's stepmother and a friend of Bernie's [Greenhouse], so we spent the day at her house. We ate well, and drank well, and at seven o'clock we go over to the hall, and there are three chairs, no piano. So I said, "Where is the piano?"

The stage manager said, "What piano?"

I said, "We are a piano trio."

He said, "No, you have been advertised as a string trio." So he has three chairs and three stands.

I asked, "Do you have a piano?"

"Yes," he says, "the piano is in the pit, but it's not tuned."

I said, "Okay, bring it up."

He said, "It is seven o'clock; there is nobody that can bring up the piano." So he looks at me and asks, "Can you play in the pit and they play on stage?"

I said, "No, we can't do that."

He says, "Can you all three play in the pit?"

I said, "No, we can't do that."

He goes down in front of the audience, and he says, "We need some strong people to help us bring up the piano."

Well, you know, you're in a university town; you immediately have plenty of volunteers. So they gather around the piano, and he says, "And one, and two, and three," and they lift it up. And he says, "Let it go," and they let it go, and the pedals fall off. So we ask if there's a tuner. Of course, there's not a tuner, and I played that concert without pedals. I played Ravel Trio without the pedals! So I really paid for the sins I had committed with the pedal before the concert, and during the concert, and into eternity. As long as I play the piano, I can sin on the pedal; it will be forgiven, because I paid it in advance.

During the Trio's first year, we came to a concert hall in Kansas, and I said to the manager, "Where is the piano I'm playing on?"

He said, "You play on this upright piano."

I said, "Do all the soloists play on this piano?"

He says, "No, for a soloist we bring a grand piano, but for an accompanist we bring this one."

Bernie Greenhouse and Daniel Guilet brought their Stradivarius cello and violin, and I played an upright!

Once we were playing the Ravel Trio and the damper pedal gets stuck. The sound just keeps getting louder and louder, and Izzy [Isidore Cohen] and Bernie look over at me like I've gone crazy or something. So we ask the audience if there was anybody who happened to be a piano tuner in the house. No such luck. Bernie likes to fiddle with things, so he gets down on the floor with his rear facing the audience, tux tails flapping, and starts trying to get the pedal to work. No luck. We call for an intermission, and luckily a man comes up and says he used to be a piano tuner and he'd give it a try. And he fixed it and we started the Ravel all over again.

And another one, which is really a funny story: I was playing with Isler Solomon in Columbus, Ohio. Again the Schumann Concerto, and in the middle of the last movement, the pedals fell off. So I had to decide: Do I stop, which meant I had to play the entire concerto again, or just suffer and play through it? [He sings the concluding section.] So I played without the pedal. And we were walking off stage, and Isler had his arm around my shoulder, and he says, "You know, Menahem, I've never heard you play so clean." So I'm suffering; I don't have pedal, and he loved it. These are all absolutely true stories.

5 Frédéric Chopin

Chopin is a composer that I feel very close to, and I play him with pleasure. His music is so complete, you couldn't add a note to it. It's perfect. The challenge for the sensitivity, the challenge to the virtuosity, the challenge to hold it together is enormous. And it takes something out of you. But in return, it gives you so much. You really feel enriched. Chopin suffered. He looked for perfection, and he wrote for perfection. He spins a line, not a passage. It's Chopin's way that when he plays the softest, he says the most important things. He presents for us a huge landscape of sounds and colors. You have to practice Chopin with your soul. You must feel the message of the music. The music is the map, and we decide what we want to say in the music.

Andante Spianato and Grande Polonaise Brillante, Op. 22

Andante Spianato

M. 3. Continue to *crescendo*.

M. 4. The second half of the measure *decrescendos*. Breathe. Prepare for the right-hand entrance.

M. 5. Right hand with beautiful full tone. The D blends and matches the decay of the B, then the line increases to the F♯ [m. 6].

Example 5.1. *Andante Spianato*, Op. 22, mm. 5–6.

Mm. 7–8. To the second E.

M. 9. *Decrescendo* from the sustained E to the D. No accents.

M. 20. Listen to the left-hand line G-F♯-E.

M. 21. A new harmonic color.

M. 25. Color.

Mm. 31–32. *Crescendo* between the B and the D♯.

M. 34. *Crescendo* the left hand; the right hand comes in *forte*.

M. 36. Pull back going to the B [m. 37].

M. 41. Let us hear the top B.

M. 44. Let it play out. Breathe before the new entrance.

M. 45. Color the B.

M. 47. *Crescendo* to the chord [m. 48].

Mm. 52–53. Still *forte* till the downbeat [D-G].

M. 67. Calm. Gentle. Don't rush.

M. 78. Hear the left-hand F♯ moving to the right-hand's F♮.

M. 96. The *fermati* are suspended in air.

Mm. 99–100. The Ds are like distant wind chimes, but treat each one a little differently.

Example 5.2. *Andante Spianato*, Op. 22, mm. 97–100.

Polonaise

M. 1. Steady! Not just rhythm but sonority.

Example 5.3. *Grande Polonaise Brilliante*, Op. 22, mm. 1–4.

M. 11. Start the second eighth *mezzo forte*.

M. 24. Use the A-A♭ to reach the forte G [m. 25].

M. 30. Two-note slurs in the left hand.

M. 31. *Crescendo* to the C [downbeat of m. 32].

M. 36. Playful.

M. 47. Steady.

M. 49. *Crescendo*.

M. 51. *Subito forte* [the second eighth].

M. 57. Like a string of pearls. Don't bunch the notes.

M. 66. A little playing with the tempo. Hurry, then stretch back to tempo.

M. 75. Start. It's the orchestra.

M. 77. Up [beat one], down [beat two].

M. 78. Big *crescendo*. Clear rhythm. Ultra *legato* slurs.

M. 85. Tone. Take the B♭ in the right hand.

M. 87. As a melody, not just a scale.

M. 88. *Diminuendo*.

M. 89. Take the A♮ in the right hand.

Example 5.4. *Grande Polonaise Brilliante*, Op. 22, mm. 87–89.

M. 92. Hear the turns in the cadenza to the F♯, the D, and the B♭.

M. 96. *Crescendo*.

M. 97. *Subito forte* on the second eighth, with pedal.

M. 103. Start.

M. 106. *Decrescendo*.

M. 124. *Crescendo* with right-hand arm weight.

M. 132. All with pedal.

Mm. 133–137. With abandon.

M. 142. Use the wrist.

M. 153. The second eighth is a start.

M. 157. The second eighth starts *forte*.

M. 160. Ease up.

M. 172. Phrase to the G [downbeat of m. 173].

M. 179. *Crescendo*.

Mm. 180–181. Hear the left-hand E♭ to the D♮.

Mm. 185–186. The trill is elegant, effortless. A little swell to the trills. Not just a doorbell!

M. 222. *Crescendo* as it ascends.

M. 228. Close.

Example 5.5. *Grande Polonaise Brilliante*, Op. 22, mm. 227–228.

Mm. 230. Phrase to the B♭ of measure 231.

M. 232. Phrase to the B♭ of measure 233.

Mm. 240–241. A two-chord cadence [B♭⁷-E♭].

Mm. 255–256. A touch of pedal to each beat.

M. 256. *Decrescendo.*

M. 257. Start.

M. 261. The second eighth note is a start.

M. 269. Less. Start.

M. 276. *Crescendo* to the top.

Deux Nocturnes, Op. 27

Nocturne in C-sharp Minor, Op. 27, No. 1

Mm. 1–2. In two beats, not four. The left hand is just a murmur.

M. 3. The right hand is super *legato.*

M. 5. The F♯ resolves to the E♮.

M. 6. A little *crescendo* up to the G♯.

Mm. 6–7. Hear the left hand moving from C♯-B to D♯-C♯.

M. 10. No stop leading to the next measure.

M. 11. *Più espresso*, and the melody is a *piano* or *mezzo piano.*

M. 13. The D♮ is a special note.

M. 14. *Decrescendo* from the C♯ to the G♯. Then the new phrase is like an after-thought.

Mm. 19–26. In the duet, each line must have a distinct color. Voice them differently from each other.

Example 5.6. *Nocturne*, Op. 27, No. 1, mm. 19–23.

M. 21. No accent on the E♮.
M. 22. The sixteenths are *un poco flexible*.
M. 28. As softly as possible.
M. 29. *Pianissimo. Misterioso.*
Mm. 29–32. Hear the left-hand line [B♯, C♯, D♯, E, etc.].
M. 44. Use that last left-hand C♯ [beat 3] to build to the next chord.
M. 48. Build with the left-hand E, G♯, B.
Mm. 49–50. Hear the left hand climbing [E♭, A♭, C, E♭, A♭, C].

Example 5.7. *Nocturne*, Op. 27, No. 1, mm. 49–50.

M. 51. Slower, and with a *fermato* over the D♭.
M. 53. *Pianissimo*, and press forward as you build—*agitato*.
M. 71. The four eighths press forward.
M. 72. Still *forte*.
M. 78. Begin as lightly as possible.

M. 83. A big *crescendo* on these first octaves. A new pedal on each of the last three octaves.

M. 84. The first note is *sforzando*. Change the pedal and catch it again.

Mm. 86–87. Delicate, not a hard sound. Slur the E to the E♯.

M. 89. The sixteenths are *dolce*.

Mm. 93–94. Pull back leading to the C♯.

M. 96. The top thirds ring; the lower ones are less, muted.

Mm. 100–101. *Decrescendo* between the final G♯ and the E♯.

Nocturne in D-flat Major, Op. 27, No. 2

M. 1. This is a reach, not a jump. And continue quietly so you can hear the melody. It's *Lento sostenuto*, not hasty, a sustained slow tempo. He asks for a *piano* but a rich *piano*. It is *dolce*, which is tender, but the *piano* is rich sounding. We will use a *pianissimo* but not here. And the left hand does not change very much no matter what you do; it always has a kind of a swing. Put the pedal down before you begin, so it opens up the sound.

M. 2. Then you open it up with that melody. It should be a *cantilena*, as beautifully as you can, *bel canto*. Tender. It's not just pulling the finger. It's the weight of the arm so that you lean in with the weight of the arm. Bring the arm all the way down into the piano; that's the sound. Your left hand is driving me crazy! It's slow, tender, reverent, continuous, with no stops.

M. 3. It doesn't get faster in the left hand.

M. 4. The B♭ cannot stick out like a sore thumb. You have to hear, "What would it be like if he only went to the A♭?" Then you go farther.

M. 5. Don't hit. Lean into it. You're on the surface of the key. Go all the way down.

M. 6. No. It doesn't wait after the A♮.

Example 5.8. *Nocturne*, Op. 27, No. 2, mm. 1–6.

M. 7. The E♭ is gentle. It's not a fast turn. And start right after the beat.

M. 8. And now reach out [G♭-G♭] with the grace note coming before the beat. There's arm weight in each right-hand sixteenth. It's like you're taking steps up; use 2-3-1-3-1-3.

M. 9. And play the G in such a way that the F is a resolution. The F has to ring so that the D♭ [m. 10] underneath blends.

Mm. 10–11. What he's doing is G♭, E♭-F, E♭-D♭.

M. 11. The B♭ resolves to the A♮ [beat 5].

M. 12. The grace notes come before the beat. But let's say you do them on the beat. Even so, the weight is on the F, the melody note. Change the fingers; use 3-1, 4-2.

M. 15. Finish. Go down to start the octave line.

M. 16. [Pressler gives a fingering for the repeated notes with 2-1 playing the second of the thirds.]

M. 19. That C is still loud. And then comes the tender answer.

M. 20. I don't like that repeated note [A♭ on the fifth eighth]; it sounds redundant. Tie it.

Mm. 22–25. Bring out those left-hand notes [E♭, D♮, C♯, D♭, C] that follow, and color the right hand. You have to play loud enough that one can hear that.

M. 25. Each right-hand note makes a *diminuendo*.

M. 26. When you come back to that F it must be something going through your heart or you have an arrow going through somebody else's heart. First of all, you have to know what that F sounds like, and then you aim for it [with the C-D♭-E♭] to get that sound.

Example 5.9. *Nocturne*, Op. 27, No. 2, mm. 23–26.

M. 30. No. Don't wait for the downbeat. Each time you sound as if the singer doesn't have enough breath.

M. 32. I put dots over those top notes; that's what we should hear.

Mm. 33–34. [Pressler's score has the D♭ tied to a D♭ on the downbeat rather than being a new C♯.]

Mm. 34–35. You don't listen. You absolutely don't listen! What happens when you have a G♯ [last sixteenth]? It goes to an A, but you go "plunk, plunk."

M. 39. Start that slowly and get faster [the last half of the measure]. I must have the feeling that each note is more than the one before. And keep your body loose so that your sonority is rich, that the weight of the arm is in these notes.

M. 41. The G♭ is a start.

M. 45. What is the dynamic? Just one *forte*. How many do you play? That F♮ is a start.

M. 46. Play that first left-hand note [D♭] an octave lower than written, but not hard, and you have to build to it with the right-hand's A♭-G-G♭. Chopin didn't have that note on his piano, and he probably thought that would be enough. But the lower note gives us more overtones. It's not an excuse; I think it will enrich it. Play the melody very deep, very rich.

M. 47. Deep, deep.

M. 50. Now, sing that in the head voice. Glide into that note. Don't hit. *Pianissimo*.

M. 51. *Crescendo* those last notes.

M. 52. Follow the line [A♭, A♭♭, G♭, F, F♭, E♭♭]. Whistle. All of that is like fireworks' colors. And sit for a split hair on the high F. And the arm must be in there [at the top]. No. Yours is like a chicken whose throat was just cut!

M. 58. Not fast—all one line.

M. 59. Go to that A♭, then grow to measure 60.

M. 60. You'll get more strength on the chord by using 2-4-5.

M. 61. Just a slight delay on that A♭.

Mm. 62–65. Can I hear that you go from a D♭ to a C to a C♭, B♭, B♭♭, A♭?

M. 63. But every note sounds the same!

M. 66. No. Resolve to that F [the downbeat]. The main thing is not the grace note; it's still the bottom note.

M. 69. More, not so soft yet. You have a long way to go to end the piece.

Example 5.10. *Nocturne*, Op. 27, No. 2, mm. 69–74.

M. 70. Now begins a thread, which is an ending duet. It's a question and an answer. You should listen to the last scene of *Aida*. [Pressler sings the tune.]

M. 75. Use the last three to close it. Lighten the left hand. Yours is accentuated one hand to the other. And why slow? Can't it be steady?

Mm. 75–76. Keep one pedal until the A♭ chord [pedal through the rest].

Mm. 76–77. Say "Good-bye" on the last two chords.

Scherzo No. 3 in C-sharp Minor, Op. 39

M. 1. Establish the tempo.

Mm. 1–8. Don't anticipate the downbeats.

Example 5.11. *Scherzo* No. 3 in C-sharp Minor, Op. 39, mm. 1–8.

M. 23. *Legato* octaves.

Mm. 27–32. Involve the wrist in playing the octaves.

Mm. 33–36. *Decrescendo.*

Mm. 39–41. Move toward the *fortissimo.*

Mm. 35–39. It moves; it sways.

M. 43. *Mezzo piano.*

Mm. 57–58. Crisp and rhythmic.

Mm. 59, 61, 63. Three different G♯s.

Mm. 68–69. *Sempre leggiero*; these are wrist octaves.

Mm. 82–83. Slur the G♯-A-G♯.

Mm. 86–87. Slur the D♯-E-G♯.

M. 98. A big breath is needed.

M. 99. Full body. Don't hit.

Mm. 104–105. Close the phrase.

Mm. 106–108. *Tenuto* chords.

Mm. 113–114. Don't rush.

M. 131. Relate the F♯ to the G♯ in measure 115.

Mm. 136–139. Exactly together.

Mm. 143–145. Over the top and down to the F♮.

Mm. 156–159. Richer chords, especially the bass.

Mm. 159–163. In time. Practice with flat fingers and *staccato*. Hear the descending scale B♭-A♭-G♭-F-E♭-D♭.

Example 5.12. *Scherzo* No. 3 in C-sharp Minor, Op. 39, mm. 159–163.

Mm. 164–167. A long line.

M. 186. The G♭ is not short.

Mm. 192–199. The phrase must have direction.

M. 200. This is almost a repeat. You must be a different person.

Mm. 224–227. Practice just the song phrases without the *leggiero*; this one is
mezzo forte.

M. 243. It is a *sforzando* in *pianissimo*. Start beat 3 without an accent.

Mm. 250–251. Don't stop in between.

Mm. 269–278. Shape six-note groups starting on beat 3.

Mm. 290–291. Use fingers 5-2 to connect the left-hand A♭-D♭.

Mm. 320–331. *Sostenuto*. [They practice *legato* melody notes with other notes
resting in the key.]

Mm. 327–328. Be sensitive to the D♯-D♮.

Mm. 338–339. *Decrescendo* to the top.

Mm. 346–347. *Decrescendo* to the top.

Mm. 348–351. Broader.

Mm. 364–365. Be careful with the *rhythm*.

Mm. 369–374. Play the octaves from the wrist.

Mm. 395–398. *Decrescendo* the phrase.

M. 398. Release the chord.

M. 440. Breathe.

Mm. 494–497. Chopin puts us in an emotional descent.

Mm. 497–501. Somber. *Decrescendo*.

Mm. 502–505. Sweetly.

Mm. 526–529. A little apprehensive.

Mm. 538–539. Evaporate.

Mm. 540–541. The A-G♯-F♯♯-G♯ has a rhythmic relationship to the principal
motive.

M. 541. The E♯ gives us water to grow on.
Mm. 542–545. Project the top from the start.
M. 552. *Crescendo.*
Mm. 567–573. Begin a series of six-note sequences starting on beat 2.
M. 573. Lean on the C♯.
Mm. 581–584. Be sure the bass sounds.
M. 585. *Meno forte.*
M. 589. Start.
Mm. 593–597. These are six-note sequences starting on the second eighth note.

Example 5.13. *Scherzo* No. 3 in C-sharp Minor, Op. 39, mm. 593–597.

Mm. 598–601. Strong rhythm.
M. 604. Use every note.
M. 605. Accent the low C♯.
Mm. 617–621. Start, and *crescendo* all the way.
M. 633. Play the low A with the left hand.

Example 5.14. *Scherzo* No. 3 in C-sharp Minor, Op. 39, mm. 629–633.

Mm. 634–636. Hold back. Broaden.
M. 647. "Out."
M. 649. "In."

Ballade No. 4 in F Minor, Op. 52

M. 1. Not too softly. The left hand is *legato*, and the D♮ resolves to the C.

M. 2. The Gs in this measure swell and stretch to the last G [beat 4]. Go up to a *mezzo piano*.

Example 5.15. *Ballade* No. 4 in F Minor, Op. 52, mm. 1–2.

M. 3. Don't stop on the down beat [E♮]; end the phrase.

M. 4. He reaches up to that G. Now swell again to open up the phrase.

Mm. 6–7. And then he says *ritenuto* and repeats it once more, and then it runs out. Use the inner line [E♮-F-E♮, E♮-F-E♮, E♮-F-E♮] to control the *ritenuto*. He unfolds it. It's like the whole thread of the spinning wheel is finished, and out comes the princess.

Mm. 7–8. Somehow you have to slip into that new tempo so that there's a connection. You have to do that in such a manner that the *a tempo* is not abrupt. And Chopin says "*mezzo voce.*" [Pressler imitates loud singing, and then sings quietly.] It's someone who speaks from the inside; he talks to one person and not to everyone.

Mm. 8–10. You must play it differently each time [C-F-E♮-B♭-D♭]. Variety is the spice of life; you must find different ways to express the repeat of the phrase.

Mm. 10–11. Give yourself room for a *crescendo*.

M. 12. And finish it.

M. 14. Now don't accent the G.

Mm. 17–18. Keep it flowing. And there must be variety to these repeated notes. Do you have another color in your repertoire?

M. 20. Bring it down.

Mm. 28–29. It must be very sensitive. [Pressler plays m. 29].

M. 30. [Pressler demonstrates the *crescendo* of the G♭s].

Mm. 36–37. Shape this left-hand phrase, and *diminuendo* into the *pianissimo*. All this left hand is *legato*.

Mm. 39–40. Create motion. Let the left hand *decrescendo*.

Mm. 41–42. Without waiting for the F♭, just a *diminuendo* [A♭-B♭-C♭]. When you wait, it's like you go around like someone advertising with a sign, "Pleasure, enjoy!" You make it so much more difficult, yes?

Example 5.16. *Ballade* No. 4 in F Minor, Op. 52, mm. 41–42.

Mm. 45–46. *Decrescendo* [B♭-C♭-D♮] as it leads to the *mezza voce*.

M. 47. Sing the C♭.

M. 49. Sing the C♮. And now *crescendo* into that B♭ [m. 50].

M. 52. Pull back to close the phrase.

M. 53. No accent on that first note [C]; it is a start. That F [middle voice, beat 5] is a horn; bring it out. Resolve the E♭ into the D♭.

M. 54. The D♭ must have a different meaning from the C [m. 53]. And the horn increases to a G♭. The F♭ resolves to the E♭.

M. 55. Hold back the tempo leading into that final G♭. And then resolve into the F.

M. 58. *A tempo*; shape the inner line.

M. 62. Push to the fourth eighth-note [the C]. Less on beats 5 and 6 to start the phrase.

M. 65. Use the broken chord to pull back the phrase before beat 4.

M. 68. Here it pushes forward.

M. 70. Slur the first two chords. And resolve. Then a new start.

M. 71. Not faster. He gives you *fortissimo*. Can you enjoy each harmony?

M. 72. Touch that downbeat in such a way that the *sforzando* is like a sigh.

Mm. 72–74. Shape the inner phrasings. All these left-hand phrases should be the same tempo. [Pressler sings these phrases.]

M. 75. It's a trill, yes? [G♭-G♮.]

M. 76. And those high Fs are like *campanelli*, and he says, "*Leggerimente*."

M. 77. Hear it restarting within the line from the D♮ and A♮.

M. 78. The left hand enters *mezzo piano*; it's on its way down.

M. 80. It's a *Sicilienne*.

M. 89. You would not have an accent on the C; it's the harmonies that change. And the C minor is a different harmony from the E♭ major, and it is in tempo.

M. 91. Lean into the downbeat [the F]. Play that tenor line like a cello.

Mm. 92–93. Here what is beautiful is that secondary line in the left hand; it gives it a different color altogether. Keep it swinging.

M. 95. Don't accent the F [beat 2]; it continues from the G.

M. 99. Finish the phrase.

M. 100. It goes to an A♮, the next one to a B♭. And then it flies all the way up [m. 101].

M. 101. Your stop [the A♮] is so exaggerated that you lose the flow.

M. 105. The B♮ is the maximum; I would say *mezzo forte*.

M. 112. I personally feel that it should not sit down at the end of each sequence. You are closing each one. Go all the way to the new entrance at measure 121. He creates a breathlessness. I feel that he repeats not in order to stop but in order to accelerate; you are not using that.

M. 117. Start the right hand with an accent. Hear the left-hand top notes ascending.

M. 121. Color the left-hand F♭.

M. 122. Voice the left hand [D♯-E♭-D♯-E♭].

M. 123. He finishes the phrase on the downbeat and starts again.

M. 122. These altered notes are emotional; he's in a dark key.

Mm. 125–126. Hear how the tenor is a countermelody to the soprano. Have a little stress on that second B♭ [beat 6].

Mm. 128–129. The alto D♯-D♮-C♯ pulls back and leads to the *pianissimo*.

Mm. 133–134. The *smorzando* slows in a natural way. Keep the pulse going.

M. 134. At the cadenza, I would like you to imagine a harp standing outside of this building, and the wind whistles through it. It's weightless, dreamy. Go only half way down into the keys. And not steady; let it move. Can your fifth finger color each one of the A♮s, like little bells? So the fifth finger stretches out to go into the keys. Now come down. This is all *pianissimo*.

Mm. 135–145. What is good is that I hear each of your entrances, but each one must have its own life. [Pressler sings the three phrases.] In order for him to lead you back home, you have to go away first; you can't be so predictable.

M. 138. Release the low G so there's a little lift before the C, and bring in that left-hand entrance with a little accent.

M. 141. With a lift before the left-hand E♭.

Mm. 144–145. Taste each G♭.

M. 152. More tone. More insistence.

Mm. 154–155. Like an improvisation.

M. 156. The right hand takes the A♭.

M. 159. With color; end it lyrically [into m. 160].

M. 166. Hear two-note slurs in the left hand [E♮-F, E♮-F, E♮-E♭].

M. 168. Down and down, *legato*. Use the right hand all the way down for more control, then use the left hand on the very last notes [E♭-E♭♭-D♭].

Example 5.17. *Ballade* No. 4 in F Minor, Op. 52, mm. 166–168.

Example 5.17. (*continued*)

M. 171. Quieter on the Gb-F resolution. Less at measure 172.

Mm. 171–172. Less on the Bb-Ab-G♮-A; it's closing.

Mm. 181–186. When he comes to this, he doesn't say, "Hello; good day; it's nice to meet you; and I hope to see you again." He doesn't say that. It's very personal, and it's very passionate, and I don't feel that you have his passion.

M. 185. Here, I need the fulfillment. There's all this expectation till he comes to this point. I'm not speaking about a tempo that you should reach or a loudness. What I speak about is an emotion that you should reach. It's *appassionato*. And push forward after the downbeat.

M. 186. Close the Gb, then start a new phrase.

M. 190. I have to hear that you are heading to Db [m. 191].

M. 191. Use wrist rotation for the top note.

Mm. 193–195. Hear the top notes, F-Gb down to Ab.

M. 195. Come in with the fifth finger on the low C and brace it with the side of the hand.

M. 196. Shape the chords to the downbeat.

Mm. 199–201. You play the *stretto* as fast as you can, but it doesn't have to be that fast. He wants it to push forward to measure 201.

M. 201. Come immediately back in.

M. 203. Make it talk.

Mm. 205–210. *Decrescendo.*

M. 211. The Coda is a *forte* but not a *fortissimo*. The tempo is too fast for you, and it's too fast for us to hear it. Try it so that we hear the phrases, so that we hear a melody. Practice the Coda *pianississimo* up to tempo for control.

Mm. 215–216. *Legato.* Use each last third to get to the *sforzando*, like a pickup. Out on the *sforzandi.* Then back in.

Mm. 216–217. Not like an exercise!

M. 218. The Ab closes to the G [beat 5].

M. 223. Begin again after the downbeat.

Mm. 224, 226. Use full arm on the downbeats.

Mm. 231–232. Push forward.

M. 233. Let me have the chord strong. Then push forward. At the top, hear the eight individual notes. Then it spins faster and faster. He writes it against the beat, in groups of four. It goes over the bar line until you show us again where the downbeat is [m. 237].

M. 236. It spins. Accent the last four notes of the run [Db-C-Ab-F]. On a given night I might *ritard* a little bit; on another night I might accelerate. There's no way of preparing it exactly.

Mm. 237–239. Start less and *crescendo* to the final chord.

Example 5.18. *Ballade* No. 4 in F Minor, Op. 52, mm. 233–239.

Berceuse, Op. 57

Mm. 1–2. There is inherent in this *ostinato* a feeling of an ending, of a cadence between the Ab and the Db. And don't play it so softly that you can't control it. You don't want to play so close to the edge that you can't control it.

Example 5.19. *Berceuse*, Op. 57, mm. 1–2.

M. 6. Somehow you must show that the second line has its own character, its own interest. They interact; there's beauty in the intervals they create together. Play the lower part darker when it comes in so that it's not an accompanied solo. It's a duet.

M. 9. Play so there's a resolution there [G♭-F]. There's pain in that second. It is as if he were stuck by a needle and then the pain is gone again.

Mm. 10–11. It takes a little longer to play the stretch up each time [A♭-D♭, G♭-C, F-B♭, E♭-A♭] as he's floating down.

M. 12. There's release when that F octave occurs.

Mm. 13–14. We should hardly be aware that the sixteenths begin. It's not an exercise.

M. 15. Barely touch the little bells.

Mm. 19–20. But resolve it before beginning the trill. Also, the trill must have life; let it swell a little before it starts down. Can we hear G♮, F, E♮, D♮, C, B♮, A♮, G♮?

Example 5.20. *Berceuse*, Op. 57, mm. 19–20.

M. 20. No. You give us G-G. You are heartless! "Bum-bum!" The second G is a new start, a new color.

M. 22. He arrives on the A♭, then he turns it around. Finish on the A♭, and then it starts again. You give me a reading, but you don't listen when you play.

Mm. 26–27. Let us hear the E♭-D♭-C-B♭ resolving to the A♭.

Mm. 27–28. Come down from the D♭—less and less.

M. 29. Let me hear E♭ to the D♭ [beats 1 and 2].

Example 5.21. *Berceuse*, Op. 57, mm. 27–29.

Mm. 30–31. The pedal has to be clearer going to the D♭, because the C and the D♭ don't like each other.

M. 31. Too fast [beat 2]. The D♭ floats up there a moment, and then it begins to go down, go down, and you can't hold it; it just continues to fall.

M. 35. With a bell-like sound. Here you play the chimes, the children's bells.

M. 36. Beat 1 is a resolution. The triplets are in the same tempo.

M. 39. To get the wrist rotation, practice the blocked sixths first. Then let the wrist settle into the key on each beat [B♭-A♭-B♭-F], and you let the hand rotate to the higher note.

M. 42. No *crescendo*. You'll throw the baby out of the cradle!

M. 43. Reach up to the F and then just like a *glissando* down. Very, very close with the fingers. And you play only with the tip of your fingers—not with the whole hand.

M. 44. It's always the low A♭ louder than the high A♭.

M. 46. He repeats the same thing, but it's in a different register, so he gives you a different quality, a different color.

Mm. 49–50. This is like the first one [m. 47], but he takes you around on a bigger circle and back to where you were. It goes out to the G♭ and back to the F.

Mm. 50–51. It is too heavy over the top. Can you play B♭-C-E♭ [last three sixteenths] into the A♭ so that we recognize we come into a neighborhood where we have been before?

M. 54. That D♭ [second sixteenth] is a resolution within the line.

M. 55. Lean into the C♭—then over the top.

M. 57. It's the same notes [second half of the measure], but give it a different color.

M. 58. It doesn't sit on that E♭ [beat 4]. It goes all the way down. No. Both notes [C♭ and A♭] resolve to the B♭, not just the A♭.

M. 62. No. Your left hand is heartless.

Mm. 66–68. You see, he stops it himself; no *ritardando* is needed.

Mm. 69–70. You're "in," then you're "out." Observe the rests exactly.

Barcarolle, Op. 60

Mm. 1–2. Put the pedal down before you begin, and keep the pedal down into the second measure; sustain the C♯ octave as long as possible. Feel a *crescendo* from the left-hand C♯ octave to the treble chord. Use all your body weight as you move from beat 1 to 2. The song is on top; the rest are textures, accompaniment. Not stiff. Keep your left hand loose, flexible. We need to hear the structure of the melody; you're playing *a piacere*, "anything."

M. 3. Blend the notes without *ritardando*. Your *ritardando* takes away from the pause that he gives you. The pause leads you; it has a life. It's not just "stop, then we go."

Example 5.22. *Barcarolle*, Op. 60, mm. 1–3.

M. 4. Inflect the accompaniment. Don't be heavy on beat 2. Hear the difference between beat 2 and beat 4 so that you have A♯-C♯ [descending], and A♯-C♯ [ascending]. Then it is a continuous motion—not one that stops here, stops there.

M. 5. Less. Leave room for the entrance of the melody.

M. 6. When the melody comes in, you have to have room to *decrescendo*. You must use your arm. These are thirds, Siamese twins; they are related; I do not hear them. Pull the sound toward the body. I should be standing on a balcony looking out above Venice. With you, I see only Martinsville!

Mm. 6–7. More melodic freedom and natural inflection without accents.

M. 7. Shape the melody—F♯, D♯-C♯, B-A♯; that's the finish. And the E leads you up to the D♯ with a *crescendo*.

M. 8. You must prepare for the first chord, and it is marked *staccato*. You must go "out" [release], then "in" [down on beat 2]. There can be pedal, but we must see the out and in. The melody sings on beat 2 just like at the beginning. Do this throughout the piece.

M. 9. Beat 4 is a "finish," and you have to place that last chord just right so that the C♯♯ goes up to a D♯ and the G♯ goes down to an F♯. Chopin is saying "and."

M. 10. I don't like your edition. There should be a tie to beat 3. The repeated note sounds so pedantic.

M. 11. Bring it down to the G♯ of beat 4, and then begin the trill *piano*. I don't think the trill should start from above, especially not this time. You already are above; you're on the A♯. Start on the G♯, with no *ritard* going into the next measure.

M. 12. More and more sound on each beat, but it doesn't move faster.

M. 13. A few more trill notes—also not from above.

M. 14. Beat one is an "out," then an "in" on beat 2. The left hand is *legato*, not "Chopsticks." Play the right hand gracefully with a little lingering at the top. Keep the top notes always clean. Play the last G♯ with the left hand; see how it helps the right hand?

Example 5.23. *Barcarolle*, Op. 60, mm. 14.

M. 15. Feel it always going back to the C♯. You can play the last G♯s [in beat 2 and in beat 4] with the left hand. Shape it differently the second time. It runs out.

M. 16. Each chord less. *Diminuendo.*

M. 17. A new sound for that C♯ minor chord. See, the G♯-A♯ grace notes show you he wants the trill from above this time.

M. 18. That left hand goes to the second F♯. Play the second F♯ with 2 and then change your finger to 1. Also, you can play the last F♯s of beats 2 and 4 with the left hand.

M. 19. Keep the left hand in control of the rhythm on the fourth beat. The right-hand's *appoggiatura* is after the left-hand's B.

M. 20. The left hand must release on beat 3; it's all right to hold it with the pedal, but the arm must release. Use right-hand arm weight as it ascends—and more alto on beat 4.

M. 21. The C♯ is a resolution from the trill; you're landing there with an accent.

M. 22. Always keep the same swing in the left hand. There's not a *ritardando*. You must express with your touch and your dynamics.

M. 23. The low point is beat 1.

M. 24. Emphasize the F♯ downbeat. Connect the octaves [G♯-F♯] with a 4-5 fingering. The double trills are fluttering like butterflies; there's movement, not static.

M. 25. Freer thirds—not square.

M. 26. No arm weight on the grace note.

M. 27. Only a little more than the first time [m. 25]. The *crescendo* hasn't started yet.

M. 28. It's a start. Up [beat 1], down [beat 2] each time [m. 29, also]. The two sixteenths and the eighth are one motion, not separate notes.

M. 30. Intensify the right hand on beats 3 and 4.

M. 31. That sigh [A♯-G♯] must be sensitive—not soft, just sensitive. The G♯ must be less. And then to start again on the E♯ you have to be less again. More trill notes, not just one. This is too loud for me; you are already at the volume of the ending of the piece.

Example 5.24. *Barcarolle*, Op. 60, mm. 28–29.

M. 32. Can I have decent sound on the first chord? With "juice"! You must show that the G♯ is the most important note. Now to make it magic, each chord must be a little less, and there's no *ritardando*. Pedal it in such a way that the C♯ remains. Hear the octave between the two hands. [They practice the chords as octaves only, then right-hand chord with left-hand single note, etc.] All the notes of the chords must be played with no holes. Bring out the top note of the chords a little bit. The *decrescendo* is gradual, measured; don't drop off so fast. And no *ritardando*. A lighter upbeat to measure 33.

M. 33. Play the last C♯ with the left hand.

M. 35. Your downbeat is too obvious. Art is never obvious; it must be innocent. The B is still a grace note—not so slow. Now the line becomes magical. It must be beautiful, but it must not be made in such a way that you say, "Attention! Now I'm going to do something."

Mm. 36–38. How many *ritardandi* in these few bars? You overdo it. You put on so much makeup that one doesn't recognize the face of the person.

M. 38. Enjoy beat 2, beat 3, beat 4. The C♯ is the central note. He was lost, going around and around the C♯, until at last he sees the door open. The C♯ is the fifth of the F♯ chord and the third of A major. How do we get to the A major? That's what I feel is missing.

M. 39. You must glide into beat 1. No false accents. In general, emphasize the quarter-note throughout this section. It's a gentle swing; don't push it.

M. 42. You have to play two voices on equal terms, but the lower voice doesn't really become equal till the C♯ [end of beat 2].

M. 43. No inner accents; go all the way to the top G♯ without *ritard*. Then, not a new start [D♯-A♯]; it is a continuation.

M. 44. Bring in the top G♯ with more weight.

M. 48. Hear the D♮ resolving to the C♯ [beat 3]. And be sensitive on that high A.

M. 51. Begin the trill on the E. That's the melody. Start in such a way that these fragments lead you all the way [F♯-G♯-A, F♯-G♯-A, G♯-A, B-C♯, C♯, C♯]. Phrase it from the second note, 2-3-1, 2-3-1, not 1-2-3, 1-2-3. It's too loud; it's too heavy-handed.

M. 53. No false accents in the left hand. The last note is a sixteenth, not a thirty-second.

M. 57. Hear the canon all the way down [B-A♯-F♯-F♯].

M. 58. Go all the way to the top note in *forte*, then immediately back to *piano*. Color that A♮. And the E [beat 3] is too heavy; it's going to the D [m. 59].

M. 59. Give that D [beat 1] a *vibrato*! That C♯ [beat 3] is a resolution; *decrescendo* a little within the *crescendo*.

M. 60. It doesn't resolve yet; keep up the intensity.

M. 62. That's ugly, ugly, ugly! That's such a glorious melody. It's not hit; it's warm and rich. It's goes down [E-D♯-D♮-B♯-C♯] so it can go back up [E-A].

Mm. 62–65. Work for the greatest *legato* possible, especially where it descends in steps [first beats of mm. 63 and 65]. For me it's too big, too heavy-handed. Do you see *forte* anywhere?

M. 64. No, it's different [beat 4]; he's trying to tell you something.

Example 5.25. *Barcarolle*, Op. 60, mm. 62–64.

M. 67. If you take a little longer going up [first half of the measure], return the time that you take. And that F♯ [on beat 2] is only a secondary voice—not so heavy.

M. 69. Finish the phrase on beat 3. Don't accent the grace notes; go to the top.

M. 70. Chopin asks a question on beat 4, yes? He has lots of pieces that do that. Don't *ritard* going into it; it keeps moving until the end. The only thing you should do is what he's asking for—a *diminuendo*.

M. 71. Work on shaping the termination of the trill. Isolate the last three trill notes and connect them to the closing [D♯-E-G♯-G♮], and then glide into the F♯ [m. 72].

M. 72. Hear A♯-B-A♮-G♯ in the lower part.

M. 74. No, you're stopping all the time. When the left hand has "*dum-pah, dum-pah*" [eighth-quarter, eighth-quarter] and you stop all the time, that's not music making. That is not on the level of a Chopin player when you do all this exaggerated waiting. The piece becomes like it's filled with plaster. Instead of seeing the arm, it's plaster here. It is wounded here; it's wounded all over the place.

M. 76. Change the pedal on each chord; we shouldn't hear any low C♯ when the bass note changes to E♯. There's no *sforzando* on beat 4.

M. 77. Take the foot off so we have that pause. No false accents on the upbeats. An F and an E♯ are different, but you play them alike [beat 3]. *Legato.* Balance the chords. Bring out some of the harmonies with supersensitivity. But yours is too heavy and sentimental. It is his genius that gives the harmonies; it is your heavy playing that makes them noticeable in a way that he doesn't. Be observant and hear the change of harmonies, but a singer would already be at the end of her breath.

M. 78. We must hear the low C♯. Nobody knows how to be freer than Chopin, and here he shows you that he doesn't want to know where beat 4 is. As an artist you are entitled to a little stretch. But if you overstretch, you're just a player for effect. This is not playing for effect; it is a most beautiful spot. It must fit like a glove.

Mm. 78–81. Breathe with the pedal release. The release is gradual, not abrupt.

Mm. 80–81. It's like a *cadenza*. It spins.

M. 82. The grace notes are melodic.

M. 83. This one trill is from above—and greater *ritardando* in the trill. You have a cadence from the last C♯ to the F♯ [m. 84].

M. 84. Now we have an even trill. Only one *forte*. The left hand has the same shape as at the opening.

M. 86. These two beats are always "out-in."

M. 87. Always voice the top notes.

M. 91. Hear the inner part, especially the third-beat sigh. A trill, not just a turn.

M. 92. Each chord must have arm weight, not harsh. You can't use all your weight, because you still have so far to go.

Mm. 93–94. Let the thumb lead. Be especially aware of sweep and shaping. Watch the descending steps; make them as *legato* as possible.

M. 100. The E♮ is a surprise; it's a change of direction. But it's not harsh. Hold back the tempo on the preceding eighth note.

M. 103. It's not quiet yet. He's still shaken by the excitement he's come through. It takes him a long time to calm down.

M. 106. The second trill starts from above [on A♯]; see how he shows you with the "preface" notes? Hear the lead-in as five notes [F♯-E♯-F♯-F♯♯-G♯].

Mm. 107, 108, 109. Hear the different harmonic destinations on the third beats.

M. 110. Place the chord, and it's as if there's a tiny *fermata* over that chord. Then start very, very light—and gentle on the descent. You have to have the feeling that the F♯ [m. 111] is a resolution.

M. 111. But it's a *forte/piano*, a *sforzando*. See how he ornaments the left-hand C♯? Now color it differently the second time.

M. 112. Almost no *ritard* going to measure 113.

M. 113. You have to learn to play an expressive thumb—not bumpy. [Pressler demonstrates the left-hand melody with thumb alone.] "Sing" each chord; your lower notes are too heavy. And the whole thing must have a swing. The right hand is a free fantasy over that melody—improvisatory, especially at places where the direction turns around.

M. 115. Work to play the left-hand A♯ together with the right-hand B♯. Take a little bit of time as you go over the top [C♯-F♯-D♯].

M. 116. Don't anticipate the third eighth. Lift the pedal for just a moment and delay before the last two octaves so there's a little breath in there. The chords are "and-out, and-down."

Interlude IV
Hotel Stories

In the beginning of the Trio, we came to a hotel in Oxford, England, and at that time, many years ago, they had a heater in the room that you had to feed with money. You had to put in ten cents, or English whatever it is; so in the middle of the night I ran out of money, and I froze. That really was bad. So I arrive for the concert, and there came Lady So-and-So; she was the wife of a history professor at Oxford who had been ennobled for writing a very famous book about the Second World War. And she said, "I welcome you, and I'm happy to have you here, and I'd like to know if there's anything that I can do for you, and I'd be happy to do it for you." And I said, "Lady ——, it's bitter cold," and she looks at me and says, "Isn't it?" That was her help. I expected she would say, "I've asked the janitor to turn up the heat"—but, "Isn't it?"

Many, many times when we played community concerts, dinner would be potato chips or whatever that was in the machine. You live with what you can get, yes? Like in the first years when we'd travel by car, and we'd stop at the gasoline station, and we'd ask the man, Where is the best restaurant? Of course he would send us to the hamburger joint that he is used to. But this one time we come into a little town; we stop at a red light, and there's someone walking. So we roll down the window to ask him how to get to our hotel, and we say, "Where is the Holiday Inn?" And he says, "Hooo, llll, iiiii, ddddd, aaay" and by the time he got out the name of the hotel, I was nearly crawling under the seat. We wanted him to stop. The light changed, and the cars in back of us are honking, and he is still telling us where to find the Holiday Inn. This is like forty years ago, and I can see that scene in front of me, how he couldn't get each word out.

6   Claude Debussy

Debussy's *Images* are for me like part of my life's circle. It started with the Debussy prize, and now he's a composer that I feel very close to and have a great affinity for. No other composer demands such constant color. With Debussy, you must fall in love with the chords. You must have a creative feeling inside of you and then try to repeat the sound again when you play the chord, until it's a part of you. Something inside of you responds to the beautiful chords while keeping a third ear on the harmony. Each piece must paint its own picture, and you must play very, very delicately. Think inside the piano—very close to the keys and softly. Sometimes think that you are wearing silk gloves.

Reflets dans l'eau, from *Images*, Bk. 1

Mm. 1–2. Your playing had absolutely nothing to do with Debussy. The man who writes this music, the *Images*, lives by shadows. There is little light and lots of shadows. You had no shadow whatever. The greatest performer of Debussy, the greatest that I experienced was Walter Gieseking. I heard him only one time in New York. Here was a man who was six foot three, enormous, playing on a miserable piano. Leaning over the keyboard and he was capable of playing from *pianissimo* down two, three, four, five levels. And that is what you fight for when you play Debussy. Take a deep breath before you begin, and put both pedals down first to get all the sonority. Then sink into those first notes, a slow attack and very lightly. Do a *crescendo* only where he has asked for it. You will like it. After all, the composer knows his piece too. What I would like you to do is to "clean" the piano; swipe the keys. It is hazy; it is a sound wave. You have to find less of a body and more of a soul. It is really no body to touch; it's only to guess, and it's hazy, and ethereal, especially in this piece. He says "*rubato*," but it's subtle—not like a Romantic composer. If it does a little bit of *crescendo*, it certainly comes all the way back down. And there's an intensity to the left-hand melody, like a golden thread.

Mm. 3–4. Take the Fs with the left hand.

Example 6.1. *Images*, Bk. 1, *Reflets dans l'eau*, mm. 1–4.

M. 5. All the way back to your *pianissimo*. You should feel like you're wearing silk gloves.

Mm. 5–8. One phrase ending with a slight *ritard*.

M. 9. No explosion and not so fast. Can you play those chords *legato*? Use small pedal changes on each chord. That third chord is a transition chord to beat 2, but you don't hear anything. The chord doesn't do anything to your insides. Can that be like water [the A♭-E♭-A♭-E♭]? [Pressler takes the slightest pause before the fourth chord.]

M. 10. You take extra time, but he doesn't give you extra time. You can't slow all the chords down. Can you do them again and taste each chord? Did you ever see a wine tasting? [Pressler looks up as if kissing the taste.] That is what I would like you to do. Taste each chord but without slowing down.

Mm. 12–13. You don't feel anything in these chords. They resolve.

M. 14. Here, too. Taste each one, not fast. Do you see a *crescendo* and *accelerando* here? Pedal every other eighth.

M. 15. And slower.

Mm. 16–17. No, there is no *crescendo*. All that is in *pianissimo* until a little swell to F major. Have a pedal change on each chord.

M. 17. And we have a finish here on the fourth chord; that's what he wants.

Mm. 20–21. He says "*Quasi cadenza*," which means that you start freer. He doesn't say "more excited." There is a swirling. And it is slow and soft, *pianissimo*, nothing. What are you playing here—Liszt? The hand stays on the keys.

Mm. 24–27. No, it's not hurried; it's leisurely—and especially the difference of going into measure 27, that E♭, the difference of the chord. And I would advise you, each time when the sweeping line goes up, feel inside of you that you go against it, that you feel you are going down, yes? The thumb must be loose.

Claude Debussy 97

M. 27. With the same pedal so we never lose the A♭. You have to be a virtuoso with your foot.

M. 28. And down. The left hand can help by taking that low C.

M. 30. The four chords go up. More impetus in the triplet.

M. 31. No. Like Mozart, eight even notes. But it's too loud. The C-D♭-B♭ is only *mezzo piano.*

M. 32. Nothing.

M. 33. And now *piano.*

M. 34. And now *pianissimo.*

M. 35. Exactly like the beginning, except the chords are broken. More fluent, more swirls.

M. 37. The left hand can take that first F.

M. 38. Hear the descending line B♭-F-D♭-B♭-F.

M. 43. Start *pianissimo*; it's not Liszt. Practice this as blocked chords. [Pressler plays the left hand while playing only the skeleton of the right hand.]

M. 50. The melody should be the same as before with slow sixteenths and coloring it to the F♯ [m. 52].

Mm. 53–54. You can divide the passage between the two hands.

Mm. 54–55. Shape the phrase to the downbeat of measure 55.

M. 56. There are rays of sunshine, but that *arpeggio* is still only one *forte.*

Mm. 57–58. And now he says, "As loud as you can play it." And rich, and we must hear each of these chords with meaning. And play out all those left-hand notes—it will take a little time. You cannot play the chord exactly in time.

M. 58. Don't overdo the slurs. Here every note is important; it's *fortissimo.* And always play that left-hand E♭ like a gong.

Example 6.2. *Images*, Bk. 1, *Reflets dans l'eau*, mm. 57–58.

M. 60. I have to hear the inner line, and the last D♭ is less. The scale is too fast; it is too loud. You must have a rhythm. [Pressler sings and taps.] Play the scales alone; you must feel the beat.

M. 62. The thirty-seconds are too fast.

M. 65. And here when you have the ending, have the feeling that it comes out of the water.

M. 66. Let me hear the left-hand second and then the thirds.

M. 67. Very, very quiet on the C minor chord—taste it!

M. 68. He restates the melody. As softly as you possibly can.

M. 69. Even less on the E♭ chord.

Mm. 73–74. Touch the top notes very lightly.

M. 75. Take the A♭ octave with the right hand.

M. 79. We must understand the rhythm.

M. 80. Like an echo.

M. 81. Set the chord underneath the D♭ with a quieter sound.

M. 91. And now nothing.

M. 93. And now the broken chord, like water playing. If anything, you should make a *diminuendo* and hold it as long as he asks you to hold it.

Poisson d'or, from *Images*, Bk. 2

Mm. 1–3. He starts with a trill, yes—a written-out trill? He says, "As soft as possible, and as light as possible," so it's very soft and very light. And take the left foot and the right foot. Change the pedal very little on each downbeat so that you create the mood of the chord, a feeling of breathing through the chord.

M. 4. And here take a pedal on each of the thirds. And now, you do the upper part and I'll play the trills. We have to hear that you are accompanying yourself, that each part is distinct and separate.

Example 6.3. *Images*, Bk. 2, *Poisson d'or*, mm. 1–4.

Mm. 5–7. A *crescendo* in Debussy is very slight, especially a *crescendo* in *pianissimo*. It never goes to a *forte*; it stays in a *pianissimo*.

M. 8. Not loud. He says "*diminuendo molto*"—and the same tempo for each beat.

Mm. 10–13. And now, play for us the duet without the inner notes. Change the pedal on each bass note.

Mm. 25–26. The F♯ and F♮—in Debussy, those are different colors.

Mm. 30–31. All these *arpeggios* are perfectly in the hand; it's very easy to play them. Drill each one. Now let's play the beautiful melody without the *arpeggios*.

M. 34. Don't hit that G; lean into it. The grace notes are not slow; it's the G that he wants.

M. 39. Divide the thirty-seconds between the two hands, because you have to get back to the next chord. The left hand plays 3-2-1.

M. 41. It's in *piano* again. [Pressler sings the tune again with the articulation.] It's always that beautiful melody.

Mm. 62–63. Lightly and with some pedal.

M. 74. Debussy gives you a little leeway, but the eighths are the same as before. He says "*Rubato*," which means "You take freedom; do what you feel like," yes? But free within the rhythm. [Pressler sings the phrase.]

M. 79. Close that phrase before going on.

M. 80. Come down [*decrescendo*] with the *arpeggio*. [Pressler has the student practice the *arpeggio* ascending as well as descending.]

M. 81. In Debussy, actually everywhere in music, the sound has to be something besides hitting the piano. It's never empty hitting. The way you do it, it's ugly. Go into it; lean into the chords. Look how each chord has its own marking. And don't play so heavy.

M. 82. The two hands are the same; they must play together.

Mm. 83–84. These notes don't belong together. The D [m. 84] must be clear.

M. 87. Not fast.

Mm. 88–93. First of all, we must hear the melody above everything. [Pressler sings the melody.]

Example 6.4. *Images*, Bk. 2, *Poisson d'or*, mm. 88–89.

M. 90. The note that we should hear is the C♯. But now you're hitting.

M. 94. It's a new start. But you're throwing away the notes. Practice with blocked chords.

Mm. 94–102. We need an evenness in these notes. [Pressler has the student practice without pedal for evenness.] Now it starts under tempo, less than the tempo, and then you push toward the end.

M. 100. This is the climax.

Mm. 100–102. Each one is less. Hear the line; it's Ds and Gs, D-G-D, D-G-D.

M. 104. Be sensitive to the E♯.

7   George Frideric Handel

The suites of Handel are magnificent; they are very beautiful, and they do demand, in a sense, the same discipline as a *partita* of Bach demands. They're less known for some reason. Pianists haven't taken to them, but Richter obviously did since he played three of them. I feel very strongly about them when I play them. The *Chaconne* is a wonderful piece, not just to learn to enrich your emotional vocabulary but also just to perform. It is something that is not done every day or by everyone.

Chaconne in G Major, HWV 442

Mm. 1–4. Theme. Always lead to the second beat. Begin the trills on the upper note.

Example 7.1. Chaconne in G Major, mm. 1–4.

M. 8. The C resolves to the B [second beat]. Begin the flourish *mezzo forte*.
M. 9. Variation 1. *Forte.*
M. 17. Variation 2. The second beat receives an accent. Follow the contour of the left-hand octaves.
M. 21. *Crescendo* the left-hand octaves.
M. 23. The left hand is not short, but *tenuto.*
M. 32. Variation 3. Begin the trill on the upper note [A].
M. 41. Variation 5. The sixteenths are *non-legato.*
M. 47. Don't rush! The F♯ is a new start within the line.
M. 70. Variation 8. *Crescendo* to measure 71.

M. 71. Each left-hand note is strong.

M. 72. *Crescendo* to the low G, then omit the final C-B-A.

Mm. 73–75. Variation 9. A lift in the left hand before the second beat.

Mm. 81–83. Variation 10. Same articulation as before going to the second beat.

M. 105. Variation 13. Same tempo, not faster.

M. 111. Each left-hand note is strong.

M. 112. *Crescendo* into variation 14.

M. 120. Variation 14. No *ritard*.

Mm. 121–128. Variation 15. A strong third beat to show the chord change. Touch the pedal to each beat.

M. 130. Variation 16. The second note in the right hand is a C.

M. 136. *Crescendo* to the low G, then *decrescendo* only the C-B♭-A.

Mm. 137–144. Variation 17. Play all in *piano*.

Mm. 146, 148. Variation 18. Play these measures as echoes.

Mm. 153–160. Variation 19. Don't play the second beats so short. Let them ring.

M. 160. End *mezzo forte*. No stop before variation 20.

Mm. 170–172. Variation 21. Take the left hand down the octave.

(*LH as edited by Mr. Pressler*)

Example 7.2. Chaconne in G Major, mm. 169–172.

Interlude V
Missed Concerts

I have had many, many travel problems, but among thousands of concerts, we missed only two. One was in Bordeaux, France. We could have taken the train, but they told us we absolutely could fly. Then it was getting later and later, and finally it was past the time you could take the train, and finally the flight was cancelled. The other time was when we were playing outside of Washington, in Rockville, Maryland, and it was the end of the Thanksgiving holiday. Something happened at the Washington airport; some airplane didn't land well, so the airport was closed, and we had to get there by car. First, we tried to get on a train; you couldn't get a train. So we rented a car, and the highway was absolutely full, and you could only go ten miles an hour. And then a rainstorm started, and we arrived too late. There were still a few people hanging around the hall, so we played the Mendelssohn D Minor Trio for them. And we came back a few weeks later to play the concert, and the newspaper headline was, "Beaux Arts Trio to Try Again."

And I had the same experience in Birmingham, Alabama, with Arthur Winograd conducting, who had been the cellist with the Juilliard Quartet. A snowstorm started in Birmingham paralyzing the city. Half of the orchestra couldn't make it, and 90 percent of the audience couldn't make it. But I could make it since my hotel was next to the concert hall, so I played a few solo pieces for the few stragglers who were there. I had to come back a few months later and play the concert.

Here is a story where I almost missed a concert. I was scheduled to perform Mozart's G Major Concerto, K. 453, with Bychkov and the Berlin Philharmonic, and the Indianapolis airport is snowed in. So I change my flight to Chicago and call the car dealer here in Bloomington. I rented a Jeep and my student drove me seven hours. And the road is closed and they tell me, "You can't get to Chicago." But the GPS shows a side road, so we take it and somehow we get to O'Hare. We get there and the captain tells us we have to de-ice, but the de-icer is frozen and we're delayed two hours to de-ice. So we arrive late, and I miss my connecting flight in Munich and have to take a later flight. But I made it just in time for the rehearsal!

8   Franz Joseph Haydn

Haydn has always been an important composer to me. His ingenuity seems to have no bounds. The Beaux Arts Trio was the first and only Trio to play forty-four of the forty-five Haydn trios, and no one has yet found the forty-fifth. We recorded twenty or twenty-one of them, and then when the rest were discovered in a monastery, we recorded those also. Recording those trios was really a lifetime experience—becoming aware of the range of his feelings, the many sides of his humor, and the depths of his humanity. Our recording won not only the *Gramophone* "Record of the Year" for Chamber Music, but we were named the "Record of the Year" for all categories for our Haydn, the first time that chamber music won that award.

The one who offered so many wonderful ideas while we were working on them was Bernie Greenhouse, our cellist. And I still remember when the Metropolitan Museum, where we played every year a series of concerts, contacted us and said they wanted us to perform all the Haydn trios during the year. And after we had played the first concert, Bernie called up and said, "I can't do it again." And it was because the cello really has very little to play; it's mostly doubling the left hand of the pianist. And I understood, and I called the director and told her that we can play each of the evenings some Haydn trios, but the rest has to be Brahms, Beethoven, Schumann, Debussy, Tchaikovsky, whatever. And she agreed and we did that, and he was happy. And in retrospect I am happy because he deserved all the accolades you can give him—not only for helping find many beautiful, valid ideas in which to express the beauty of the Haydn trios, but him being what he was, giving the [Beaux Arts] Trio the richness of his sound—he had the most beautiful sonority—but also the richness of his soul. He had a beautiful soul. I loved him very, very much, and I still do.

Piano Sonata in E-flat Major, Hob. XVI:52, Mvt. 1

Haydn wrote the E♭ Sonata late in life, and it's full of adventure; it's full of virtuosity; it's full of beans—it doesn't show any age. I felt that would be the right piece for me! [Pressler played it in his 1996 Carnegie Hall debut recital.] I *still* feel that way and I love the piece, so that's why I play it. I hope you love this Sonata. He's way ahead of Beethoven and even Mozart in sophistication. It's an unbelievable piece. Regarding the style, we don't play Haydn as loudly as Beethoven, although we're close in this Sonata. It's never heavy-handed.

Mvt. 1. *Allegro*

You're inconsistent in rhythm. There are many places where your octaves would be helped by using the fourth finger.

M. 2. Don't end the phrase with an accent. It closes.

Example 8.1. Sonata in E-flat Major, Hob. XVI:52, mm. 1–2.

Mm. 3–4. If these end with a *staccato*, there is no relation to measure 2.

M. 5. If this is the first piece in a recital, then I would suggest you play those thirds with both hands. Otherwise, you will always worry, and in the worry, the rest of the sonata will suffer. It will relieve an enormous amount of worry for you.

Mm. 6-7. We must hear a difference between the D, the Db, and the C.

Mm. 6–8. Hear the harmonies. Practice the left hand blocked so that when you play it broken, you can hear the changes.

M. 8. Without accenting the Ab. It doesn't get as loud; it stays *piano*. Also, the chords are too short. I would say to play them as sixteenths. How would you play a thirty-second note? It would be over before you start. Would you like to see the fastest gun in the West? Would you like to see it again?

M. 10. Hear the left-hand D [beat 1] going to the Eb [beat 3]. Then we feel we have reached our goal.

M. 11. There is a relationship between a D and a Db, between an A♮ and an Ab [m. 12]. Within music there are relationships; each one knows his neighbor.

M. 15. Beat 1 would be the end of the phrase.

M. 16. Finish [beat 1] and start [beat 2].

M. 18. The left-hand A goes to the B♮.

M. 20. The G goes to the F [top line].

M. 21. The F goes to the E♮ [beat 2]. Bring out the left-hand's Db, but not the G.

M. 22. Finish on beat 3.

Example 8.2. Sonata in E-flat Major, Hob. XVI:52, mm. 21–22.

M. 24. Practice just the skeleton [the chords] to hear the relationships.

M. 25. Close. Finish [on beat 3].

M. 31. Play 5-4-5-4-5 in the left hand.

M. 34. Gentle.

M. 35. Don't end the right-hand thirds with 1-2; use 4-2 so that the hand is open. The four-note slurs are like a question, "May I join you? Okay, come with me [m. 36]!"

M. 40. Bring it down, a natural coming down.

Mm. 44–45. Bring it up a little [F♯] and then bring it down. Resolve. And don't use 5-5-5 in the left hand. Play 3-4-5.

M. 46. You inner ear must tell you how to play this new key. It's not the same way as before [in B♭ major at m. 27]. He may have been an old man at the time, but he was full of beans.

Mm. 48–49. You have all these deceptive cadences. The resolutions get a different color.

M. 53. Hear the right hand, then the left hand. The canon is here.

Mm. 53–54. Hear the line descending; the G [beat 4] goes to the F [beat 1], to the E♭ [beat 2], to the D [beat 3], to the C [beat 4].

M. 54. No false accent on beat 2.

Example 8.3. Sonata in E-flat Major, Hob. XVI:52, mm. 52–54.

Mm. 61–62. Hear the resolutions in both hands. [They practice the left hand.]

M. 63. The left hand not so short.

M. 64. From a sensitivity point of view, the D♮ is important. The F♯ closes with the G.

M. 68. Now you have the E major. [Pressler whistles it.] All of a sudden you have "Three Blind Mice."

M. 115. He's laughing, like the basso in the opera. You're too serious.

M. 116. Too heavy-handed. Very little pedal. Clear, transparent, like fresh water flowing from its source in the mountains, like the mountains where Haydn lived.

9 Franz Liszt

Liszt is undeniably a master of the piano. He wrote many great works, the Sonata chief among them. His organization in that piece is unmatched by anyone. And his demands on the pianist and even on the piano itself elevated the piano to a tremendous height. He is what you think of when we say *virtuoso*; he was a tremendous showman. There was a time in my life when Liszt played a great role, but now I find some of his rhetoric a little pompous. It's true, and it's actually because my wife disliked hearing me practice Liszt. And years ago I played a great deal of Liszt: the B Minor Sonata, the *Dante* Sonata, the E♭ Concerto, the *Mephisto* Waltz, many things. I still love certain works, and I love him as a man who was such a wonderful encourager and supporter of other composers. Liszt, like Rachmaninoff, wrote music to fit his own hands, and we must often find *our* way to play the pieces.

Grande Ètude de Paganini No. 2 in E-flat Major [*Andante Capriccioso*]

M. 1. We have to have a sense of dynamics that is better. The introduction must go up to the B♭ chord. Measure 1 begins; this is the first level.

M. 2. This is the second level.

M. 3. Now start and go all the way. Warm it up as you go—and not too loud.

Example 9.1. Paganini *Étude* No. 2 in E-flat Major, mm. 1–4.

M. 4. *Cadenza*. Start in *pianissimo* so that there is a rise. And the slower you start, the faster you can finish. [They drill the last five ascending chords.] Now let me have your thumbs only [the repeated notes]. Now practice the right hand as written with the left hand playing the thumbs only. After the *fermata* he has sequences starting on the C♯, yes? Once we recognize those sequences, we build on them, growing as it descends. Once you start that B♭ [the trill], don't play like the Jolly Green Giant. Play it with a little *sforzando*, and then start the trill softer. There is an elegance in that gesture; it's B♭-B♭-B♭. Release the pedal so the rest can be heard. Experiment with dividing the chord between the hands. You could even play the last B♭ with the left hand if you want.

M. 5. I would like for you to pull each finger out. [They drill the passage adding one note at a time.] There can't be a gap between the hands; you have to wait imperceptibly for the other hand to be there. Lean into the top E♭; linger just a tiny bit. Each of the chords is long, melodic.

Mm. 5–6. The first phrase is open [ending on beat one]; the second one [mm. 6–7] is closed. Release the pedal after the chords so that the run can be clear. You can't have a gap in the run.

M. 8. In the left hand, can I have a special color on the C♭? That's the only time you have that, so naturally you should do something special. I'm still not happy with the scales; the transfer of the hands is anticipatory, and the motion is not smooth.

M. 9. It's *poco*. Not so much.

Mm. 9–10. Here again you have the open one and the closed one [mm. 10–11]. And in the chordal progressions, the middle voices are interesting.

M. 10. Divide the scale between the hands.

M. 12. Let me hear the voices of the last chord resolving to the downbeat [m. 13]. The top F goes to the D, and the middle D goes to the B♭.

M. 13. The passage is too loud. Lean on the first chord a little more; you are hitting it.

M. 14. Now the passage is more but not that much louder.

M. 15. Each time is a little more.

M. 16. The left hand is too harsh.

M. 17. Each octave passage is more than the one before; it's B♭, then D, then F [m. 18]. There's no new accent on the right-hand entrance; it's part of the scale.

M. 19. Can I have a little more strength in those top three As? And let us hear that they're descending.

M. 21. Let me hear the G octave; it relates to the E♭ [m. 20]. Release the pedal after each flourish.

M. 22. Let me have that D in the bass for the cadence.

M. 23. Both hands must be together on the flourish, and the right hand must lead. Can you make a *diminuendo*? Give me the B♭ a little bit more so we resolve to the E♭ chord.

Mm. 24–26. The left hand is one rise.

Example 9.2. Paganini *Étude* No. 2 in E-flat Major, mm. 24–26.

M. 30. Take only three notes in the left hand [beat 2], and play the G with the right hand so you play a strong chord. On the octaves, keep the arm moving in one direction; don't fall on the lower note.

M. 32. Start the octaves less each time [mm. 33–34].

M. 34. More than before; the A♭-F-B is more than A♭-F-D♮ [m. 33].

M. 38. Hear it going from C to C.

M. 41. The B♭ chord is the resolution.

M. 42. Finish it on beat 2.

Mm. 43–44. Hear the right-hand notes, D-C♭-B♭, and then the tops of the chords A♮-B♭. Use the wrist for those octaves.

M. 44. It's one sweep. You hesitate.

M. 46. Don't *diminuendo*; hear it needing to resolve to E♭.

M. 66. Coda. The C♭ is a surprise, it's always gone to a B♭. Play it once to a B♭ to hear the difference.

M. 69. Take the foot off before the flourish.

M. 71. Start a little slow, then faster and faster.

M. 72. Don't start the chords so loudly; you don't have that much strength.

M. 73. The E♭ must be juicy, rich. The whole body must be ready to come into that chord.

Grande Ètude de Paganini No. 3 in G-sharp Minor [*Allegretto*], "La Campanella"

In "La Campanella," Liszt uses the piano in the most glorifying way a piano can be used. The sounds that he elicits from the keyboard are magnificent and beautiful, and so attractive that there is no audience that will not react to it. Liszt created so many beauties which have become meaningful to the majority of the audience that loves music.

Mm. 1–3. Keep the pedal down. First of all, you give the little bells a color and a direction. Either they come or they go, depending on how you want the piece to start; they don't just stand still. That is the introduction; those are the bells that are going to play throughout the piece.

Example 9.3. Paganini *Étude* No. 3, "La Campanella," mm. 1–4.

Mm. 4–5. Let the wrist help you. Think *rotation*—not a *jump*. The pedals should only be an eighth. Don't linger past the rolled chord.

M. 6. Shape the melody. It always moves to this point [the A♯], and then it comes down. The A♯ in measure 8 is always less.

M. 12. When he reaches the highest note, change the pedal. The tune is starting again. *Leggiero*.

M. 20. It goes away.

M. 23. The timing must be consistent. Yours has a kind of haste.

Mm. 27–28. Let's hear it going up to the C♯, then down to the B, then the A♯, then the G♯.

M. 29. That F♯ is the end of the phrase—less.

M. 32. Now the tune begins on E, so it's less than when it began on F♯ [m. 30].

M. 41. Suspend it a little; then it comes to life again when the theme comes in.

M. 51. A new pedal as the new theme starts in triplets.

M. 60. The fingers push themselves out of the key with a little wrist bounce. [Pressler demonstrates a brushing or plucking effect on the key and then within his other palm.] No, don't pull out. Push against the key so that you have strength if you need it.

M. 61. A little accent on the fourth eighth-note to enforce the meter.

M. 71. It's a duet, but the left hand is the lesser voice.

M. 77. Very, very close. Completely within the key, not above at all.

M. 80. And we're glad to hear the theme again. It's more reflective this time.

M. 95. Very close fingers, and lean into the thumb.

M. 97. Push out again.

M. 112. Always get new wind. Let it soar, not walk.

Mm. 121–122. On the octaves, use 4-5-4-5-4-5 so that you relax.

Mm. 123–125. This is not the climax of the song. The climax is at measure 127. Are the bass notes all the same? No, you have to go according to the harmonies. Otherwise, it's tasteless, it's noise. If that's what you're looking for, you achieved it! What you do is impede the beauty of that song. It's like an orchestra where the trombonist says to his wife, "Did you hear my solo—wah, wah?" "Yes, I heard your solo."

Example 9.4. Paganini *Étude* No. 3, "La Campanella," mm. 121–125.

M. 127. Here is the climax; it's the second phrase of the tune.

Mm. 131–133. Now you still have the strength you need for the coda. He provides the shaping for the melody; it's up to C# and D# and then down to C# and B.

Mm. 134–135. It goes up to the C#, then down to the G#.

Piano Sonata in B Minor, S. 178

Liszt here is at his best. Everything that he represents is in the Sonata: the amorous, the religious, the showman, the influence, the example, the role model—everything is here. This Sonata can have an enormous impact on a musician, not just for an audience. It is really a great piece and demands everything from you, and there is always so much more that can be found. The variety he expresses is unbelievable. And there is the role of the fugue, because we know that Bach is the emperor of the fugue. But the fugue in Liszt's Sonata is a remarkable piece of appreciation of the role of a fugue in building something important. Just as Bach's fugues sometimes reach the monumental, so Liszt succeeded in writing a fugue that is important and gives the Sonata an aspect that, without the fugue, it never would have.

M. 1. Do the second G less than the first.

M. 2. Have you ever been to the Grand Canyon? In the Grand Canyon you see all of a sudden the earth is opening up. It would be worth going to the Grand Canyon in order to play the Liszt Sonata, that you see the earth opening up.

Example 9.5. Sonata in B Minor, mm. 1–3.

M. 4. Now that we've done it the first time, these Gs are less.

M. 7. Then it's even less.

Mm. 8–9. Be more careful to control the sound, not just blaring. And it's one *forte*, a good *forte*.

M. 10. What is missing in the theme is the rhythm. You are not giving full value to the dotted half.

Mm. 9–10. No, they're not all equal; the A♯ is not as loud as the G and D. And the triplet is too fast. It's triplets and eighths. It's not how fast you can play it; it's how fast he's asking for.

Mm. 11–12. Now we have the sequence. If the first is like this [Pressler sings the phrase, measures 9–11], then the second is less.

Mm. 14–15. The bass is a strong statement.

Mm. 14–17. Which is more, the first time or the second? Yes, it's absolutely the second one.

M. 17. Can you play *piano*? And the *arpeggio* down is a *diminuendo*. And what do the bass and treble do? [Pressler plays the F♯-G, G-A♭, F♯-G, G-A♭, G♯-A, A-B♭, G♯-A, A-B♭, A♯-B, B-C, A♯-B, B-C.] So that you hear the *arpeggio* down and you respond to it with the chords.

Mm. 17–19. Look, he says *piano* [m. 17], he says *piano* [m. 18], he says *piano* [m. 19]; how many times can he say it? He's trying again and again to go up until he breaks out here [m. 25], yes?

M. 26. That is no rhythm! [Pressler sings it in rhythm.]

M. 32. Not everything is on the same level. The D chord would go out of the key and the diminished chord would come into the key. It is always a *forte*; but what is most important is the agitation of all the rhythms.

Mm. 45–46. But that is only *piano*. Play once the right hand and close the phrase. And the left hand has the one third going up and the other third going down. Play it so that we have a difference, yes? The second one is never accented; it's a quarter and an eighth, and on top we have the *arpeggio*.

Mm. 47–48. Save. Not too loud yet.

Mm. 51–54. It doesn't have to go that much faster; it's just *più agitato*. Play only the single notes. Play the two-note slurs in both hands with the same inflection in each.

M. 55. And whatever tempo you build up to, that is the tempo of this section. You go so fast you make it impossible for this to be the crowning achievement of this section.

Mm. 56–67. What is bad about it is we hear an octave exercise. Play the first entrance [m. 55], the second one [m. 61], and the third one [m. 67]. Now play the very beginning [mm. 8–11] and now this place [mm. 56–60]. [Pressler taps the identical tempo for each.]

Mm 58–60. The three eighths [D-B♭-F♮] are preparation for the lowest note. Use your arm to shape these motives.

Example 9.6. Sonata in B Minor, mm. 58–60.

M. 72. Come down so it can build again.

Mm. 79–80. If you can do the *accelerando*, do it—as much as you have the strength, yes? But if you go so fast in the beginning [mm. 51–54], you make it impossible for this to be the achievement. And take a little time on the last one [F-E♭ in m. 79]. [Pressler demonstrates and emphasizes the E♭.] Now when you practice, it is important to hear yourself play and build the piece so that you really feel when you get here that it was really a big curve—not an octave exercise, but an emotional outburst.

M. 78. Go.

Mm. 81–82. It's not the *pizzicato* [A♮] that is important; that's the same *pizzicato* as in the beginning. What's important is the bass melody [mm. 83–86].

M. 86. Come down.

M. 92. Down.

M. 93. And this should be the softest.

Mm. 95–100. Build each entrance.

Mm. 115–116. An echo! Not slower. Resolve. Come down.

Mm. 117–118. Don't accent the eighth notes.

Mm. 118–119. He's coming down.

M. 119. And less and slower, and less. What do you feel when you play that chord [A♯ diminished]? It's a question mark.

Mm. 120–124. And he asks the question. [Pressler plays these measures.]

M. 122. The quarter is not so short.

Mm. 124–128. And he answers. [Pressler plays these measures.] But up to this point, it's like a question.

Mm. 124–125. Can you feel what that opening does?

M. 132. The grace note is not so long. The B♮ is the note you want.

M. 139. Go to this C. He increases to the C, but it is still gentle.

M. 140. Slowly.

Mm. 142–143. The second chord would be less.

Mm. 144–147. Hear the resolutions.

Mm 153–155. You play all the F♯s just the same; they should each be different. [Pressler plays the measures to point out the different colors of the underlining chords.] You must feel when the F♯ has a D under it, or a C♯, or a B, yes?

Example 9.7. Sonata in B Minor, mm. 153–155.

M. 154. This G has a pull to it.

M. 158. And that [the C♯] would be a little longer than the G [m. 154], right?

M. 162. You don't feel the magic; it does not envelope you, and you certainly don't envelop us. What does this chord [B♭ major] do to you? [Pressler plays measures 161–162 and measures 163–164 several times.] Let me hear that it does something for you. Surprise us.

M. 163. A different color, not twice the same way.

M. 165. The last chord is less; they can't all be the same. The E resolves to the D.

M. 171. We must hear each F♯.

Mm. 179–182. All of the right hand is a scale, yes? As lightly as you possibly can. And it comes down and finishes on the D [m. 182]. [Pressler plays the scale outline.] And the left hand plays the theme.

M. 182. And it goes up in a different key, yes?

M. 184. Again, as light as you possibly can.

Mm. 185–186. And finish on the E.

M. 190. You should not start very loud. You slowly build.

M. 203. We should hear the F, the F, and the F.

Mm. 204–205. The octaves culminate on the downbeat. Don't hold back the phrase.

Mm. 205, 207. Each one comes down.

Mm. 206–207. Again, the octaves culminate on the downbeat.

M. 208. Start less.

Mm. 221–231. This section must have meaning. All this effort and then the composer writes C#-B, C#-Bb, C#-A, C#-G#, et cetera, to C#-F#-E# [mm. 228–231]; this is a Herculean effort. [Pressler sings it with all the swirls.] Each of the distances is different. The further you go away from the C#, it requires a little bit more time. Only a pianist could play it exactly in tempo, and that is not a complement. Then he culminates with fire on the diminished chord, yes?

Example 9.8. Sonata in B Minor, mm. 228–231.

M. 231. That chord is too soon [the third beat]. [Pressler sings C#-F#-E#.]

Mm. 232–234. Can I have the difference between A-E-A-E?

Mm. 236–237. What is this? An exercise? Czerny? [Pressler plays the passage bringing out the line and leading into measure 238.] Isn't it a bridge?

Mm. 239, 241. Can you hear the difference between these two *arpeggios*?

Mm. 242–243. And now hear G♮-F# and B-A in the left hand, not the jumps [C#-G and D#-F#]. You have big hands; you should easily do that.

Mm. 244–245. Listen to the left-hand melody, and it comes down with charm to the A.

M. 249. A different chord than before.

M. 250. Start from nothing.

M. 254. Continue that same speed. Otherwise, it's simply too fast and has no connection.

Mm. 271–275. Here the right hand gives you all the cadences, but then it's "Ya! Da!" [m. 276].

M. 276. Not fast.

M. 277. It's like the beginning of the Sonata, but you are so fast at this point that it's not talking anymore; it's not the same piece; it's meaningless. It sounds like you don't know what to do with this place, so it's better to get it over with. [Pressler plays the theme, mm. 277–279, in single notes like in the opening.] It's the same, yes?

Mm. 291–292. Go.

Mm. 296–299. The last chord is "out" each time.

M. 300. He says, "*Ritenuto*," which you do. He says, "*Ed appassionata*," which you *don't* do. Now how can one learn to play this place passionately? After you have heard this [Pressler sings the chords of mm. 296–299], it's like fate is knocking at the door. And there is a person who's begging.

Mm. 301–304. The fate again.

Mm. 305–309. This is a great moment. [Pressler plays these measures.]

M. 323. Come down.

M. 325. Slower.

M. 348. What does this say to you? He says, "*Dolcissimo*." How tender can he get? And then he says, "*Con intimo sentimento*." Were you talking intimately there? Absolutely not!

M. 351. Even less after the trill.

M. 387. He shows you he wants it to start slowly with the eighths and then get faster towards the end.

M. 393. Slow it down.

Mm. 394–395. The left hand is important too. That is the climax; it's like the brass follows the outline.

M. 396. And slow.

Example 9.9. Sonata in B Minor, mm. 394–396.

M. 397. Come down.

M. 399. Not too fast [the turn].

Mm. 407–408. And now, each one is a little less. Can you hear the resolution? Each one is tension and release, tension and release.

M. 410. Plaintively.

M. 414. Instead of a finishing chord, he extends it.

M. 459. When you come to the *fugue*, not fast. It must talk.

M. 710. Here he tells us there is hope for humanity.

Example 9.10. Sonata in B Minor, mm. 710–714.

The most important part for me was not that you couldn't play the piece. I don't think there is anything in the piece you cannot conquer. What was missing was the reason for that piece to be, not just to show your *octaves* or where you play some thirds, where it ends up being an exercise in a few different forms. You must traverse it in front of us, and with us, and take us through this enormous canvas. It is from dust we came, to dust we go, but not before going through heaven, through hell, and find in the end that phenomenal transfiguration—when it becomes all of a sudden transformed, that somehow he has found his final journey into peace. When that last chord comes before the *pizzicati*, it should be a spiritual enlightenment. From the beginning there is an intensity of each theme built out of one little seed. There must be an immense emotional range and a sense of mystery.

Figure 1. Daniel Guilet, Menahem Pressler, and Bernard Greenhouse forming the Beaux Arts Trio on June 19, 1959. IU Archives, P0023936.

Figure 2. Menahem Pressler with a student at a piano in 1973. IU Archives, P0027422.

Figure 3. Menahem Pressler, October 2003. IU Archives, P0070637.

Figure 4. Menahem Pressler, publicity photo. IU Archives, P0070644.

Figure 5. Menahem Pressler, publicity photo. IU Archives, P0070645.

Figure 6. Pressler in his Indiana University studio. IU Archives, P0070650.

Figure 7. Bernard Greenhouse, Daniel Guilet, Arturo Toscanini (*seated in high-backed chair*), Pressler, unidentified woman. IU Archives, P0070654.

Interlude VI
Funny Stories

In Amsterdam, we played a concert in the chamber music hall in the Concert-gebouw. Alfred Brendel, who is also a Philips artist, played a concerto in the big hall, and he came to our concert after his concerto. After the concert, the director of Philips Records took us all out to dinner, and after dinner they bring the dessert menu, and I see "Beaux Arts Trio." And I say to the waiter, "What's that?"

He says, "I don't know."

I said, "Who does know?"

He says, "The cook, the owner."

So I said, "Could you ask him?"

He says, "Sure."

So the cook comes out and says, "Yes, it's named for my favorite group."

I say, "What is it?"

He says, "It is three different, very exceptional sherbets, wonderful fruit that you can't find everywhere."

And Brendel says, "Do you not have anything named for me?"

And he says, "Not yet."

And I actually have that menu.

One time a fan asked me, "Who does your arrangements?" And I answered, "We're so poor we just do the composers' arrangements."

And one time someone said to me, like someone had said to [Jacques] Thibaud, "Your group is so good, I hope it grows and grows and grows!"

The Trio was rehearsing and Bernard Greenhouse, the first cellist of the Trio said, "Menahem, you are too loud." We tried it again and he said the same thing. Then the third time I didn't even play, and he looked at me: "You are still too loud!" I protested that I didn't even play. "Yes, but you *looked* too loud!"

I sometimes have a dream that I have to play a concert and I haven't restudied the piece. I'm sweating blood thinking of the passages that I ought to be playing. "I know this piece, but I haven't played it in years, and now I have to play it."

Actually, a very true story, and I don't know how this dream happened—it's terrible. I dreamed I would be playing with Stokowski, and I lost my pants! In my dream, I never even had a hope that I would be playing with Stokowski; that would be such a great thing. And what does fate do? I actually get an invitation to play with Stokowski conducting the New York Philharmonic in the Pension Concert, one of the great affairs of the year. But I tell you the truth: because of the dream I wore not only suspenders but a belt. What kind of a crazy dream is that? Really a crazy dream.

10 Felix Mendelssohn

Mendelssohn, when you see his works and the enormous perfection of his writing, he's a master. His preludes and fugues are not often played, but should be. His *études* also should be played. Obviously, I have played the two trios many, many times, and they are such great music that you could play them every day. Mendelssohn is still very underrated as a composer and as a pianist too. In Leipzig, Mendelssohn is all around you. He was the director of the Gewandhaus; he founded with Schumann the conservatory there. He brought Bach back through the B Minor Mass. Bach was forgotten, even though Bach came from Leipzig. Mendelssohn discovered the richness, the virtuosity, but mainly the depths of feeling in the Fourth Concerto of Beethoven, and played it, and we owe him a debt of gratitude for that. Nobody at that time played it; they thought it wasn't great music.

Rondo Capriccioso, Op. 14

The *Rondo Capriccioso* is a beautiful piece to play, a wonderful piece to play, and many pianists have played it with great pleasure. It shows a great deal of the transparency and beauty and the lightness that Mendelssohn was capable of.

M. 1. Now to begin with, it is something very gentle. When he starts the first chords, he's actually giving us something like an accompanist gives for a singer to introduce the mood. You played much too loudly, and much too big, and much too heavy. You should very lightly introduce the song.
M. 3. I don't think it needs that big a *ritardando*. From that point on yours becomes a heavy sounding song.
Mm. 3–4. Hear the A♮-D♯ resolving to the E.

Example 10.1. *Rondo Capriccioso*, Op. 14, mm. 1–4.

Example 10.1. (*continued*)

Mm. 5–6. You *crescendo* the D#-E-E too much.

M. 7. And that, which is so beautiful, it could be two clarinets. When it joins, shape it beautifully [B-B#-C#-A-G#]; let it flow.

M. 13. It's too accented. Follow the contour of the line.

Mm. 15–17. Hear the two lines, top and bass, and the Es are too exaggerated. Don't play *fortissimo*; just think clarity, yes?

M. 18. Each group of three right-hand notes leads to the next beat.

M. 23. Think of a new instrument down there [G♮-F#-G♮-E].

M. 25. Less sound; *diminuendo* so you bring it to a conclusion.

M. 26. More *ritard*; you have to lead into those two *fermati*.

M. 27. *Presto.* What I would like is no pedal and as softly as you possibly can play. Only pedal a little bit on the first E, nowhere else. And I would like that your arms be completely free.

Mm. 27–28. The slur [E-D#-E] diminishes each time. Don't accent the last E; make it softer.

Example 10.2. *Rondo Capriccioso*, Op. 14, mm. 27–30.

Mm. 32–36. Can you hear the sequence [B-A#-B and A-G#-A]?

Mm. 38–39. Listen to the G-F♮-E-E♭ *diminuendo* from a *mezzo pianissimo* to a *pianissimo*. But you're starting from a *piano*.

M. 50. Less, then measure 52 is the least; follow it all the way down.

M. 59. The A♮ is less again.

M. 71. Color that E.

M. 74. The B is a new start.

M. 82. Make the Ds longer.

Mm. 91–95. You have to hear the line coming down.

Mm. 97–99. Now, for the octaves, what I would like is the arms to be very light—and lead with the left. Begin them very, very light.

M. 100. The octave Ds should not end with an accent; you go thump on the last note!

M. 101. The cadence chord [G major] should not be so short.

M. 117. Surprise us with the A major.

Mm. 124–127. *Pianissimo*, and he does have a *crescendo*, but at the maximum he is *piano*, certainly not *fortissimo*.

M. 133. Help out with pedal in this section.

M. 138. No, don't give the same weight on a C♮ that you do on a C♯ [m. 136].

M. 150. You actually are doing what is written, but it is too dry for my taste. Pedal where you have the melody [mm. 150–151], then take your foot off for the rests [mm. 152–153].

Example 10.3. *Rondo Capriccioso*, Op. 14, mm. 150–153.

Mm. 156–157. Block the pattern so the hand can learn to stay close to the key.

M. 177. That C♯ goes on up into the air. Take a little time there.

M. 179. Sssh!

Mm. 183–188. That's too much pedal. You practice so well and then you put on all that pedal. You have to go on a diet, a pedal diet!

Mm. 191–193. And the higher you go, the more pedal you can take, because there will not be so many overtones, yes? So when you go to the top, take some pedal.

Mm. 196–197. Like it's the end of the piece. Finish!

M. 206. You have to switch the brain at this point. Take a second so that the brain will do it for you. And also, not that it starts to induce fear, but on the contrary, you release because you know you can play what's coming.

Mm. 211–212. If you do the pedal as indicated, be sure that you play the repeated Gs very quietly; it's *pianissimo*.

Mm. 217–226. Do for me once just the sixteenths, listening to it "run out." Now let me have just the eighths. Shape the *decrescendo*. Now do once just the thirds. Now play it all together again.

Mm. 223–226. Now give us the feeling that it runs out; it finishes, and then comes the surprise.

Mm. 227–237. Yes, pedal, but not like someone who is in a shipwreck and is holding on to a piece of wood! Now I would like to hear the left hand alone shaping the line. Bravo! That is what I want. Now I would like to hear the right hand with half the weight of the left hand.

Mm. 227–233. Pedal on beat 1, and release on beat 2.

Mm. 234–236. Here you must change the pedal on beats 1 and 2.

M. 237. Don't accent the last note [B]; finish there. Then start with less so you have power to finish strong.

11 Wolfgang Amadeus Mozart

I feel that Mozart and Schubert are actually the most difficult composers to perform. There's no hiding, which means you can't use the pedal to the extent that you blur a passage. And then, because it is so pure, so natural, depth has to be created by your view into the depths of the piece. Schnabel's remark about the piano sonatas is still the best: "Too easy for children, too difficult for artists." And since years have gone by, I still feel the closest to these two, Mozart and Schubert, but it is in Mozart where you rediscover how deep your feelings are, because his demand to you as a musician is very strong. His demand to you as a pianist is equally strong, and his demand to you as interpreter of the music in a sense develops further and further throughout the years. The moments of joy, the moments of pain, the moments of love are stronger now than when I was younger. It started that way, but they became stronger, and now they are much, much stronger. It is with a reverence, with a love, with a sense of responsibility that I share my love for Mozart by playing him, through knowing him, and through teaching him. It is a joy to teach Mozart and to be aware of what it is in you that creates that devotion.

Piano Sonata in B-flat Major, K. 281

Mvt. 1. *Allegro*

M. 1. Be sure the trill connects into the second beat. Ease out of the trill with a decrease of speed.

M. 3. The two chords must relate to the trill and the scale. Full sound on the G and the F, not so short, and with a touch of pedal. The thirty-second figure must be played with a relaxed hand; start the F with a down wrist.

M. 4. Relate to measure 2 still with a full sound.

Example 11.1. Sonata in B-flat Major, K. 281, mvt. 1, mm. 1–4.

M. 7. Strum the chord.

M. 9. The pattern leads to the B♭ on beat 4.

M. 12. The second eighth is a new start.

M. 14. Have a slight break before bringing in the ultimate B♭-D-F-D.

Mm. 16–17. Bring each hand to a close with no extra space between the octave leap.

M. 17. Move the phrase forward through the Cs.

Mm. 18–20. We have the question and answer.

Example 11.2. Sonata in B-flat Major, K. 281, mvt. 1, mm. 18–21.

M. 22. Not heavy.

Mm. 22–26. Practice the skeleton chord progression.

M. 23. Use the wrist at the middle of the run.

M. 29. *Diminuendo* as the line descends.

M. 35. The D must relate to the previous E♭—not so short.

Mm. 35, 37. Stroke the left-hand notes, G-C-C.

M. 41. Play the graces on the beat.

Mm. 42–44. Play the trills as triplets.

Mm. 48, 50, 52. The left-hand starting notes not so loud. The scale must sound free.

Mm. 61–62. Connect the left-hand thirds.

M. 67. We must hear that last B♭. The chord is crisp and not too loud.

M. 68. The second figure is an echo, and slightly slower.

M. 69. This figure descends and leads us back to the return.

M. 72. Close the figure with a relaxed hand.

M. 109. Close the phrase, *diminuendo*.

Mvt. 2. *Andante amoroso*

M. 1. Swing in one, not three beats.

M. 7. *Diminuendo.*

Example 11.3. Sonata in B-flat Major, K. 281, mvt. 2, mm. 1–8.

M. 12. Just *mezzo forte*. Press into the right-hand E♭.

Mm. 14–15. Longer chords.

Mm. 16–23. In four-measure groups. Don't take time to breathe between every two measures.

M. 17. Play the grace note on the beat.

M. 25. Play the F♯-G as even sixteenths.

M. 27. Not loud, just a *mezzo forte*.

M. 33. Play the A♮-G as even sixteenths.

M. 42. Come out of the trill with a C-D to lead to the E♭.

Mm. 45–46. Close the phrase, resolve.

Mm. 47–48. Connect the right-hand octave leap [B♭].

Mm. 48, 50, 52. Play different B♭s according to what follows. How many B♭s do you have in your palette?

M. 53. Start the G♭ from the key.

Mm. 59–61. The left hand could help.

Example 11.4. Sonata in B-flat Major, K. 281, mvt. 2, mm. 59–61.

M. 99. *Decrescendo.*

M. 101. *Decrescendo.*

Mvt. 3. *Rondeau: Allegro*

M. 1. Keep an even tempo throughout and relax the arms.
Mm. 3–4. *Decrescendo.*

Example 11.5. Sonata in B-flat Major, K. 281, mvt. 3, mm. 1–4.

M. 7. Play the graces on the beat.
Mm. 7–8. Connect the trill to the B♭ with no holes.
M. 17. And close the phrase.
Mm. 39–42. Play ending notes [D-E♭ or D-E♮] to the trill each time.

Example 11.6. Sonata in B-flat Major, K. 281, mvt. 3, mm. 39–42.

M. 43. Not all the same. Tell the story.
Mm. 52–54. The left hand is smoother, not so accented.
M. 55. The accents belong to the right hand only.
M. 56. Play the left-hand *staccato* very easily, not overdone.
M. 68. Voice the outer lines.
M. 70. Roll all the way from the bottom to the top; open the door.
Mm. 75–77. Shape the left-hand three-note figures.
Mm. 113, 118. Play even sixteenths, not smears, that lead into the trill easily.
M. 123. Play the left-hand passage lightly and with control.
Mm. 159–160. Slower; time is needed to close the entire movement.

Wolfgang Amadeus Mozart 129

Piano Concerto in C Minor, K. 491

Mvt. 1. *Allegro*

Mm. 100–103. You hear what the orchestra plays; it's fate that he's concerned with. Yours sounds like, "My daisies, oh my poor daisies." There are no daisies; I need more character. Use your arm on the Gs to bring you up to begin the scale. The scale is too mannered for my taste. It's a bridge; make it smooth, very natural with a sense of direction. Even if you do it with a philosophical bent, it's serious, but still not ponderous.

Mm. 102–103. Stay up all the way; don't diminish.

Example 11.7. Concerto in C Minor, K. 491, mvt. 1, mm. 100–103.

Mm. 105–106. Now close it.

M. 108. Now it starts.

Mm. 109–110. The left hand diminishes and goes out.

M. 110. It's the variation, but without exaggeration.

M. 112. A hair of delay. This fifth is not what you'd expect.

M. 117. Reach up to the G.

M. 118. You finish your phrase and the orchestra starts something new.

Mm. 123–125. That sounds so gingerly. That octave leap is daring; it's a trapeze artist.

M. 131. I want you to take the E♭ with the left hand so that the leap will be secure.

M. 135. This is different from before [mm. 131 and 133]. Before, the sixteenth pushed forward into the chord, but here it must feel completely different to find that B♭ chord.

M. 136. Don't hit the chord.

M. 139. Don't hit that D; finish it, then start a new scale.

Mm. 140–141. The last notes of the scale prepare us for the long note [B♭].

M. 146. There should be a different touch for the chromaticism. If you pull back the time like that, then you must go back to tempo in measures 147 and 148; otherwise, you have set a new tempo.

Mm. 153–154. Go up the second time.

Mm. 155–156. Be aware of the cadence in the left hand.

Mm. 167–168. It's a sequence; the second time is less, yes?

M. 169. Use the last four left-hand notes to lead to the next measure.

M. 175. Mozart writes the trill into the line.

Mm. 178–179. Change the dynamic. The last note is light; close it.

M. 186. The G closes the phrase.

M. 198. Start.

M. 221. I would play this one less.

Mm. 239–241. Emphasize the lower notes, but don't exaggerate the leap from the C. Make a nice cadence.

Mm. 241–244. Until now you are surrounded by the orchestra, and you play every bass note with them; but here you are alone, and it should not sound so notey.

Mm. 242–243. Open, then close.

Mm. 248–249. Sing, then close.

M. 250. Not short in the right hand.

M. 254. Let us hear the richness of the chords. Keep the shoulders loose.

M. 256. Not rushed.

M. 260. Come down to that B♭.

Mm. 261–262. [Pressler adds scale passages to "fill it out."]

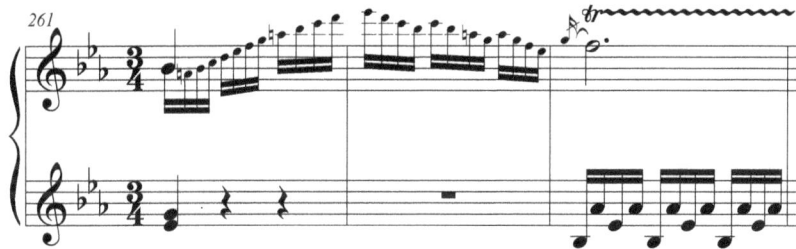

Example 11.8. Concerto in C Minor, K. 491, mvt. 1, mm. 261–263.

M. 263. Start the trill from above.

Mm. 283–284. Resolve the B♭ to the A♭.

M. 293. Still *piano*.

M. 299. Make no *crescendo*.

M. 300. The sixth is too soft for my taste. And now go up to the B♭.

Mm. 309–310. I play the F♯, C♯, and A with the left hand to emphasize those notes, if it helps. It needs more articulation, but you can use the pedal.

Example 11.9. Concerto in C Minor, K. 491, mvt. 1, mm. 309–310.

Mm. 317–318. Again, the left hand can help on the D, A♮, and F♯.

Mm. 322–323. Follow the line down.

Mm. 330, 334, 338, 342, 346. Play all those ending chords so that each one has a reason for being there. I'd like a *sforzando* on each of those chords.

Mm. 332–333. Hear all the Fs.

M. 347. Use the right-hand notes [A♭-G-F] like a kind of melody.

Mm. 353–354. Not loud; close the phrase.

Mm. 355–361. The chords must seem connected. I need the scales to have a little bit more burnished sound, a little more bronze.

Mm. 389–390. Let the sound bloom; lean into those upper notes. It doesn't have to be so dry; you can use some pedal.

M. 391. Let it close.

M. 409. Close to a cadence.

M. 411. With emotion, but not sentimental.

Mm. 413–414. This one is less.

M. 415. This is the third sequence. If you start this measure too loudly, it is like "gilding the lily."

Mm. 415–416. Start each chromatic scale from the G.

Mm. 417–418. Take us up to the climax and then back down, because then you have the bassoon entrance.

Mm. 421, 423. I play both those Cs with the left hand.

Mm. 425–426. Lead with the thumb.

M. 435. That G is a finish.

Mm. 435–436. Don't accent the low Gs; it's like a trill.

M. 444. More as he takes over; really pull out more stops there. He moves in; he doesn't wait.

Mm. 449–451. No *diminuendo* to the C; then make a *diminuendo* to the D.

Mm. 452–453. It sounds too small, and the left hand is only one quarter. The right hand is "out" on the F.

Mm. 467–470. [Pressler suggests using scales and broken chords to embellish the cadence.]

Example 11.10. Concerto in C Minor, K. 491, mvt. 1, mm. 467–471.

M. 471. Begin the trill from above.

M. 522. Make a *diminuendo* with those notes, C-E♭-G-C.

Mvt. 2. *Larghetto*

M. 1. Begin with rich sound—rich but not hard. He repeats the B♭s to keep it alive and give it a rhythmic impact. It must have broadness, outlook, dignity, beauty, and it's one large phrase, not torn to bits.

M. 2. Enrich the cadence. Hear the alto G going to the F, the tenor E♭ to the D.

Example 11.11. Concerto in C Minor, K. 491, mvt. 2, mm. 1–2.

M. 3. Make it a beautiful sonority.

M. 4. The Ds have a swing to them. Less, end in *piano*, and out.

M. 9. Out on the E♭.

M. 10. Out on the F.

Mm. 14–15. [Pressler recommends adding trills to the B♭ and the A♮ and then connecting notes down to the B♭.]

Example 11.12. Concerto in C Minor, K. 491, mvt. 2, mm. 14–15.

M. 17. Play it with a richness.

Mm. 23–24. The last notes must flow into that G. You are composing that bridge.

M. 24. The A♭ must top the G, yes?

M. 25. When you have thirds, they take on a new richness.

M. 26. You have to play the E♭ in such a way that it deserves a D.

M. 35. The left hand is too short.

M. 38. A different touch from measure 37.

M. 49. Each scale is a *decrescendo*.

M. 50. The left hand is not short.

M. 57. Reach up to the E♭.

Mm. 57–58. Resolve the diminished chord [beat 4].

Mm. 72–73. [Pressler demonstrates additions to the cadence by including trills and additional connecting notes.]

Example 11.13. Concerto in C Minor, K. 491, mvt. 2, mm. 72–73.

M. 80. More sound; the E♭ is the climax.

M. 83. *Diminuendo* the scale.

M. 84. More sound on this closing idea; I don't hear you. Use the weight of the arm; especially the E♭ has no life.

Mm. 86–88. What is the left hand saying? [Pressler plays the chord progression to hear the shaping.] You must feel how the melody works with the harmony. It's not what someone tells you; it's what you feel inside.

M. 88. Close on beat 3.

Mvt. 3. *Allegretto*

Mm. 16–17. Many good things. What I object to is that somehow throughout the piece you don't find new sounds or know how to manipulate the tempo a little bit better. The development in those variations must be the focus. In this first one, although it's the same tempo, one must feel the sense of *virtuosi* and how much agitation there is.

M. 16b. [The second endings are measures 16b, 24b, and 32b.]

M. 17. Use your arm; you sound so lighthearted. The end of the measure comes down a bit.

M. 20. Come down so that the A♭ [m. 21] is a beginning.

Example 11.14. Concerto in C Minor, K. 491, mvt. 3, mm. 17–20.

Mm. 21–23. Bring the left-hand E♭ into the D [m. 23]. The right-hand figure propels you forward.

M. 23. The Ds are so dry! It's like the desert all of a sudden; the desert wind has taken hold, and it's only the bones we hear.

M. 29. I don't hear the first note.

M. 40. The Gs are like a signal.

M. 42. While the scale is going up, it's *non-legato*.

M. 43. Now it's *legato*.

M. 45. Start. The scale is *non-legato*, and color beat 3.

M. 46. It starts from below and goes up.

M. 47. *Legato* again. Use the last note of the group to send it back up.

M. 57. Give yourself a little bit more on the low notes.

M. 60. Have a clear E.

M. 61. That's a surprising harmonic exchange!

M. 62. Go up.

M. 64. And don't play it so mighty that the entrance gets dwarfed, so that they fight with each other.

M. 65. Give the chords enough weight.

Mm. 69–71. Be careful that you don't swallow the left hand.

M. 72. Take the last half of the bar with the right hand.

M. 84. The Cs are a new beginning.

M. 87. Have a free arm and a clear sound on the chord.

Mm. 104–105. What kind of mood is that? It's warmer and happier, and what he wants is a warmer and happier sound; it sings more.

M. 106. The A♭ is "out", but the F is "in."

M. 107. You can have pedal on each note, but don't hold the pedal through.

M. 108. This is "out" and "in."

M. 110. For the bass A♭ to the treble E♭ you must position your body so that these two notes are solid.

M. 111. Let that be more blooming and not so dry.

Example 11.15. Concerto in C Minor, K. 491, mvt. 3, mm. 105–112.

Example 11.15. (*continued*)

M. 121. Always when he uses chromaticism there is a sadness. It doesn't skip.

M 124. It's okay to come into the chord with a slight *sforzando*, but sustain the chord.

M. 127. Finish on the C, and then give us more *crescendo* so there is a sense of daring there.

M. 128. You want to free yourself after the A♭ so you can come in with movement. Open up the sound.

M. 130. Close it down, and then open it again [D-E♭-F♮].

M. 131. The thirds are *legato*, and be careful that they are not so bangy that they take away from the G.

M. 134. Less on the B♭.

M. 139. Don't hit the G and F♯; make a line.

Mm. 141–144. Are you aware of the line the scales make? Bring out those lowest notes.

Mm. 142–143. Isn't A♭-G different than A♭-A♭ [mm. 141–142]?

M. 150. The left hand closes.

M. 152. The E♭ is less than the E♮. Your sound is too harsh.

M. 159. The D♭ is long, and also the D♭ in measure 160 and the C in measure 161. That variation has a sense of hopelessness, because he doesn't resolve it for us. I love playing it, because there's a quality that's so deep and an expression of his personal feelings in some ways so formal, like Bach.

M. 172. Change the color! The oboe and the flute had these melodies, and then it is your turn to imitate or do better than they did. Play the upbeat in such a way that you set up a slight pause on the C major [m. 173].

M. 173. The Gs are plaintive.

M. 176. Those bass notes are so short; are they quarters or eighth notes?

M. 177. Not faster.

M. 179. *Diminuendo* the G to the F♯, and not faster.

M. 180. Swell the D⁷ chord and then out on beat 3.

M. 189. The A is "up" so that it can come down to the D [m. 190].

M. 191. The D-E-F belongs to the next.

M. 192. "Out" on the B♮.

M. 194. Can those be bright and shiny? And playful like a little laughter.

M. 198. I wouldn't play these so short.

M. 208. The left hand must be exactly even; you know the orchestra has those same eighth notes.

M. 212. Have a sense of coming back down.

Mm. 219–220. [Pressler inserts a mini *cadenza*.]

Example 11.16. Concerto in C Minor, K. 491, mvt. 3, mm. 218–220.

M. 221. Outwardly, it's a dance. After all, it's in 6/8, but the words that he uses are not so happy. Give it a tiny bit of sadness that the *chromaticism* implies.

M. 224. Color the major chord.

M. 227. Be careful that you don't play so carelessly; it opens up here.

M. 230. There's a breath there; take off your foot. The D is "out."

M. 236. Close the phrase.

M. 240. It's a written-out *accelerando*.

M. 242. "Out" on the Cs.

Mm. 246–247. Give us the Fs, then start less.

M. 249. Close it.

M. 250. The grace notes are on the beat.

M. 257. The left-hand C is just a quarter.

Mm. 258–259. Lighter on the Cs.

Mm. 265–266. Close the phrase.

M. 282. Surprise. It's a deceptive cadence.

M. 285. Play the last two chords with the orchestra. It's as if the curtain goes down on a tragedy, a grand tragedy.

Piano Sonata in D Major, K. 576

Mvt. 1. *Allegro*

Mm. 1–2. To the D, to the F#, to the A. This fanfare culminates in measure 2. Keep moving forward and *crescendo* to measure 2. The As don't *decrescendo*.

Example 11.17. Sonata in D Major, K. 576, mvt. 1, mm. 1–2.

M. 4. Close the phrase.

Mm. 7–8. Close the phrase, but not too softly.

M. 11. Hear the slur in both hands, the left-hand E to F♯ and the right-hand C♯ to D.

M. 15. That *arpeggio* [e minor] must be more daring.

M. 16. End big, then contrast.

M. 18. Close.

M. 21. The E♯ is less than the D♯ [m. 20].

M. 23. Use the left-hand three-note figure to *decrescendo*.

M. 24. Start less and build to the end. Yours sounds stuck in the same dynamic. The left hand should lead you forward.

M. 26. Still building.

M. 38. Shine over the top.

M. 41. End big.

Mm. 42–43. I would lead to the downbeat with the chord not so soft.

M. 46. Graceful.

M. 50. A surprise. Let the right hand take time around the pattern.

M. 51. Go up so you can come down in the next measure.

M. 57. Have a presence, *mezzo forte*.

M. 65. Bright, not hard.

M. 68. Less the second time.

M. 69. Feel that F♯ leading to the G of measure 70.

Mm. 72–73. Lighter on the second note [B♭-A].

Mm. 73–74. Again, lighter on the second note [C-B♭].

Mm. 77–78. *Diminuendo* to B minor.

Mm. 111–117. I don't find that you're sensitive enough to the difference between C to G [mm. 111–112] and C to G♯ [mm. 112–113], and from D to A [mm. 113–114] and D to A♯ [mm. 114–115]. And the line is growing from C to D to E to F♯ to G. I don't hear that you play with the awareness of an artist, yes?

Example 11.18. Sonata in D Major, K. 576, mvt. 1, mm. 112–118.

M. 115. The left hand has to get out of the way.

M. 135. What is the difference from the previous time [m. 131]? It's a different chord.

M. 137. The F♯ is not short.

M. 139. Not heavy.

M. 142. More right hand than left hand.

M. 150. Start new.

M. 153. Start, so that measure 154 is higher.

M. 154. The second half of the measure comes down.

M. 155. The D is "out" and then a new start so that we have ups and downs.

Mm. 159–160. A natural ending, not so obvious, maybe just a little "and out."

Mvt. 2. *Adagio*

M. 1. Make your ornaments not so bumpy, aria-like.

Example 11.19. Sonata in D Major, K. 576, mvt. 2, mm. 1–4.

M. 6. Start the right hand less, and open up the distance; it's an E♯ rather than E. This must touch you very deeply, then move to the A [m. 7].

M. 8. My question is, "Is the E-C♯-A going up or down, or is it staying on the same level?" You want it to go up, so fine, let's do that. But it starts from wherever you left off; the cello leads us to the new pattern.

M. 10. Hear where it is going. The left-hand thirds lead us to F♯ [m. 11].

M. 12. Finish the phrase, the F♯ resolves on the E.

M. 13. Twice you have played that chord so blah. It has an accent on it, it is a surprise, it is an emotion; it has always been an A chord until now. Use the wrist for it [the sixty-fourths] so there is direction, then it comes down to the A [m. 14].

M. 14. Then it goes up again to the G♮.

M. 16. Link to the F♯ minor key with the *chromaticism*.

M. 17. It's magic, so different from the previous theme. Paint a picture with these notes. The left hand is strumming, bowing. The E♯ resolves to the F♯; the B♯ resolves to the C♯.

M. 18. Sink into the C♯.

Example 11.20. Sonata in D Major, K. 576, mvt. 2, mm. 17–18.

M. 20. The right hand cadences, then the left-hand entrance renews it.

M. 23. Swell the measure. Again, *chromaticism* leads to the new idea.

M. 24. The right hand spins.

M. 31. Control the left-hand entrance; open the door.

Mm. 33, 37. These should not sound the same. There should not be the same weight on the notes.

M. 43. Listen for the leaf to spin downward from C♯ to G♯ to E.

M. 44. The dotted eighth must be very exact. Pedal to color the top of the line.

M. 45. The left hand colors, fills in, and expands the right-hand E.

M. 50. Reach up to the C♯.

Mvt. 3. *Allegretto*

M. 1. You're right that it says *Allegretto*, meaning it should not be too fast, but it has no spark. I think just a little bit faster would give you the possibilities of sparkling. The right-hand fourth note [D] can't bang.

M. 7. No accent—it's coming down A-F♯ [m. 5], G-E [m. 6], to D, C♯, B, and A.

Example 11.21. Sonata in D Major, K. 576, mvt. 3, mm. 5–8.

M. 9. And start.

Mm. 13–14. The left-hand eighths are too short.

M. 16. Less, but still loud!

M. 26. Give the long note more life. This begins a section that goes up [m. 28] and should keep going up [m. 30] and only comes down in measure 33.

M. 34. This has both sides to it; it is "finish" and it begins a phrase.

M. 40. Now, sparkle.

M. 45. Sparkle.

Mm. 46–48. Listen for the two voices.

M. 49. Sparkle.

M. 52. The C♯ finishes; the E is a new start.

M. 56. Finish gracefully.

M. 62. *Crescendo* all the way up.

M. 69. This is the top.

M. 70. Now it comes down.

M. 84. Not too much; this is only the start.

M. 85. And grow.

M. 87. And more.

M. 88. This is the top.

M. 94. The C♮s are sharp notes.

M. 95. Again, that first note [F♯] is long; it's a complete contrast from the Cs [m. 94].

M. 99. Contrast, surprise!!

M. 125. Again, it's an ending and a beginning.

Mm. 161–162. *Decrescendo* without much *ritard*.

Mm. 184–189. More on the B so the phrase can *diminuendo*. Then play the final chords with charm, not heavy.

Example 11.22. Sonata in D Major, K. 576, mvt. 3, mm. 184–189.

Interlude VII
Stories about Pianists

When I was young, I heard Ignaz Friedman. He still remains in my mind as one of the great pianists. Even today, when I hear a recording of him playing Chopin, or Mendelssohn's *Songs without Words*, I find it to be incredible, wonderful playing.

Sviatoslav Richter was one of the greatest pianists. We played four times during his festival in Moscow at the Pushkin Museum. He was a great icon in my life. I was very surprised and honored that he spoke about me in his diaries. Once we were playing in Menton, France, and he was playing in Italy, just across the French border. We were able to hear him play, and afterward I went and spoke to him. He was not very happy about the way he played. He told me he would love to go to France, but he had no passport. You know, it was before September 11, and they didn't check very carefully at the border, so I said, "Why don't you come with us?" So he was lying in the floor of our car, and we took him across to France! I asked him whether he knew the Schumann trios; he said no. He came to our concert the next day, when we did one of the Schumann trios. Then he invited us to his festival near Tours and also to Moscow.

He was enormously hard on himself. His talent was so big; he reached out further than most of us. His repertoire was bigger than any other pianist's; he played more than Michelangeli or Pollini. Only Andras Schiff has a larger repertoire nowadays. Richter said he would like to play duets with me, but we were never able to schedule it. I was very surprised when a student of mine showed me Richter's memoirs where he mentioned me:

> A magnificent programme! Whenever these artists perform, it's a real artistic event. Pressler is particularly close to me as a musician. He captivates with his sincerity and, it seems to me, the music gives him immoderate pleasure. For him, giving a concert is a source of genuine happiness, and for this I envy him enormously. Initially, one was rather put off by his superfluous gestures (expressive of his enthusiasm), but after five minutes you no longer noticed (and in any case he does it with total sincerity).[1]

When Artur Rubinstein came to hear our trio for the first time, he told me backstage that when he was told the Beaux Arts Trio was the greatest, he was sure they had to be three Japanese musicians. Instead we were three old Jews playing!

With Rubinstein, the beauty of his playing was so natural that when you heard him, you felt, "Yes, that is the nature of the piece; that is the way I would like to play it." The reason Rubinstein's Chopin is beautiful is his relationship with the composer. No teacher can do this for you.

I studied one summer in France with Robert Casadesus. You know, of course, that Casadesus devoted himself to Debussy and Ravel and Fauré, but the German masters also played an immense role in his work. I admired him so much as a pianist, as an artist, and as a man. He was very helpful with fingerings. I still use his fingerings to the "Appassionata." Casadesus once commented he hadn't heard a trio play so beautifully since Cortot-Thibaud-Casals!

After Casadesus, I spent a very intense summer with Egon Petri in Oakland at Mills College. His first question was to ask me why I wanted to study with him since he thought I seemed "finished." He knew I had already won the Debussy Prize and made my debut with Ormandy and the Philadelphia Orchestra. Petri's approach was very different from mine. He filtered everything through his brain and only then came the heart. His passions were controlled, thought about. But me, I'm very emotional, and I make a lot of motions at the keyboard. He watched me play, and then he asked, "Why is your nose so close to the keyboard; does it smell good to you?" So he would make these remarks, and I respected him for it. Even in my disagreement with him, I found my own answers.

I remember Rudolf Serkin performing the Brahms D Minor Concerto in New York; it was one of the greatest experiences of my life. He did not have what I would call a beautiful sound, certainly not that night; what he had was an intensity. He was like a knight on a white horse, and he guarded and defended Brahms in the most vital way. The performance was unforgettable because of his enormous intensity and love for the music.

Note

1. Bruno Monsaingeon, *Sviatoslav Richter: Notebooks and Conversations* (Princeton, NJ: Princeton University Press, 2001).

12   Serge Prokofiev

To me, Prokofiev's music is incomparable; it's both exciting and colorful. By learning so much of his repertoire—recording all the sonatas for MGM and playing the Third Piano Concerto many times and editing the Ninth Sonata for Leeds Music—his music had an enormous impact on me. Everywhere you look, there is melody.

Prokofiev was a great, great composer, and like in the case of Rachmaninoff, he was a great, great pianist. All of the things he wrote, he played. I feel, however, that he is being played too much for the effects that he created and not enough for the beauty that he created. He's also not played for the depth of feelings that he had. He wrote for himself as a pianist, and he wrote for himself as a composer who wanted people to love and appreciate his music. He was lucky because there were quite a few great pianists who would take those sonatas and make them their own, and then of course, with Horowitz's blessing, everybody played the Seventh Sonata, and played that last movement, which is wonderful and, as far as the composition is concerned, is so outstanding. To play that, you feel that inner excitement that made Prokofiev one of the great composers that we know. We name him next to a Mozart, Beethoven, Brahms, Schumann. He is one of the great composers in music.

Piano Sonata No. 4 in C Minor, Op. 29

Mvt. 1. *Allegro sostenuto*

It's brooding. There are many, many, very interesting and beautiful ideas here, but each of your phrases is slowing down. Very often when you play so slowly, there is no motion. It doesn't feel like a first movement of a sonata; it's an *Allegro*. The memory for a piece like this is really not that difficult. You've got to make the effort. Do it four bars at a time, eight bars at a time, redo it and redo it, and you'll see that a piece like this will come much faster than a piece like Mozart which goes this way around and that way around, and as soon as you ask yourself, "Which way is it?" it's too late. Here, once you have committed it to memory—memory of the fingers, memory of the ear, and memory of the mind—so you know "Now I'm going to this key and now I'm going to that key," it's really not that difficult.

M. 1. Hear the cadence in the opening figure; we have to have a sense of finishing. He is explaining to us the piece. I don't hear your low C. It's not so fast; it's *molto sostenuto*. There is a bite there, something that is very much Prokofiev, and somehow that's missing. Your beginning starts off with some dust, and I always feel we should take something and clean it up. Use *una corda*; the intention is the darkness.

M. 2. Voice the A♮-G♯ line.

Mm. 3–4. The melody continues from the D to E♭ and finishes on the C.

Example 12.1. Sonata No. 4 in C Minor, Op. 29, mvt. 1, mm. 1–4.

Mm. 6–7. The Gs are too loud as a continuation of the melody.

M. 7. Where does he have the accent? If it was on the chord, it would be on the top. You have the accent on the C, and that's a finish.

M. 12. Finish with a surprise. First there is a finish, and at the same time there is a deceptive cadence because you expect a C in the bass. Don't make a *crescendo* when it goes up in a *pianissimo*. Play so it is not dirty in the pedal.

M. 17. Now really finish. We expected this C minor chord six bars earlier, but he prolongs it six measures because of the deceptive cadence. He is looking for that cadence and he finds it here. Use the *sostenuto* pedal to sustain the C minor chord. You realize you must play the chord first and then put the pedal down, yes? Your *appoggiaturas* are too much together with the melody, and the melody should be louder than the upper note. It's "tee-yum, tee-yum."

Mm. 19–20. Shape the three *sforzandi*; bring them down.

Mm. 23–24. Bring out the left hand as a melody [E♭-D-C-D-E♭, etc.].

M. 28. The A♭ and B♭ are more than the G [m. 27].

Mm. 29–31. No, the left hand should be clearer; the right hand is too intrusive.

M. 32. The left hand is the main voice, then the right hand catches up to it [m. 34] and has the climax [m. 35].

M. 35. No *diminuendo* yet.

M. 37. A firmer bass. Which is the first voice? Yes, the left hand.

M. 40. All the time I need that chromatic scale in the left hand.

Mm. 55–59. That phrase has two cadences; the bass G goes to C [mm. 56–57] and the E♭ goes to A♭ [mm. 58–59].

M. 61. Finish.

M. 71. If it were a G♮, your inflection would be right, but the minor must be colored differently.

M. 77. Why is the last one long? All the last notes have the same value.

M. 89. In a sense that downbeat should be an ending, and then you have the theme again.

Mm. 92–93. Look at the line; the right-hand A♭ resolves to the G.

Mm. 109–111. The *appoggiaturas* can sound more beautiful.

Mm. 113, 115, 116. I would play the higher notes less loudly.

M. 117. There should be a wait, just a comma, before this measure, and the thirty-second run is from nowhere. In the left hand, the top note [beat 3] should be the softest. He has a pedal point—always the G, always the G.

Mm. 122–124. Give us the pedal point.

M. 125. I don't know why you hit the C♯ so loud; sing it.

M. 126. This is your climax, *fortissimo* and *pesante*. You were louder before when it was just *forte*.

Mm. 129–132. It must become very clangorous, grander and grander.

Example 12.2. Sonata No. 4 in C Minor, Op. 29, mvt. 1, mm. 129–132.

Mm. 133–136. Let me have the bass notes alone, and now the *chorale*.

M. 137. Take a breath when you have this quarter rest. You can see this as an ending and a beginning. He opens it with that G major chord [m. 136], then he resolves it with the cadence.

M. 143. Beat 3 is two eighth notes.

M. 149. Finish on the downbeat. Again, the melody is the lower note of the thirds, not the *appoggiatura*.

M. 150. Be a little sneaky with your left-hand chromatic line; go up and down.

M. 153. Play the sixteenths with firm fingers.

M. 155. G is the note that he wants.

M. 157. Give more on the G so it can come down to the F♯.

M. 159. Surprise us with that chord [F♯ minor]. Can you feel that that's something special to you? Go from the G [m. 157] to the F♯.

M. 162. Come way down with transparency; is that triple *pianissimo*? Prepare the right-hand fingers on the keys one after the other, like a *glissando*. I don't hear enough of the left hand.

M. 183. Finish. Now we begin the rise to the very end.

M. 188. It doesn't stop on the downbeat after the trill; that's just part of the gesture. It goes all the way to beat 2. If you didn't have the trill, it would be just a two-note slur; play it that way.

M. 196. Too fast. Eighths are eighths are eighths.

M. 197. This is the most.

Mvt. 2. *Andante assai*

The main thing is that first of all you control the layers, beautiful layers of different sonorities. Always hear the ones that are the main voices.

Mm. 2–3. The melody must be very *legato*.

Mm. 5–6. Resolve to the A♭, then the line continues to come down to the G and the F♯ before the left hand *crescendos*.

Example 12.3. Sonata No. 4 in C Minor, Op. 29, mvt. 2, mm. 1–6.

M. 8. The left-hand E♭ increases to the E♮.

M. 12. The left-hand thirds *decrescendo* into the downbeat.

M. 13. Play the low third in such a way that you put the arm in the direction in which you're going. Your arm pivots on that low third. Pluck those left-hand *staccato* notes, but with the high A not too loud.

Mm. 13–21. [They practice the right-hand and left-hand melodies omitting the accompaniment notes.]

M. 19. Same tempo, not faster.

M. 22. Maintain the triplet.

M. 24. Like a funeral march.

M. 25. It's too loud and much too free; it's an accompaniment. The left hand is the leading voice. Change the pedal with the melody, generally twice per measure. If you touch the pedal lightly, it will not harm the harmonies. [They practice the melodies alone with pedal.] It is better to let go of the fifth finger of the right hand and play 1-2 to avoid accenting the accompaniment notes with the thumb.

Example 12.4. Sonata No. 4 in C Minor, Op. 29, mvt. 2, mm. 25–26.

M. 29. Your accompaniment is too loud, and you accent the second beat.

M. 33. All the trills and broken chords are not the primary voices.

M. 62. Not faster; think the same sixteenth from before. [Pressler uses the metronome to compare measures 54 and 62.]

M. 70. Just a tiny bit of pedal on the "*sec*" chord.

M. 81. I think you are a little short with the pedal. This section can take longer pedals.

Mm. 86–87. Sensitive, you are going from the C into the C♯.

M. 87. The trill is soft, but with substance; it runs out.

Mvt. 3. *Allegro con brio, ma non leggiere*

Mm. 1–6. What is missing for my taste is that you don't have any kind of a picture in front of you when you play the piece. When I hear you play the piece, I can imagine an acrobat coming on the stage [mm. 1–2], and he makes a summersault [mm. 3–5]. That's what I'm missing; we have really a character study there. And when someone hears you, he doesn't have to know that you're thinking of that. It doesn't matter; you're thinking of it. And he will find his own picture in your playing. But if you play like you did, there is no picture for you; there's no picture for the listener; and there's no picture for anybody. Let me hear you go for a *fortissimo* [m. 2] that is very powerful. What's missing is that the right hand in the end hasn't got the strength that it needs. If the first bar stretches a little bit, it's all right. Inflect it down and then up into that D♭ chord [m. 6].

Example 12.5. Sonata No. 4 in C Minor, Op. 29, mvt. 3, mm. 1–6.

Example 12.5. (*continued*)

M. 18. We need a difference between the *forte* and the *piano*. Before that, it's right and it's wrong. Yes, you can inflect a little down, but you're already playing your *piano* there.

Mm. 25–35. [For security, Pressler has the student practice left hand alone, then right-hand blocked chords, then the left hand as written with the right-hand blocked chords.]

Mm. 38–39. It must be very even.

M. 82. Climactic on the Cs.

M. 83. Clear, even, like a clarinet *glissando*.

M. 84. It's a new world. The curtain comes up. It's springtime; the flowers are beautiful. It's in a new key. The left hand is like strings, not excited. With you, it's "From eight o'clock to ten o'clock it's this, and from ten o'clock to twelve o'clock it's that, and from twelve o'clock to two o'clock it's that." It's just a day of work. Open the curtain to something romantic.

M. 87. The trill is actually like a *vibrato*.

Mm. 89–92. Two voices. Practice the left-hand part with two hands, each line as beautiful as the other.

Mm. 106–107. Can you play *legato*, especially when you have the half steps? First of all, it's too loud; second, you're playing *non-legato*. Practice just the top notes.

M. 146. Bring in each new voice, but lighten the upper note so there's less accent on the interval of the seventh.

M. 153. What's *precipitato*? Precipitate, rushed, dash, just move!

Mm. 162–166. Not *rallentando*; he already writes it in slower values. There's a difference between this and the previous measure. [Pressler sings "Yah-ta-da" in *forte* with *staccato*, and then in an expressive *piano*.]

Mm. 165–166. Resolve it. No, don't fall asleep.

M. 177. You can actually play that B [beat 3] in the right hand.

Mm. 186–189. The accent is all in the left hand. The right hand is brilliant, but it's only a trill. Don't make it sound labored.

M. 208. Not so notey; have a feeling of going all the way.

M. 211. Accent those second eighths [left hand].

Mm. 222–223. You must get in with the thumb [left hand] in such a way you can get out with the thumb. It would help if you don't see the leaps in reference to the left hand but rather that the right hand guides you with a feeling for the *octave.* One can have a strong feeling for certain distances, certainly for *octaves.*

Mm. 224–225. The chords, the B and then the C. You have to have power, your maximum, so that all your weight is in there.

Example 12.6. Sonata No. 4 in C Minor, Op. 29, mvt. 3, mm. 224–225.

13 Sergei Rachmaninoff

Rachmaninoff's piano music is appetizing and challenging and desirable. You like ice cream? Then you'll like Rachmaninoff. Rachmaninoff is an immediate, great pleasure on a number of levels. Like Liszt, the piano sounds remarkably beautiful. His invention of melody has a direct appeal, and many great pianists, himself the greatest, have taken up the cause, not only to present his music but to present themselves. In Rachmaninoff, you present yourself as well as that beautiful music with the hope that that beauty is going to shine on you, as it did on Horowitz, on Cliburn, on many who have played his music and have given us the great pleasure of seeing and hearing.

His four concerti and the *Paganini Rhapsody* are wonderful—such a magnificent blend of virtuosity and lyricism. The character pieces, the preludes, the two sets of *études-tableaux*, offer so much—so much color, so much emotion, a longing, a melancholy—with such lush harmonies. Because he wrote to fit his own hands, we have to sometimes find other ways to play those notes, dividing passages or chords between the hands. The *études-tableaux* have a twofold intention: like Chopin's *études*, he writes them to tax the pianist's technique to the fullest, but they also have a design and a beauty that asks something of your spirit, of your emotion.

Étude-Tableau in A Minor, Op. 39, No. 6

M. 1. Before you begin, you must know where you are going. You see that he has *Allegro*, then he gets faster and faster until he hits the *Presto*. You've got to get to the *Presto*, so you have to know what is your *Allegro* and what is your *Presto*.

Mm. 3–4. The second one begins with a *diminuendo*, so the second *sforzando* is less than the first, because he is on his way down, yes?

M. 5. This is the bottom.

Example 13.1. *Étude-Tableau* in A Minor, Op. 39 No. 6, mm. 1–5.

Mm. 6–10. You must show the outline of the melody, A-B-C-B-C-B-A. [Pressler sings the melody.]

M. 10. Close it.

Mm. 16–18. Can we have the sequence D-C-D-C, C-B-C-B, B-A-A?

M. 19. Each time he has the three against four, which gives the scale more impetus.

M. 22. The first *sforzando* is not so much.

M. 24. Now more.

Mm. 28–34. Use the motion of your hand to show us the melodic notes.

Example 13.2. *Étude-Tableau* in A Minor, Op. 39 No. 6, mm. 28–34.

M. 34. I would like it to start a little under tempo.

M. 35. You must drive to the C.

M. 36 Wait, then start with a real *pianissimo*, or you can try starting *piano* and then going down. Give it a character; it's a march.

M. 46. Now let me have the right hand from the "point of departure" where the *accelerando* and *crescendo* begin. But why are certain notes longer than others?

M. 52. Why so long [Cb and Bb]? The *forte* announces that the excitement has reached a peak and goes back down again.

Mm. 56–58. Very little pedal!

M. 59. When you get there, you must play as softly as possible. Practice each group so that the wrist snaps to the last note in one motion.

Mm. 59–65. Practice the left hand alone. That is not clean! And all of it is *piano*. Less right-hand thumb.

Mm. 63–64. Pedal with the slurs; get off the pedal on the left-hand eighths.

M. 66. Connect the G♯ and E with a pedal.

Mm. 70–75. Pedal with the bass note. I want you to play that *fortissimo* with a kind of violence. The left hand goes up to the A♯ [G♯-D♯-A♯]. There are three of those and then three that come down.

M. 76. Less pedal.

M. 77. How do you interpret that "*a tempo*?" He is referring to the *Presto*, not the *Allegro*.

M. 80. *Diminuendo* to the C; it's a resolution.

M. 81. Only *mezzo forte*; it's not that loud.

M. 93. This should be like in the beginning [m. 1].

M. 97. Play the third finger on the Bs.

M. 106. This is less.

M. 112. Resolve to the *pianissimo* [m. 113].

M. 117. Just the opposite of the opening; this one is less, then he builds to the last chord.

M. 119. Do this one in octaves.

Example 13.3. *Étude-Tableau* in A Minor, Op. 39 No. 6, mm. 117–121.

Interlude VIII
Honorary Citizenship in Magdeburg, Germany

When I left Magdeburg, it was right after the Kristallnacht; it was a very diffi-cult experience. My father's clothing store was destroyed, and only my closest family—my father and mother, and my brother and sister—escaped. I knew that all my other relatives, my grandparents, aunts, uncles, and cousins, died in con-centration camps, but I did not know where or how. Now when I came back for this affair, it was something very special. The entire hall, which was the opera house, was filled, and the audience showed me an extraordinary warmth before I played a note. And I was quite tired because I had been to the Hochschule für Musik in Detmold to give master classes and played a concert, went to Hamburg to play a concert, then to Berlin, and then came to Magdeburg. And when I ar-rived, there was a luncheon with all the officials, and the concert started at five thirty. And so I had just half an hour to rest, and then I went to the piano, and I played really well. There was a warmth from the audience like when the news-paper said, "A son returned home." So it was very special. At the end of the con-cert, the mayor comes and wants to go on stage, but the audience won't let him, so I played an encore. Then he forced himself up, and he says, "He'll play after that." And they gave me this trophy that's big just to hold it. And the stage was filled with flowers. And there were three German students who each brought a rose onto the stage. It was very touching. And then the applause, and the televi-sion, and the radio.

And then the next morning was the ceremony to lay the commemorative stone at the cemetery, and that was also special, because, first of all, the Germans keep good records, so I found out exactly the date my four relatives were transported to Auschwitz and killed there. And the mayor was at the ceremony, and the in-terior minister from the province. And a brass band was there playing funeral music. There were over a hundred people, and Daniel Hope, my violinist, drove from Antwerp to be there. It was very touching. And I was told that you must pay for the stone, and I said okay. Then I was told that the students, thirteen and four-teen years old from the high school that I was expelled from because I was a Jew, paid for the stone, so my money went for other people who don't have it. I was deeply touched; I was deeply moved. And it seemed as if the circle closed itself, that one could forgive in that sense. These people who have nothing to do with it feel responsible for it. It was only the fourth time since the war that they have awarded the honorary citizenship, so it was really quite, quite special.

14 Maurice Ravel

With Ravel, like Debussy, you are conscious of what the chord does to you; you really can taste the chord and the beauty of the harmonies. So Debussy and Ravel, even though they're very different from each other, both come in this same category. They are very, very special, and I immediately react if I hear a piece by Debussy or Ravel.

To say at my age now that I love Ravel would be an understatement. I can tell you that Ravel has given me some of the most intense emotional feelings of any composer; those feelings are emotional, are sexual. He is writing in a way that takes your whole being, becoming a partner with him. To go through a piece like "Ondine," his "Scarbo," his *Valses Nobles et Sentimentales* is like that. But even when you go through a piece like his *Sonatine* you discover that everything that came later is already in that piece. And when he has this G and an A♭ together, to me it is always like those who are drug takers who take a little needle that goes into your skin and then you take it out, and the pain that you feel in that moment is in this piece, and he evokes it so strongly. Yes, I have to thank him for some of the most intense moments in my musical life, and this is saying a lot, because I am speaking after having a Mozart to live with, a Bach, a Beethoven, a Schumann that I adore, and then of course all the other names that we have. But he and Debussy have created a world in which I love to live—and without which I would not want to live. And I really mean that.

Sonatine

Mvt. 1. *Modéré*

M. 1. *Diminuendo* between the F♯ and C♯. Show the octave doubling of the melody.
Mm. 3–4. *Subito pianissimo*, then it's even more *pianissimo* to begin the ascending line.

Example 14.1. *Sonatine*, mvt. 1, mm. 1–5.

Mm. 5–6. Carry the phrase over through the F♯-C♯. Sing there; it's now *mezzo forte* and it goes up.

M. 9. More intense than the rhythmically less active version in measure 7.

Mm. 11–12. Contrast the register changes.

M. 13. The lower voices *diminuendo*; they're like different instruments from the melody.

M. 19. Keep the focus on the melody; keep the bass *pianissimo*.

M. 23. A very special moment.

Mm. 24–25. Be a "painter." Think the thirty-second notes of the opening to keep the eighth notes from compressing.

Example 14.2. *Sonatine*, mvt. 1, mm. 24–26.

M. 29. [The second ending is measure 29.]

Mm. 34–37. You could use a redistribution of the left hand's upper notes to make it more smooth.

Mm. 41–42. A greater *diminuendo* here.

M. 43. Begin with nothing.

M. 47. The right hand can take the F♯s.

M. 55. A more crashing C♮.

Mm. 57–59. Have a more natural *rallentando*; the melody leads. Never stop before the downbeat.

Mm. 78–80. The sixteenths are almost like the previous eights.

Mm. 86–87. A slow *arpeggio*.

Mvt. 2. *Movement de Menuet*

Mm. 1–3. *Pizzacato* lower voices.

Example 14.3. *Sonatine*, mvt. 2, mm. 1–4.

M. 12. *Pizzacato* left hand C-F.

Mm. 13–15. The low notes are accented like a plucked harp string; everything else is *pianississimo*.

M. 17. The grace notes are just like those in bar 16.

Mm. 18–20. The plucked Fs return.

Mm. 27–39. Follow the dynamic plan precisely.

Mm. 28, 31. The right hand can help.

M. 35. Arrive at the climax like a full orchestra, all together. If the cymbal player enters early, he's fired!

Example 14.4. *Sonatine*, mvt. 2, mm. 33–38.

M. 38. Don't stop before measure 39.

Mm. 53–54. Now the accompaniment is *legato*.

M. 58. The C♭ is "a little bitter."

Mm. 70, 72. Hear the "bite" between the C♯ and the B♯.

Mm. 79–80. More *crescendo*; plan how you will reach the *forte*.

Mvt. 3. *Animé*

Mm. 4–5. Let the right hand help with the sixteenths.

Example 14.5. *Sonatine*, mvt. 3, mm. 4–5.

M. 9. A big *crescendo*.

Mm. 10–11. The left hand is *non-legato*. Follow the line down.

Mm. 16–17. A big *crescendo*.

Mm. 22–23. Another big *crescendo*.

Mm. 33–34. Hear the second B as a kind of resolution of the first.

Mm. 37–38. He asks for a *decrescendo* on beats 2 and 3.

Mm. 39–40. Glide from A♯ to the B [m. 40].

Mm. 42–43. Glide into the *a tempo*.

Mm. 47–53. Feel this as a *hemiola*. Lead with the melody.

M. 53. Hear this G♯-E as the most intense iteration of the descending gesture.

Mm. 54–55. Grab the left-hand chords. Play each one *non-legato* with a separate pedal.

Mm. 60–64. All these lower quarters [A-G♮-E] are *non-legato*.

Mm. 71–72. A big *crescendo*.

Mm. 78–81. Now the quarters are *legato*.

Mm. 80–90. *Pianissimo*.

Mm. 94–95. No stopping before the downbeat.

Mm. 95–99. Shiver, but shiver quietly. It's like you're out in the cold with a wet shirt.

Example 14.6. *Sonatine*, mvt. 4, mm. 95–99.

M. 106. Begin *pianissimo*! Use a flatter hand so you don't grip the notes so much.

M. 112. Hear the right-hand melody, but play out the left-hand second with a bite.

M. 119. Again, the bite on the second.

M. 120. Start *pianissimo* again.

M. 127. A little more.

M. 131. Still more.

M. 135. You've reached the climax.

Mm. 135–139. *Diminuendo* with the left hand playing *non-legato*.

Mm. 139–140. No stopping before the downbeat.

Mm. 142. Use the *ritard* to glide into the G♯ [m. 143]; it's not jagged.

Mm. 145–146. The rhythm is clear, but it's still a glide into the F♮.

Mm. 154–156. Let us feel the *hemiola*.

Mm. 159–160. Project the "ta-da" [F♯-C♯] each time.

Mm. 159–172. Pay attention to the clear terraces according to Ravel's *forte-fortissimo-fortississimo* indications. Note the corresponding register changes.

M. 172. The left hand crosses over. [Pressler uses the thumb on the F♯ and 3-4-5 braced on the C♯.]

Miroirs

Noctuelles

Mm. 1–2. Let us hear the flickers of top melody [E♭-B♭-C-E♭-F-E♭-B♭].

M. 3. You've reached a *piano* by this point.

Example 14.7. *Miroirs, Noctuelles,* mm. 1–3.

M. 17. Swell to the G and away.

Mm. 21–22. Resolve the F♯ to the F♮.

M. 31. Give this a new color. Yes, even orange, if orange has a meaning for you.

Mm. 35–36. Keep the pedal till the sixteenth rest. *Decrescendo* the last few notes.

Mm. 37–38. Orchestrate. The Fs are horns; the chords are clarinets and bassoons.

Example 14.8. *Miroirs, Noctuelles,* mm. 37–38.

Mm. 41–42. Now the chords are clarinets.

Mm. 42–44. Now we have the high winds.

M. 47. These are the strings.

Mm. 51–52. Now we have the full orchestra.

M. 61. The C major is like an afterthought.

M. 63. Swell to the next measure and away.

M. 64. No pedal on beat one. A new start on beat two.

Maurice Ravel 161

Mm. 74–75. These sixteenths are in a new register, so they require a new color.

M. 88. Touch the C♯ in a new way. It's as if you discover that note.

M. 115. The G♯ is a new color change.

M. 120. Show us the *chromaticism* between the two hands. [B♭-A♮-A♭-G♮-G♭, etc.]

M. 131. *Decrescendo.*

M. 132. *Decrescendo* and away.

Oiseaux tristes

M. 2. Let us hear the B♭-A♭.

Example 14.9. *Miroirs, Oiseaux tristes,* mm. 1–3.

M. 7. Sinister.

M. 14. The right-hand thumb is the important note.

M. 15. This is the echo.

Mm. 23–24. The B♯ glides into the C♯.

M. 31. The left-hand thirty-second notes must be clear.

Mm. 32–34. Color the D♯s.

Example 14.10. *Miroirs, Oiseaux tristes,* mm. 32–34.

Mm. 35–38. How many shades of *sombre* do you have? Distant and more distant.

Une barque sur l'océan

Mm. 1–2. Not too slowly. Keep touching that F♯ pedal point.

Mm. 4–5. This is one phrase.

Mm. 6–7. One phrase.

Mm. 8–10. One phrase.

M. 11. A new color.

M. 24. Take the B-G with the right hand.

M. 26. Take the first three notes with the right hand.

Example 14.11. *Miroirs, Une barque sur l'océan*, mm. 24–27.

M. 33. These are brassy chords.

M. 37. Take a little time before measure 38.

Mm. 38–48. Change the pedal with each low G♯.

M. 39. Terrace the changes of register.

M. 55. *Crescendo* the two-note slur [G♯-A♯].

M. 56. *Decrescendo* the descending two-note slur.

M. 60. Have a slight *crescendo* into measure 61, then *subito piano*.

M. 65. Phrase the last two eighths into the next measure.

M. 69. Take the first two notes as a right-hand octave.

M. 71. Switch hands on the first two notes.

M. 87. Take the A [last eighth note] with the left hand.

M. 93. Take the A [last eighth note] with the left hand.

M. 97. Take time into measure 98.

M. 106. *Crescendo* the left-hand broken chord.

M. 112. Color the register changes.

M. 117. Have a swell to create a sweep.

M. 125. Not too slowly.

M. 126. The E♮-C octaves are horns.

Mm. 128–129. The horns continue.

M. 132. *Diminuendo* up to the melody.

Alborado del gracioso

M. 1. The left hand sets up three beats in the first measure, then two beats in the second.

Example 14.12. *Miroirs, Alborado del gracioso*, mm. 1–4.

M. 5. *Crescendo* into the *forte* [m. 6].
M. 14. Try it with the *sostenuto* pedal.
M. 18. Play the As with the left hand.
M. 19. Play the Gs with the left hand.

Example 14.13. *Miroirs, Alborado del gracioso*, mm. 18–19.

M. 21. Pull back a little bit as this phrase closes.
M. 23. *Decrescendo* the thirds.
M. 24. Less.
M. 30. *Crescendo.*
M. 31. No accent on the C minor chord; it's a resolution.
M. 34. A breath after the *forte.*
M. 36. A breath before starting the *fortissimo.*
Mm. 53–58. With pedal.
M. 54. Not rushed.
M. 56. *Decrescendo* as the left-hand line comes down.
M. 59. This is more subtle, less points.

(more subtle, less points)

Example 14.14. *Miroirs, Alborado del gracioso,* mm. 59–62.

M. 64. *Decrescendo*; bring it down.

Mm. 69–71. *Decrescendo*, then *fortissimo*.

Mm. 76–79. The treble chords are cymbals.

M. 83. Ease into the treble chords; it's not a hit.

M. 126. Keep the pedal.

M. 130. Yield a little.

M. 134. Sneak in with the chords.

M. 150. *Decrescendo*.

M. 151. Now it's *mezzo piano*.

Mm. 158–159. *Crescendo* to the second chord.

M. 163. *Decrescendo*.

M. 178. It's *piano* with no *crescendo*.

M. 181. Lift the pedal as it ascends.

M. 185. Bring in the pedal.

M. 186. Touch the pedal on each eighth.

M. 190. Less. Continue the touches of pedal.

M. 192. Take the F♯ grace in the left hand.

M. 197. This last chord is accented, but it's less loud.

Mm. 207–208. Dry and *staccato*.

M. 213. Play the first three notes of the run in the left hand.

M. 219. A big *crescendo* into the *fortissimo*.

M. 225. Accent the chord. Then start again with the last three sixteenths.

M. 227. Back off a little so you can push to the ending.

Interlude IX
Through Hell and Back

The period of December 2014 and January 2015 and the months following was a most dramatic time in Menahem Pressler's life. On December 19, Sara Pressler, his beloved wife of fifty-five years, passed away. While grieving her death, he traveled to Berlin to honor his commitment to perform Mozart's A Major Concerto, K. 488, with the Berlin Philharmonic in a New Year's Eve concert. However, stepping off stage following his performance, he experienced shortness of breath and pain in his left side. In typical Pressler fashion, he attempted to brush it aside and go on with his schedule. On his flight back to the States, he was constantly bothered by the recurring pain but again blamed it on the ill-fitting seat belt. By the time he was home, he was in a great deal of pain. When he was examined in Indianapolis, he was told he had suffered a serious aneurysm, quite possibly during the flight home, but there was nothing they could do; it was too risky to operate.

It just so happened that his close friend who is head of the cancer clinic in Indianapolis has a son who had studied medicine and worked with a leading cardiac surgeon in Boston, one of a handful of US surgeons approved to perform special non-FDA procedures in life-threatening cases. So immediately Menahem traveled to Massachusetts General Hospital where Dr. Virendra Patel, MPH, determined he was a good candidate for a delicate and innovative stent grafting procedure known as a fenestrated thoracic endovascular aortic stent graft. This procedure involves taking precise measurements of the heart, which are then used to modify the stent so it will fit properly into the aorta of the individual.

The surgery was performed only eight days after the Berlin concert. The coincidence that Pressler's friend knew of Dr. Patel in Boston, who is allowed by the FDA to perform this procedure only when there is no other option available, is truly amazing. Altogether, Pressler was in the hospital and rehab for three months, and the surgery was a success largely due to his own determination to push himself forward each day in recovery. After these three months of recuperation, he reintroduced himself to the piano by spending a full month practicing only finger exercises, his own exercises he had assigned to so many of his students. This was in preparation for an all-new program of Schumann lieder he was scheduled to perform soon.

Less than six months after his graft, on July 15, 2015, Pressler performed a Schumann program, the *Dichterliebe* and the last songs of Schumann, at Wigmore Hall in London with baritone, Matthias Goerne. One week later they performed the program again at the Verbier Festival in Switzerland. Pressler invited Dr. Patel, his wife, and three daughters as Pressler's guests to the London concert to celebrate his return to the concert stage. In Pressler's words, "God gave me the gift of music, and he gave Dr. Patel the gift of healing. The world is a better place for having a man like him in it."

15 Franz Schubert

Schubert, like Mozart, is difficult to play because of the purity of the line and the beauty of his melody. Schubert gave the world something that even Beethoven didn't have—this overflow of melodies, a feeling that either in life or in heaven, the angels must dance. Schubert's music is intimate. Schubert always felt he was living in Beethoven's shadow, and it was actually Beethoven's death in 1827 that freed Schubert—one of the titan's pallbearers—to compose his own monumental piano statements in what turned out to be his final year of life. At my age, when playing the big B-flat Schubert Sonata, it still shows me how far I have come walking up the mountain, how far I am from the top, and how much climbing should be done.

He has become even more of my ideal for the next world; he has brought me closer to that point. When I play him now, and when I hear him now, the feelings I cannot explain to you are of such purity that I wonder, What would be a world without music? Like Nietzsche said, it would be irrational to live in such a world. We live in a world where each of us who is learning his music or playing his music or teaching his music is continuously playing it anew, because to play him is an enormous challenge each time again. Because it is to climb the highest mountain, and to climb the highest mountain on one day means you have the dreadful task to climb it again the next day. Everything hurts, everything bites, but you still have the feeling that you want, you must, and you will climb that mountain. That is Schubert. That is close to heaven—nearly, you could say, as close as it gets. Of course, there is the man who guards the doors of heaven, Ludwig van Beethoven, but I think even he would agree that if you have that kind of beauty in your life, you are entitled to the entrance, and he will open the door.

Sonata in A Minor, D. 784, Op. 143

Mvt. 1. *Allegro guisto*

Mm. 1–8. You must pay close attention to his dynamic markings; with you a *fortissimo* becomes a *mezzo forte*, and a *piano* becomes a *mezzo forte*. There's no *crescendo*. It's the mystery. It's dark; we don't see anything. We feel something, but we don't see anything. The dynamics point you to the inner meaning of the piece.

Mm. 2–3. Have a feeling of release in both hands on the A. It's closer to a sixteenth than an eighth; there's more air in there.

M. 3. Put the left-hand thumb on the A so it can reach the other notes.

M. 4. Move "out," and leave the phrase open.

M. 8. Close the phrase.

Example 15.1. Sonata in A Minor, D. 784 (Op. 143), mvt. 1, mm. 1–8.

M. 9. We all have memories which stay with us as long as we're alive. I heard this
played by one of the greatest of all pianists, Sviatoslav Richter. He played this
like a man that's carrying the weight of the whole world on his shoulders.
And I thought I was on the Volga, although Schubert was on the Danube.
What I want is that you give the weight.

Mm. 9–10. Hear the relationship between them. The second is less and *decrescendo*.

M. 15. [Pressler gives fingering for *legato* octaves.]

Example 15.2. Sonata in A Minor, D. 784, (Op. 143), mvt. 1, mm. 15–16.

Mm. 18, 20, 22. Can I have all three strata [*forte, piano,* and *pianissimo*]?

M. 19. The last note is *mezzo forte*.

M. 20. *Piano*, but not *pianissimo*.

M. 22. It's a controlled trill; always know the rhythm. 1-2 seems to be the best fingering for you. Do the trill exercise on these notes every day for ten minutes.

[Pressler also has him hold the second finger down while repeating the thumb and *vice versa*.]

M. 25. Use 4 on the last E [of the trill]. Have a big *crescendo* during the last two beats into the *fortissimo* of measure 26.

M. 26. Can the right hand play 5 on the A and then substitute a 2?

Mm. 27–29. It's a phrase, but you play an exercise. Go down a little with the line and come up with the line.

Mm. 32–33. Keep going; have direction.

M. 34. Still in *fortissimo*, but treat these as two-note slurs—and all the ones following. Give it life.

M. 44. The As remain loud so the *piano* [m. 45] will be a contrast.

Mm. 47–50. Each one gets progressively less.

M. 53. The arms have to swing.

M. 55. That's *piano* and there's no hit.

M. 60. The B descends to measure 61.

M. 61. Go all the way down.

M. 68. Voice the C♯; hear the left hand.

M. 72. A little different the second time. Orchestrate it differently; bring out the left-hand D♯-C♯ with a little bit of color.

Mm. 75–76. Don't neglect the rests.

M. 79. That must be frightful; it's a frightening moment.

M. 90. Both notes are *fortissimo*.

M. 96. It's coming down.

Mm. 98–99. Not slower.

M. 104. Very light in the left hand, and you have the rotation to help you. The tempo is as the beginning.

M. 110. Yes, slurred, so less on the second note.

M. 114. Use the fourth finger on the black keys, and practice just the thumbs alone.

M. 116. When you come to the lowest note [F], use the arm to push yourself out.

M. 120. Push yourself out of the chord.

Mm. 122–123. Take off the pedal for the rests so we can hear the right hand clearly.

M. 126. A clearer change from A major to F major. What special color can you give us for that change? *Diminuendo* to measure 127.

M. 127. Color it. [Pressler plays the right hand gently and expressively.] Play once with just the sixths. And now play just the thirds and fourths.

Mm. 138–141. The chords are *legato*. [Pressler gives a fingering, 4-2-1, 5-3-1 changing to 4-2, 5-3-1 changing to 2-4, 5-3-1.] Bring out the top note. Keep the arm free. Don't hit; it should glide. The motion of the hand helps it to be *legato*.

Example 15.3. Sonata in A Minor, D. 784, (Op. 143), mvt. 1, mm. 138–141.

M. 141. Now it's happy. It should have a lilt in that register. Change fingers on the repeated notes. You'll never be able to play this section well with your fingering. You need to change the fingers.

M. 146. It's so loud. With you it's like a squawking; it doesn't have a lilt.

Mm. 158–163. Change the fingers on the repeated notes.

Mm. 162–163. Use 4-3-5-4, yes?

Mm. 171–172. Play the B and C in the right hand.

M. 175. Play like a cello.

M. 184. Close it.

M. 190. Use the fourth finger for the last E.

Mm. 193–194. Feel the direction.

Mm. 199–200. Again the two-note slurs.

M. 203. Lean into the B♭.

M. 217. Let us hear and feel a difference with the E♮.

M. 237. Play it with your body, not just your fingers.

M. 247. Let me hear the difference. Not *crescendo*, but the contrary.

M. 260. *Pianissimo*; it's like an exhaling.

Mm. 268–269. Do a little *decrescendo* from the E to the C♯.

Mm. 270–271. In *fortissimo*, with the arms free. The arms control it.

M. 278. That's a different terrace of sound.

M. 282. Not slower.

M. 285. Less; no *crescendo*.

M. 286. Now frightening. But when you hit the piano like that, it's like a Karate chop, and I don't want you to do that. It's a musical expression, a tremendous expression. Play it with your body.

M. 290. Less than before. You have to control the hand and the keys—stay in the keys. Everything is relaxed, including your back.

Mvt. 2. *Andante*

Mm. 1–2. Phrase over the top. It's a four-measure phrase.

M. 4. Use the wrist to follow the contour of the notes.

Example 15.4. Sonata in A Minor, D. 784, (Op. 143), mvt. 2, mm. 1–4.

Mm. 7–8. Hear the two cadences.
M. 15. Use the wrist.
M. 29. Beat 2, *mezzo forte*, and then begin the *decrescendo*.
Mm. 31–32. Lilting.
M. 34. Wrist.
M. 39. Keep the left arm loose.
Mm. 52–53. It's bird-like.

Example 15.5. Sonata in A Minor, D. 784, (Op. 143), mvt. 2, mm. 52–53.

Mvt. 3. *Allegro vivace*

Mm. 1–2. [Pressler gives a left-hand fingering.]

Example 15.6. Sonata in A Minor, D. 784, (Op. 143), mvt. 3, mm. 1–2.

M. 30. *Crescendo* to the *fortissimo* [m. 31].

Mm. 32, 34. Clear rests.

Mm. 44–45. Follow the right-hand line [B♮-A-G♯-A]

M. 47. Start *forte*.

M. 48. Now *mezzo piano*.

Mm. 69–70. *Crescendo*.

M. 126. *Fortissimo*.

M. 128. Now *mezzo forte*.

M. 131. Not so much slower than Tempo I.

M. 160. In tempo.

M. 168. The A♭ is a surprise.

M. 169. It's *a tempo*.

Mm. 174–177. Follow the notes that are on the beat [D♭-E♭-F-G♭-A♭-D♭-G♭-F-E♭-D♭-C-G♭].

Example 15.7. Sonata in A Minor, D. 784, (Op. 143), mvt. 1, mm. 174–177.

M. 178. Color the chord.

M. 184. *Decrescendo* from E to C♯.

Mm. 193–194. Close the line to the downbeat of measure 194.

M. 225. *Mezzo piano*.

M. 226. Now *piano*.

M. 227. Let it swing.

Mm. 258–259. Don't rush.

Sonata in A Minor, D. 845, Op. 42

Mvt. 1. *Moderato*

M. 1. First of all, it has to be in 2, not in 4, and the touch must imply Romanticism. Can it have a much more, how shall I say, silky sound? Subdued, soft.

Example 15.8. Sonata in A Minor, D. 845, (Op. 42), mvt. 1, mm. 1–4.

M. 9. It's such a beautiful reaching out.

M. 10. Don't accent the downbeat; it's a curve.

M. 10–11. Expectant.

M. 19. Keep the momentum through the Es till the downbeat [m. 20].

M. 20–23. Don't accent against the accents, only where he has it.

M. 24–25. *Crescendo* through the *sforzandi.*

M. 26. It's more serious; it doesn't bounce.

M. 27. *Decrescendo.*

M. 29. A little *crescendo* into the *forzando.*

M. 50. Set up the cadence on beat 3.

M. 52. A little more voicing of the left hand.

Mm. 53–54. Follow the line, G-G♯-A.

M. 55. Color the minor chord.

M. 56. Let's hear the left-hand movement again.

Mm. 57–58. Follow the line, A-A-B♭.

Mm. 64–67. It's not just a restatement; it's magical.

M. 73. No, that's a surprise between the G and the A♭.

M. 77. A sense of real release. A very light slur.

M. 78. A slight swell; follow the contour of the melody.

M. 86. If he hadn't given you the accent on the D, the stress would have been on the C. Feel the difference. This accent is the first of four, so it has to be more.

M. 89. The E major is a surprise, like "Yes."

M. 92. Notice that the left hand is only an eighth. He sends it out—like when he has it the other way around [m. 94], the right hand has an eighth.

Mm. 93–94. The *pianissimo* statement is the echo.

M. 105. *A tempo.*

M. 115. Voice the left-hand melody.

M. 116. Now the right hand answers.

Mm. 115–117. [Pressler suggests a fingering for the right-hand mordants.]

Example 15.9. Sonata in A Minor, D. 845, (Op. 42), mvt. 1, mm. 115–117.

M. 118. He reaches out and over the top.

M. 119. Pull back a little bit to get into F minor.

M. 120. A graceful ornament in the left hand.

M. 123. Not a huge *crescendo*, only a little swell.

M. 128. A smooth descending scale, not like you're counting.

M. 131. Change the fingers on the repeated Cs.

M. 147. Use 3-1-2 on the ornament.

M. 150. Finish.

Mm. 155–157. The left hand sounds too heavy, and the thirds don't sound together.

M. 163. The right hand can help the left-hand thirds.

Example 15.10. Sonata in A Minor, D. 845, (Op. 42), mvt. 1, mm. 163.

Mm. 180–183. No, don't compete; only do the indicated accents.

M. 185. And more, and more.

M. 215. The B minor is too loud.

M. 233. The F is something you have not had before.

M. 237. Be surprised; we expect an A minor chord.

M. 248. It's naked; we need a more *legato* touch.

M. 273. The left hand is not good; the B-C-B needs to tug at us a little.

Mvt. 2. *Andante poco moto*

We see that we have so many variations—you have the one in sixteenths, and the one in thirty-seconds, and the rhythmic one and the contrapuntal one, and then you have the very fluid one—so I would suggest that the tempo of the theme is a little too fast. It is more important. Its step is like in a ballet, how the dancers come in front of the stage. I think *gracioso* is the right word to describe this mood. You have to see tonally how you are going to play each variation so that there's a contrast between each.

M. 1. In a sense the upbeat is flat. Give that dot a little air.
Mm. 3–4. Since it holds [m. 1] and then it holds [m. 2], now it must go forward. Finish [m. 4].

Example 15.11. Sonata in A Minor, D. 845, (Op. 42), mvt. 2, mm. 1–4.

M. 7. Lead it down from the B in the right hand to the A and G in the left hand so that you have two melody lines.
M. 11. The B is more than the top G, but the G should not disappear.
Mm. 15–16. Cadence. Follow the voice leading.
M. 18. Resolve to the second beat.
M. 20. You should give the alto C and G more than the soprano E and D.
M. 22. Resolve to the second beat.
Mm. 23–24. Follow the lower voice all the way down [Eb–D–G].
M. 24. I would think you could have a better *pianissimo*. It's a long piece, so give us as much tonal variety as possible.
M. 25. I don't like the short trill.
M. 28. Resolve to the D minor.
M. 29. That's more than an accent; that's a *forte piano*.
M. 33. Variation 1. Close to the downbeat [m. 34].
M. 35. Cadence [to downbeat of m. 36].
M. 37. The ornament comes before the beat, not on the beat. Close again going into the next measure.
M. 40b. [The second ending] Certainly not an accent on the third beat.
M. 42. Close the ornament on the C.

M. 43. That's Schubert at his best when he closes a phrase like that. [Pressler sings the phrase.] And it should be *legato*.

M. 46. The C is a resolution.

M. 47. Use the wrist to reach out from the A [beat 3].

M. 53. Play *legato* in the left hand. Just like when you play the single notes, slur the first three.

M. 57. Variation 2. It's a little fast. It's dance-like and very happy. [Pressler has the student begin the theme and then start the variation to have the same tempo.] Change the tone quality. It's not light enough; it doesn't drop like rain from your fingers. Use 1-3-2 on the mordent. When you have the three notes, pull it toward you.

M. 60. He wants more brilliance in the upper octave and charm in those *staccato* notes.

M. 61. With the same fingering and with a light arm.

M. 62. Start less as you go up to the top. Somehow shade going to that Eb; it's something new.

M. 63. The *ritardando* is not as natural as I would like it; you stop too quickly. And the *a tempo* not so *staccato*.

Mm. 65–66. The G-G is less than the A-A [mm. 64–65]. It's the way you touch it; reach out to the high G and to the high A, and connect it with the motion of the wrist. And the left hand continues to dance.

M. 71. No *ritard*.

M. 72. *Leggiero*.

M. 75. [Pressler provides a fingering for the right hand.]

Example 15.12. Sonata in A Minor, D. 845, (Op. 42), mvt. 2, mm. 75.

M. 78. Out of the C major comes the dark C minor and then he resolves it [m. 79].

M. 79. Your *ritard* is too slow, and the *a tempo* is too fast; it doesn't make any sense.

M. 81. Variation 3. You accent the thirty-second note. None of these repeated Gs is unimportant; they are the heartbeat. Don't let any notes disappear.

M. 85. The accent tells you the second note is less each time. The first is the tension; the second is the resolution. Tension, resolution, tension, resolution. But the left hand is the main voice.

Example 15.13. Sonata in A Minor, D. 845, (Op. 42), mvt. 2, mm. 85–88.

M. 93. The left hand is lighter on the second note each time, just like the right hand in measure 85.

M. 96. Use the wrist to release the G major chord.

M. 97. Be careful that the repeated notes are continuous.

M. 99. Although you go away from the G, it stays steady.

M. 106. Variation 4. I don't feel that the left hand is supplying the affinity to the theme; it runs. The long note has a dot over it, but you make it too *staccato*. You make me too aware of the short note; I hear accents all over the place. And the right hand must be very light so that you draw circles with your hand or with your arm. The hand goes up and down, over and over. The fingers remain close to each other. Yours sounds like you are jumping over hurdles all the time.

M. 108. The second E♭ [left hand] is already less, then both hands end on the A♭ [m. 109]. The right hand phrases from the second sixteenth to the accent so that it hangs together.

Mm. 109–110. The same thing that you sang romantically, whispering, now you play dramatically.

M. 110. Don't just play the accent with your muscle. The accent is different depending on where you are. Certainly, the accent is less when you are coming down. You should have a feeling for that F♭; it doesn't belong in there.

M. 113b. [The second ending is measure 113b.]

M. 114. Now the right hand accompanies.

M. 115. Let the ear be satisfied. First it was B♭ [m. 114, beat 3]; now it's A♭.

M. 117. Close both hands on the E♭.

M. 120. And then all of a sudden he has an accent on the upbeat.

M. 121. You must finish it. It doesn't have a *sforzando*, but it's *fortissimo*. The last note doesn't have a *staccato*; it's a wedge, an accent, as if it's a downbeat.

M. 122. *Leggiero*. Be sensitive with your pedal, because the notes in the left hand are a little on the short side.

M. 128. On the way up is a *decrescendo*, so each one is less so that you end *pianissimo*.

M. 130. Let me hear the D♭-C.

M. 134. We've been building to the F; now close it down. It's interesting that he has that *forte piano* on that F.

M. 135. Variation 5. The repeated notes should be like stones skipping over the water, but yours is up and down. We must feel the meter. It swings on the first note; hear the relationship of the three notes within each beat. The repeated notes run out, like a basketball. That would give you an image, like dribbling a basketball.

M. 136. I need four horns. It needs a little bit different sonority in your sound, not so short and stuttering. It's "bwa, bwa, bwa," not "dk, dk, dk." The repeated notes should have a bounce to them.

M. 139. There's a cadence on the downbeat.

Mm. 142–143. A more beautiful ending to the phrase.

M. 143. We don't know there will be that E♭ [right hand]. Feel it, do it, say something.

M. 144. You must let it run out [on beat 2].

Mm. 146–147. The ending of the phrase must always be beautiful and artistic.

M. 155. There's a resolution there, C minor to G major. I would like you to bring out the E♭ and the D in those two chords.

M. 159. The Gs diminish.

M. 160. The thirty-seconds are like a bird. It has a lilt to it, a niceness to it.

Mm. 162–163. It's like a discovery; you all of a sudden are in D♭ major. Usually he brought us right back, but here he all of sudden says, "Oh, those flowers are also quite beautiful." The *ritardando* is spread out over both measures; otherwise, he would say *a tempo* earlier.

M. 165. Be careful with the register, *legato*. That should be heavenly, not so hard!

M. 168. That B♭ has that kind of sadness, a kind of melancholy. Here, too, bounce it out.

M. 168. Why is it all of a sudden so short?

Mm. 168–171. The two notes need greater sensitivity—the D-C [m. 168], E-F [m. 169], A-G [m. 170] and A-G [m. 171].

M. 169. After your E-F, fade the repeated notes.

Mm. 170–171. The right hand also has a melody. Finish it on the fourth sixteenth [m. 171].

M. 171. You can use the left hand to get that first C [beat 2]. Now he transfers it to the lower register.

M. 179. Close it to the C [m. 180].

M. 180. Now open it to the C [m 181].

M. 181. Close it. This is in a German way, "Goodbye, *Lebevohl*." It's a very beautiful, very touching ending.

M. 183. Come all the way down. Be very close in the key.

M. 184. With very glittering light, and so that the E-F-E is more than the C.

Mvt. 3. *Scherzo*

Mm. 1–4. Put those Es in the left hand. For each motive, there is one motion for all three notes. I don't hear you doing the repeated notes well, especially in the left hand.

Mm. 3–4. You have to prepare the *fortissimo* with a *crescendo*.

Example 15.14. Sonata in A Minor, D. 845, (Op. 42), mvt. 3, mm. 1–5.

Mm. 8–10. This answers the first phrase. *Decrescendo* as the line descends.

M. 10. Don't rush into beat 2.

M. 13. Feel the chord *crescendo* into the *forte piano* [m. 14].

M. 14 It was a *forte piano*, so this is now *piano*.

M.15. Resolve the left-hand chord to the C major chord [m. 16].

M. 16. Go down.

M. 17. A special touch on that A♭; lean into it.

M. 20. The F resolves to the E without taking time after it.

M. 22. The Gs come from nowhere; this is a new start.

Mm. 25–27. You don't have to rush it.

Mm. 29–31. Let the left hand help with the thirds.

M. 32. I want the difference between the *piano* and the *pianissimo*.

Mm. 33–35. Again, let the left hand help.

Mm. 36–41. Now this could be angry or dramatic or whatever, but this one [m. 42] is relaxed; it is like a waltz.

M. 37. I wonder, if that were orchestrated, how that person playing the second beat would feel, because you play with no inflection on that note. He has to work for a living. As a conductor, I would have to talk to him. I would throw him out.

M. 49. Change the pedal so the D♭ can disappear.

M. 57. No, that's so loud! That left hand enters where the upper horn has decreased to.

M. 58. Play the left-hand E♭s with 3-2. You can make it easier by playing that C♭ in the right hand. The C♭ must connect to the B♭. It should be the left hand that we listen to.

Mm. 62–63. Come down. The left hand has to be very precise because you are splitting some of these chords. You need to have something special in the sound here. Voice the upper notes of the left hand and the upper notes of the right hand. Practice the left hand alone so you can hear how you balance the chords.

M. 68. Yes, a *ritard*, but still in the swing.

Mm. 78–79. Close it all the way before beginning the *forte*.

Mm. 79–83. [Pressler gives a fingering for the thirds.]

Example 15.15. Sonata in A Minor, D. 845, (Op. 42), mvt. 3, mm. 79–83.

Mm. 87–92. It's still not clear; all the notes are not sounding.

M. 92. Finish it there on the E.

Mm. 101–102. Why does it get loud before the *fortissimo*? To the contrary, you would go down; you would get out of the way.

M. 106. Hold the left hand so you can resolve it. The rests are not for the left hand.

Mm. 110–111. Resolve the F to the E.

M. 112. The Es should be tied, not repeated.

Mm. 122–126. A big *crescendo* to the top.

M. 127. It sways like a hammock.

M. 135. [The second ending is measure 135.]

M. 136. Trio. What is missing is the character of the waltz.

M. 140. And when you put that F with it, it's so refreshing, as if a breeze blows. I don't hear all the Fs. There should be some independence in that line as if an instrument were playing it.

Mm. 148–149. Be careful that you bind the D to the F.

M. 150. Take that G with the left hand.

Mm. 159–163. Go up; I want to enhance the positive nature of the phrase.

Mm. 166–167. Go down; I want to enhance the negative aspect.

Mm. 178–178. Color the second G-A.

Mm. 180–181. Now a different color. I have to see that the piece has become a part of you and that you listen and create.

Mm. 181–182. We have to know this is the last one, the ending.

Mvt. 4. *Rondo*

M. 1. Not "tak-a-tak-a-tak-a-tak-a." It should sound like a melody, not an exercise. It's *pianissimo*, not an aggressive sound. The many notes are not to be disturbing; the E is just the harmony. He has the word *legato* there, and he's referring to the melody. Try for a *legato* feeling, not the feeling that it's running away from something. It's not so restless. It could even be faster and not be restless.

RONDO

Example 15.16. Sonata in A Minor, D. 845, (Op. 42), mvt. 4, mm. 1–8.

Mm. 13–14. Now when you have the thirds in the left hand or when he holds the notes [mm. 35–42], that should enrich your texture. I don't find that rich enough. What it also does is to slow you a little bit so you can take a breath. There's a cadence in the thirds.

M. 15. Now this is the second time; it's a variation of the very same melody.

Mm. 26–28. *Legato* over the top, and there's no *crescendo*.

M. 33. This is another variation.

M. 35. And now for the first time you have longer notes that give a firmer harmonic base for the melody.

Mm. 36, 38. The left-hand Es are not short notes.

Mm. 45–46. Close it.

Mm. 49–50. Only one accent; the second note [E] is less. But I don't like that much *diminuendo*. It's still in *forte*.

M. 53. When the upbeat has the *forzando*, you can take a little more time.

Mm. 57–58. Use 5-4, and less on the A. Inherent in it is a *decrescendo*.

Mm. 63–64. That is the finish.

Mm. 65–70. It *crescendos* because of the movement of the bass. This phrase stays open.

M. 68. The B♭ holds for the whole bar; you take the hand off too early.

Mm. 75–76. This phrase closes.

Mm. 83–84, 87–88. Echo. It's like on the organ when you push the stops in and you get a different sound. That's what I want here.

Mm. 89–90. Make a *diminuendo* going up.

Mm. 107–114. I would do the left-hand accent on the first beat of each measure.

Mm. 108–109. It's a half note and a quarter, two-note slurs. There's no accent, but you lean against it so there's less on the quarter.

Mm. 114–115. Finish the phrase [on the E].

M. 119. When it starts on a B it's not the same as when it started on an E [m. 115]; it's less.

M. 127. The *piano* is not so busy; it's still *legato*.

M. 137. Play the C♯ [right hand] with more understanding of it.

M. 143. The fingering that's given for the trill is good [right hand 2-3-1, left hand 3-2-1]. It lets you go in and come out.

M. 144. If you would play the last octave [B] with the left hand, you could get out of it, but it's still in *fortissimo*. You have to find the time to take a breath; otherwise it's hasty.

Mm. 144–148. Use the wrist to get the high notes.

Example 15.17. Sonata in A Minor, D. 845, (Op. 42), mvt. 4, mm. 143–146.

M. 152. Now let us hear the difference between a B♮ and a B♯.

Mm. 155–157. The *pianissimo* suspends in the air.

M. 158. The left hand should have a rocking feeling.

M. 173. It should be louder when you come in with the thirds.

M. 177. You have a *fortissimo* and then a *crescendo* to a *forte*. What is obviously forgotten here is that it starts in a *piano* [m. 187].

Mm. 179–180. It gets louder with the octaves.

Mm. 189–190. Don't sit down on any of the chords.

Mm. 190–191. Give me an ending.

M. 193. The E starts at least in *forte*.

Mm. 193–207. Let us hear a *decrescendo* the whole way up and the whole way down.

M. 208. Here you are *pianissimo*. When you have no more bass, clear the foot to prepare for the new entrance [m. 209].

M. 209. Release the arm and play *legato*.

M. 241. I get the feeling you are running from someone who is going to attack you. I get frightened myself, and I think I am looking at someone who is running away. It's not to run away from; it's to be enjoyed.

M. 254. Cadence and take a breath.

M. 255. Now we have the major; it's a different attitude.

M. 262. I would use 5-4 for the octaves [D-B]. It's the ending.

M. 289. Let's move with the ear to the left hand, not "dot-e-dot-e" in the right hand.

Mm. 310–311. Close it.

M. 313. Enjoy that B♭.

M. 348. The two notes can be separated if you want, but not *staccato*.

Mm. 357–358. Close it.

Mm. 361–362. Why not 5-4?

Mm. 377–380. *Crescendo* through the *forzandi*.

M. 396. Close it.

M. 421. Finish it; take a breath.

Mm. 457–460. You can take a little time for emphasis.

M. 462. Kind of a suspense here, waiting for something to happen.

M. 500. Sit on the B♭ just a little.

M. 501. Come down and play it lightly. The *accelerando* is very gradual all the way to the end.

M. 529. The two notes in the left hand are a tympani.

Mm. 542–544. Let it run out.

Impromptus, D. 899, Op. 90

No. 1. *Impromptu* in C Minor

You're not able to do yet what Schubert does, to use one theme and to give it enough variety of touch, of expression, and tempo. You have to know how to feel that, like a poet, to give the piece a sense of continuity so that we will want to hear it. Otherwise, you are playing the same thing again and again.

M. 1. Not heavy on the B and even less on the C. [Pressler sings B-C, then B-C-D.]

M. 2. When you play these *staccati* in the beginning, it's a little dry. The *staccato* quarter has to be longer than the sixteenth.

M. 3. Shape the E♭-D-C; *legato*.

Example 15.18. *Impromptu* in C Minor, D. 899 (Op. 90), No. 1, mm. 1–5.

Mm. 5–6. Now let me hear the difference between the single voice and the chords. That's so many voices, four and sometimes five voices to be exact.

M. 13. No, not heavy on the D.

Mm. 14–15. You shouldn't spell; you should say the word. You are accenting every note.

M. 23. What about the dots on the left hand?

M. 29. Now the biggest. [Pressler has the student practice measures 29 to 31 "with the dots."]

Mm. 35–37. Now move. It must contrast to the previous motives.

M. 42. Not single notes; you're spelling.

M. 44. You pedal badly; the left hand must be clean.

M. 45. Not single notes in the left hand. Transfer the weight from one position to the next; use rotation.

M. 54. Why do you hesitate? You have a cadence to the A♭ [m. 55].

M. 59. Don't hit. It's not just *pianissimo*; it's a feeling, an expression.

M. 65. Why do you hit that chord? And take the pedal off; the chord holds just a quarter note.

M. 74. Don't hesitate before the A♭ [m. 74].

M. 87. The Gs *dimenuendo*. Keep the arm hanging loose and free. The arm has no motion; it doesn't do anything. The wrist is a little higher, and the octaves are done by the wrist, like "The Erlkonig." It's like you have a whip, and the notes are played by the end of the whip.

M. 94. Those accents on 1 and 3 are important.

M. 95. You understand that this is the same. The arm is loose and the wrist is playing the repeated notes. You're sitting on the C too long.

M. 103. Lightly change the foot on each beat to gradually thin out the sound.

M. 111. Does the left hand have to be so *staccato*?

M. 112. Why are you all of a sudden so fast?

Mm. 124–125. There must be a consistent beat. [They practice getting from the triplets into the sixteenths.]

Mm. 125–126. Swell a little bit into the E♭.

M. 134. Don't let the left hand suddenly push you so fast.

Mm. 140–141. You have to feel each note of each chord. Hear the voices moving within the chords.

Example 15.19. *Impromptu* in C Minor, D. 899 (Op. 90), No. 1, mm. 140–141.

M. 142. Play eighths in the right hand, not quarters.

M. 145. But when it changes to minor, you must feel something different.

M. 148. Now the entrance nice and soft.

M. 152. A feeling for that B♮, for the major.

M. 153. We must hear the melody in the left hand [B-G♯-A]; you're accenting every chord.

M. 163. The accents on beats 1 and 3 set up the cadence.

M. 168. Release the pedal so the C doesn't hold over.

M. 176. You are holding that C in the bass!

M. 186. That *fortissimo* is not enough.

M. 191. Don't wait before the C [m. 192].

Mm. 192–193. Change the fingers; use 1-2-1-2, anything. Let it run out, less and less.

M. 196. More; it's not a *sforzando*; it's a *forte piano*. Go up to a *forte*.

M. 200. There's an E♮; it changes everything.

M. 201. Now less.

M. 201. Now a *crescendo* but not from the first note.

M. 203. Come all the way down.

You have come quite a long way, but there's a long way to go. I want you to practice it with a metronome. When you come to the places that go faster, go a little faster, but come back to what that metronome is. You are playing it as if he says *animato* or *con moto*. He pushes by having single notes, triplets, by having sixteenths with the same melody. It's always the same thing, only that Schubert knowing, writing, feeling there has to be emotion in a piece like this. You can't stand still, but it can't run away. You have a certain amount of freedom to push the tempo but then to come back.

No. 2. *Impromptu* in E-flat Major

M. 1. Now the first thing is the position of your hands. Your hand must go up to turn toward the B♭, and then turn the other direction to come down. You see, when you would be in a pool and have to swim fast, you give a kick in order to push yourself into it, and this is that motion which pushes the hand into the direction in which you play. The wrist makes a circle, and always the fingers go to the bottom of the keys. And the other thing is, I don't want the left foot down. Let's try the metronome at 69. The other is too much of a suffering tempo, or an apologetic tempo. It has a spirit of elegance and a spirit of virtuosity and beautiful *perlé* playing. And you use the wrist to connect. Right now it sounds like an exercise, not an *impromptu* of Schubert. Sometimes we play an *étude* to learn some particular thing, but generally we play pieces because they say something, not just to overcome a technical problem.

M. 2. Now the arm changes direction to come back up.

Mm. 3–4. Then there are little leanings into these upper notes with a loose arm. It must have freedom of motion. [Pressler gives a fingering for the right hand.]

Example 15.20. *Impromptu* in E-flat Major, D. 899 (Op. 90), No. 2, mm. 1–4.

Mm. 6–7. Then F-C; the arm turns again, yes? The arm doesn't go up; the wrist brings you to the C, and to the F [m. 7]. And when you play F-C it's more than when you play B♭-F. There is no verve in your playing; it's like someone talks with no inflection.

M. 9. It's louder this time. "Louder" is not a good word for a teacher to use, but "contrast." There are three times [mm. 1, 6, and 17].

M. 24. Come down.

M. 25. And now for the first time you have a *pianissimo*; it's a different terrace of sonority, yes?

Mm. 29–32. Your pedal is too deep. You can't use so much pedal when you are in the lower register; it begins to swim.

M. 51. A nice B♭ in the left hand.

M. 52. Don't raise the elbow: just raise the wrist. And make a circle.

Mm. 62–68. [Pressler demonstrates a fingering to avoid 1-2-3, 1-2-3.]

Example 15.21. *Impromptu* in E-flat Major, D. 899 (Op. 90), No. 2, mm. 62–68.

M. 74. More.

Mm. 77–79. The *sforzandi* are leading you to the *fortissimo* [m. 81]. They form a *crescendo*.

Mm. 80–82. A big *crescendo*.

M. 82. It's a warm chord; it's not hit.

M. 83. Lean into the left-hand chord; it's a half note.

M. 85. *Piano*, it's an echo.

M. 103. Here you have a *sforzando* in *fortissimo*, but you played a meek *sforzando*.

M. 116. Schubert has an accent on the D♯ and before on the A♯ [m. 112]. Every time he changes direction he wants us to hear it and you to feel it.

Mm. 123–124. *Decrescendo*; hear the resolution.

Mm. 143–144. Resolve to the C♮.

M. 151. It's a very strong accent. Can we have the *fortissimo*? It's a different world; with you there's not much of a difference.

Mm. 152–153. Resolve to the A♯.

M. 153. I would suggest you use the thumb on the G. Otherwise, it sounds like someone has been wounded in the war and has a scar, a sign of a handicap.

M. 165. Let me have the C♭ in your left hand.

M. 167. Let me have that top B♭ [left hand], and don't stop the trill. Play it in such a way that you bind these two chords.

M. 194. Bring out the C♭.

M. 212. The C♭ again.

M. 263. Start *mezzo forte*.

Mm. 282–283. Not slower.

So you have the arm motion, the hand, the fingers touching the bottom of the keys like in our exercise, and you have different dynamics so it doesn't sound like "you heard it once, you heard it a hundred times." It's always fresh, and especially when he goes into a different register. And you have the difference in the various touches. And then in the right hand you have the two-note slurs [mm. 143–144 and mm. 152–153]. And then you have the *accelerando* for the last seventeen bars. And at the end you take no prisoners.

No. 3. *Impromptu* in G-flat Major

You come in so late with the melody notes. When there is no note in the accompaniment, the melody has a note, so it is continuous. And you play so many single accented notes. Play the long line. These notes are very soft and fluid, like water drops.

M. 1. How loud should the melody be? When he wants it louder, doesn't he tell you louder? Then it should start *pianissimo*. Play it as softly as you can play it; control it. And the eighths, although they're soft and subdued, they are clear, like a waterfall. Let us hear the freedom. [Pressler suggests that the quarter equals 84.] The first three notes are missing already. And there's no accent on those right-hand G♭s.

M. 3. When you go from a G♭ to an F, can you glide down? It's one direction through the four notes with the weight of the arm controlling it.

M. 4. Go up a little more for that *crescendo*. Let me hear the third [A♮-F].

Example 15.22. *Impromptu* in G-flat Major, D. 899 (Op. 90), No. 3, mm. 1–4.

M. 6. Come down to the G♭.

M. 7. You take too long to get to the A♭. You have to prepare the hand.

M. 9. That would be a start. Start less.

Mm. 9–10. But you're stopping before the D♭.

M. 12. Go up to that F♭, but then don't come down so far you don't have room to be softer at measure 13.

Mm. 13–14. I would say bring it up to the D♭.

M. 14. Do you have a *diminuendo* there? That means the previous sequence must be more.

Mm. 15–16. It must close to the G♭ [m. 16].

M. 16. The *crescendo* opens it up.

M. 21. Hear the E♭ going to the D♭ [m. 22].

Mm. 21–24. I want you to practice E♭♭-C♭-A♭ to the D♭, C♭-A♭-E♭ to the G♭, and F-B♭-A♭ to the G♭. The three notes guide you to the last note, yes?

Example 15.23. *Impromptu* in G-flat Major, D. 899 (Op. 90), No. 3, mm. 21–24.

Example 15.23. (*continued*)

Mm. 21–22. Go up to the Db. And still you are late to the Db.

M. 24. How will you get to a *forte* [m. 25]?

M. 25. *Forte*, but not hard. And more in the left hand.

M. 31. Come down to the Db [beat 4], all the way down.

M. 34. Bring it down.

M. 38. The *pianissimo* is in measure 39, not here on the Bb.

M. 44. No, it's not "dah-dah" [beat 3]; it's slurred.

M. 49. *Crescendo* to the G♮ to make room so that the next one can come down.

Mm. 51–54. That line in the bass Eb-Db [m. 51], Cb-Bb [m. 52], Ab-Gb [m. 53], F [m. 54]; I don't hear anything of that line when you play.

M. 52. When you play the left-hand line, you slow down your right hand enormously. Between "nothing and too much" there is the right way.

Mm. 53–54. That takes too long to get to the Cb [m. 54].

M. 55. The return. Relax your body, especially your neck.

M. 65. Play *espressivo* the *nachschlag* of the trill.

M. 72. Take time to mold the line.

M. 80. And that's the most.

M. 83. No, twice you go to Cb [mm. 81 and 82], and now you succeed to pass over it to the Eb. That's the ending in a way, so you can stay very slightly longer on that Eb, and it has to have a limpid sound; the arm is completely loose when you play that note.

So there's much work to do. The first thing is that you practice the singing line, the right hand, and in a tempo that is the tempo of a melody. You practice it so that you can play as *legato* as possible and be observant to the dynamic markings. Then the accompaniment; right here is where you learn to accompany. And then you are able to sustain the melody. Then you practice the dynamics. The image could be like water. It's a very, very beautiful accompaniment and a beautiful melody.

No. 4. *Impromptu* in A-flat Major

Mm. 1–4. You don't free your arm when you play; your wrist stays in one position. It should bring you from one position to the next to the next; it's the most natural way of playing. And what is not good is when you play the repeated note. The wrist pivots on that repeated note; everything is loose and free. The chord is the resolution, and the wrist gives you that chord for free, but you don't get it for free.

Example 15.24. *Impromptu* in A-flat Major, D. 899 (Op. 90), No. 4, mm. 1–4.

M. 47. The melody is a *mezzo piano*.

M. 68. Let me hear the F♭ in the left hand.

M. 77. That upper F is a note that, if you miss it, it's like seeing a person's underwear rather than his tuxedo. But you can prepare it. Think from the F to the F; that's your problem. Now it's already a little better.

Example 15.25. *Impromptu* in A-flat Major, D. 899 (Op. 90), No. 4, mm. 76–79.

M. 100. Still *fortissimo*.

Mm. 102–103. Hear the cadence with a little *ritard*, then back in tempo.

Mm. 104–105. Don't stop before the chord.

M. 106. Have a little *ritard* going into the new section.

M. 107. This section is restless. He is writing Scriabin here, although he didn't know it.

Mm. 123–124. [The second ending is measures 123–124.]

Mm. 127–128. It cannot be that stiff going up; free the wrist.

M. 141. You should vibrate inside with this theme.

Mm. 167–172. Start a little slower. Don't use your arm, just the wrist.

Mm. 201–202. Keep going till a little *ritard* in measure 202.

M. 203. Flatter fingers for a less notey sound.

Mm. 276–277. "Hook" the chords.

Interlude X
A New Love

What is really remarkable in my life today is having found the woman that I love, Lady Annabelle Weidenfeld. To have been able, through circumstances, to find a person who is everything to you, of whom you can really say, "She is my life," is truly remarkable. To have found a person like this, I thank God for it, because it is like the luck of—who is the luckiest man in the world? I think it is Menahem Pressler!

What I have said now is absolutely the truth. She means everything to me, and I mean everything. In life, to be alone is lonely; we all need a partner. I am lucky; I found that. I found it late, really late, but that doesn't make it less meaningful or precious.

She was always there in my life. She was organizing the Trio's concerts in London for the management office there and later brought us many times to Spain. Of course, I didn't have any kind of designs on her; I was married. And I had a very fine wife, as you know. I loved Sara, and she was tremendously supportive, and she helped me in my professional life too. As you know, for many years all students had to have an interview with her. She would tell me, "This one may play octaves well, but he is not a person you should take." And I would listen to her; oh yes, I would listen.

Annabelle has had her own full life for many years. I knew her all these years, over fifty years, and we never got together, of course, until her last husband died. And I never even imagined that it would come to this that it has. And now I feel I am in a new life, having passed through this miracle of a surgery and coming out on the other side. And in this new life, which has brought us together through circumstances after our spouses had died, I am very lucky. And that is very true.

16 Robert Schumann

Schumann is played too little because he is not completely understood. His genius and romanticism are so young and pure that I feel a tremendous thrill each time I play or listen to his music. Those fortunate few who are tuned into him receive a beautiful message. In chamber music, we have only nine trios. The Beaux Arts Trio recorded them twice, and we added the single pieces that Schumann wrote for trio. My relation to him has continued, it has been enriched, it has been deepened, and each time I play or I teach his pieces, I feel the enormous fantasy, the enormous beauty, that this man could imagine in music. I only hope that I may open the door to the listening student that he will be enchanted and will all his life have that feeling when he opens that music that life is beautiful, that life is desirable, and with Schumann it is most desirable.

Piano Sonata No. 1 in F-sharp Minor, Op. 11, *Grosse Sonate*

Mvt. 1. *Introduzione: Un poco Adagio—Allegro vivace*

Mm. 1–5. Very free, turbulent. Feel the tension of the repeated As and F♯s. Give dynamic room for a full, resonant baritone.

Example 16.1. Sonata in F-sharp Minor, Op. 11, mvt. 1, mm. 1–5.

M. 6. Start the phrase and build.

Mm. 12–13. *Fortissimo*, but not hard.

M. 13. Transfer the sonority from the right hand to the left hand.

M. 14. Start quietly.

M. 20. Squeeze the harmonies in each right-hand chord. The last left-hand note is like an afterthought.

M. 26. Close the phrase. The bass fifth is only a reminder of the opening.

M. 31. Begin the theme *mezzo forte*.

Mm. 33–38. *Legato* octaves; use the fourth finger on the black keys.

Mm. 37–38. *Molto ritard*; return to F♯ minor. The *ritard* doesn't conclude until the E♯.

Mm. 48–52. The *accelerando* is an outgrowth of the whole mood.

M. 51. Schumann restates the previous measure.

M. 52. Take time on the last three eighths, and still *fortissimo*.

M. 53. Present the motive in *pianissimo*. Pluck the tympani notes. Lift before the slur.

M. 54. Breathe before the right hand enters. The right hand is light, not a heavy chord.

Mm. 56–57. Answer with the left hand. [Pressler shows the student a fingering for the left hand.]

Example 16.2. Sonata in F-sharp Minor, Op. 11, mvt. 1, mm. 53–58.

Mm. 57–58. Ease into the cadence.

Mm. 70–72. *Crescendo* to the climax.

M. 73. Spread the slur.

Mm. 73–74. *Pizzicato* left hand from the wrist, not cramped. This can be with touches of pedal.

M. 76. Accent the *pizzicato* motive.

M. 96. The last eighth starts the phrase.

Mm. 106–107. Bigger circles; these are two-measure groups.

M. 114. The Fs are horns. The fourth eighth begins a variation of measure 106.

M. 123. The theme is a *legato* line and a repeated-note line in each hand. Stay in the key for the repeated notes.

M. 126. A sensitive resolution to C♯ minor [third eighth].

Mm. 134–135. The new phrase in *a tempo* is not so fast. Make sense after the *più lento*.

Mm. 145–146. Settle and *diminuendo* until the downbeat [m. 146].

M. 146. Play the drone fifth with a slight accent. Luminous right hand, rich sixths, with the three-part chords balanced over the bass. Swing open to the E of measure 147.

M. 147. The alto voices answer the melody of measure 146. The C♯ closes.

M. 150. The C♯ closes the phrase.

Example 16.3. Sonata in F-sharp Minor, Op. 11, mvt. 1, mm. 146–150.

M. 152. The right hand takes the F♯.

M. 159. *Decrescendo* as in measure 157. The E is an ending and a beginning.

Mm. 168, 170. Accent the left-hand A.

M. 178. [Second ending]. Ease into the F♯ minor.

M. 183. Not lazy.

Mm. 194–196. It's a music box.

M. 206. Start again on the B.

Mm. 208–209. Swell to prepare for the *fortissimo*.

M. 211. Even more on the F♯.

Mm. 223–224. The lowest point of the piece.

M. 242. A new start.

Mm. 239–242. Lead the left-hand sixteenths to the eighths.

M. 246. How unexpected that A♯⁷ chord is!

M. 250. The last two sixteenths must relate to the previous sixteenths.

Mm. 261–269. The chord progression is important, not just the rhythm.

M. 270. Ease into the intro theme with a *ritard*, broaden. The bass is *mezzo forte*.

Mm. 281–282. Ease out of the *più lento*.

Mm. 298–300. It's the music box again.

Mm. 329–332. Pull back. It's victorious.

Mm. 333–334. Full body in the chords.

Mm. 345–352. It's as if he is remembering what happened before.

M. 396. The second theme is despair, not hope.

M. 404. The end of the piece before the Codetta begins.

M. 406. The downbeat is an ending and a beginning.

Mm. 418–419. Play these two chords especially *legato*.

Mvt. 2. *Aria*

M. 1. Swing in three, not in six, with a clear difference between melody and accompaniment. Hold it together with not so many breaths.
M. 5. Breathe before the new phrase; express the *forte* intensely.

Example 16.4. Sonata in F-sharp Minor, Op. 11, mvt. 2, mm. 1–5.

Mm. 9–14. *Legato* melody. Use the four on the black keys. Catch the low note in the pedal.
M. 10. Be easy on the three A#s [fourth eighth].
Mm. 12–13. Use a clear connecting pedal catching the bass note each time.
Mm. 16–27. The right hand colors the melody. Move and shape the phrases.
Mm. 18–19. The left hand can help with the sixteenths [A-C and D-A].
M. 27. The downbeat A needs more sound. Prepare it with more *ritard*.
M. 42. The right hand takes over the melody on the E, but don't make it noticeable.
Mm. 44–45. You may prefer to divide this up between right hand and left hand.

Mvt. 3. *Scherzo e Intermezzo*

M. 1. Clearly this is a fast and playful character. Answer with the right hand. The right hand can play the upper note [F#] but it must match the left hand.
M. 4. The right hand can take the B.

Example 16.5. Sonata in F-sharp Minor, Op. 11, mvt. 3, mm. 1–4.

M. 9. The eighths are not short. Prepare the right hand during those eighths.

M. 10. The right hand plays the Bs as an octave.

M. 11. The right hand plays the Es as an octave.

Mm. 10–12. Lean into the *sforzando* chords.

Mm. 18–19. The right hand helps with the Fs and B♭s.

M. 20. A new idea enters in the bass.

Mm. 27–31. Broader, not faster.

M. 51. Have a clear *pizzicato* in the left hand, *legato*-loving thumbs in the right hand.

M. 81. The G is a big deal.

Mm. 94–95. The D-C♯ is a clear answer.

Mm. 131–132. Pull back.

M. 146. This ending must lead to the new idea in measure 147.

M. 147. It's a *Polonaise* dance in the bass.

M. 150. The last-chord pickup puts it back into the character and tempo.

Example 16.6. Sonata in F-sharp Minor, Op. 11, mvt. 3, mm. 147–150.

M. 162. "Pixie-like," not fast.

M. 167. The chords are as if the expressive *recitative* is reacted to by the orchestra.

M. 168. The *quasi Oboe* line *decrescendos* while the left hand holds the chord.

Mvt. 4. *Finale: Allegro, un poco maestoso*

M. 1. Even though it's *fortissimo*, it's an upbeat and the beginning of a long phrase.

Mm. 1–6. Be aware of the rhythmic tension; don't give in to the feeling of two. He doesn't affirm the 3/4 until the cadence in measures 7 and 8.

M. 8. The *sforzando* closes the theme; then the next section is *legato*.

Example 16.7. Sonata in F-sharp Minor, Op. 11, mvt. 4, mm. 1–8.

Mm. 8–9. Shape the four eighths.

M. 13. Build to the *fortissimo* [m. 14].

M. 14. Stretch this climax.

Mm. 16–17. A pompous interruption.

Mm. 24–28. All these little motives build a sweeping theme.

M. 44. The downbeat is the focal point of the phrase.

Mm. 47–48. Color these chords.

Mm. 84–85. Glide through this progression.

Mm. 86–89. It dances.

Example 16.8. Sonata in F-sharp Minor, Op. 11, mvt. 4, mm. 86–89.

Mm. 106–125. Sing and conduct this section until it feels right.

M. 133. Pull back.

M. 134. Sing the A and begin moving forward. The right hand soars to the high A.

M. 142. Start.

M. 158. Pull back.

M. 159. Like a *glissando*.

M. 171. *Crescendo* instead of *decrescendo*.

Mm. 172–173. *Crescendo* to the G♮s.

M. 184. Start.

Mm. 205–206. A new character.

Mm. 232–233. Shape these chords.

M. 320. Voice the left hand.

M. 322. More.

M. 323. Pull back slightly.

Mm. 351–352. A very touching theme.

M. 397. Don't be so sudden with the *Più Allegro*.

M. 423. *Tranquillo*.

M. 429. The thumb melody begins.

M. 437. A *fermata* over the *sforzando*.

M. 457. *Crescendo* to the *forzando*.

M. 461. Take time on the eighths.

Faschingsschwank aus Wien, Op. 26

Schumann is one of the composers whom I don't experience that much in chamber music, so at my Carnegie Hall recital [February 1996], I wanted to play a piano piece by Schumann because I adore him. I think he is one of the truly great geniuses. But I didn't want a piece that was being played continuously by everyone, such as the *Carnaval*, the *Kreisleriana*. So the *Faschingsswank* was the piece which I took up, and it led me to a discovery. I think it's a very beautiful piece that deserves to have a life. Schumann's Op. 26—that's Schumann at his wonderful time, at his strong time, and he's writing music that is unbelievably passionate and wonderful. It's a masquerade, and each one is a different picture. They're romantic. The curtain goes down and another comes up, or fireworks spinning, or anything you can imagine. They are characters; he wrote about them, and he put them into notes.

Mvt. 1. *Allegro*

Mm. 1–8. You have the two chords, and then these eighth notes must get you to the next. What I would like you to do is play just the chords [mm. 1–8]. Now play just the eighths to the next chord so that you hear that the B♭ major becomes the F major. I need juicier chords; can you grab the chord? They can't be flabby. Be careful that it's not so fast that I can't hear the chords.

M. 4. No, this is not a finish chord; there is one terraced line that reaches the top in measure 8.

Sehr lebhaft

Example 16.9. *Faschingsschwank aus Wien*, Op. 26, mvt. 1, mm. 1–8.

M. 9. Now, if the preceding was B♭, this is now G minor; it has a different sound, a different color. And the Gs must be clear, and the first one leads to the second.

Mm. 9–12. Your chords must be the same tempo as the eighths. You give *your* tempo and you follow *your* tempo, whatever it is. You could play it faster or slower, but there must be control within that beat.

M. 13. Here we have a "start." That is less. The right hand can play that last G.

Mm. 24–25. So we have the feeling we are in a carnival; we see so many people and so much is all around us, but there is also that which holds it together. The melody is not B♭-A [with an accent on the A]; it goes to measure 26. He shows you with the accompaniment. Now do it again without making a false accent, and make a swell.

M. 26. You do see a *sforzando*? Don't play so fast that you run over that.

M. 36. Begin this phrase less.

M. 38. He closes, then he interrupts himself [m. 39] to have the new dynamic.

M. 45. Surprise us with that A♮—it should have been an A♭.

Mm. 55–58. Less and less.

Mm. 53–61. A phrase like this with descending sequences, it gets less. You must follow his outline.

Mm. 60–61. It finishes.

M. 75. The right hand plays the last D.

M. 77. This time bring out the second voice. Enhance the harmonies.

M. 87. Let us follow what we see in the music. He has a syncopated note and puts the other one in the phrase mark. Each slur must end less. Notes are played not by the fingers but by the wrist. It is always one motion, "in and out," "down and release," that binds the two chords. It is true that when the hand goes up to the E♭ or B♭ it is more difficult. You have to release the pedal or the notes will bite each other. The A♭ and the G bite each other. The B♭ and the C bite each other.

Example 16.10. *Faschingsschwank aus Wien*, Op. 26, mvt. 1, mm. 87–90.

M. 95. Here the left hand takes it.

M. 96. Here the right hand takes it.

M. 102. Now we begin a different sound.

M. 103. It's always a *diminuendo* between the long note and the short one, but never hard.

Mm. 114–118. Catch the low note in the pedal.

Mm. 117–118. Make a *crescendo* and have a *subito piano*, then a color change for the treble chords.

Mm. 151–154. Follow it through; come down. The left hand doesn't stop on the long notes.

Mm. 159–160. This is more; this [mm. 161–162] is less. There's a different color between G-C and D-G. Follow the outline of the phrase; it all comes down [mm. 159–166].

Mm. 167–174. Hear how one hand complements the other.

Mm. 175–176. You're stopping it with an accent on the G [m. 176].

M. 198. Start *mezzo piano*.

M. 206. Reach a *forte*.

M. 207. Begin *mezzo forte*.

Mm. 269–272. Make a phrase. If there is a point, then you must have a recession. It's different; we're in B major. When you play, I feel that it's a Sunday afternoon and all the good citizens of the town come, and they're very polite, and they greet each other, but they have actually no interest in each other. What is missing is the exuberance that he has here. All the citizens are there, but not all are dressed alike. Some wear red and some wear green, and there is something in the air that is happy.

Mm. 276–277. Those are the tympani. Take a pedal on the third note [downbeat of m. 277].

M. 293. Can you imagine "La Marseillaise" being played? It's certainly not slower.

M. 323. Push forward.

M. 324. Start *mezzo forte*.

M. 332. Here I would advise you to start softly so that you go from the F to the G [m. 333] to the A♭ [m. 334] to the B♭ [m. 335].

M. 340. No, a different color. You jump by pushing out. When you jump up, it is not the same as when you jump down; the high A♭ is gentler.

Mm. 353–355. Less and less.

Mm. 356–361. Now let's hear the note that's interesting, the inner line that the right-hand thumb plays, the C♭, C♮, D♭, D♮, E♭, E♮, F.

M. 367. Maybe it's personal, but I feel this one less [m. 366, beat 1]. That chord has a special sensitivity. You just passed by it; what I would like is that you feel it.

M. 388. That is like a canon, but you have too many wrong accents. It's always lighter on the second note.

M. 402. All of a sudden you jump into something that has clouds, and then when you go to the next chord [m. 404], it's clear.

M. 411. Finish, take the rest, then start the next.

M. 423. The same as before—finish.

M. 464. Now the Coda. No, don't use the middle pedal. The same shaping as before.

M. 481. A new color on the *pianissimo*.

M. 490. You're awaking; start a little under tempo.

M. 497. I didn't hear the F in the left hand.

M. 521. Speed up, but not immediately.

M. 529. A start.

M. 535. If you get that fast, you can't finish the piece; nobody could. So get faster, but not so fast that no one could control it.

Mm. 537–538. With a little more pedal, like Brahms. You do have to be able to play those notes.

Mm. 539–540. A real ending.

Mm. 543–545. You're still in a *fortissimo*, not a *piano*. And the ending is interrupted by the horns [the G♭s].

Mm. 548–550. Hold the pedal all the way through the three chords. That is an exalted and excited ending.

Mvt. 2. *Romance*

M. 1. He has the same melody three times with some small changes, but you must decide which is the most, which is the least. You have to be the one to make it interesting. A lot is your imagination, how you present it. Hear the opening D followed by the alto E♭. You must speak the words.

M. 2. Give a good cadence there, then color the D.

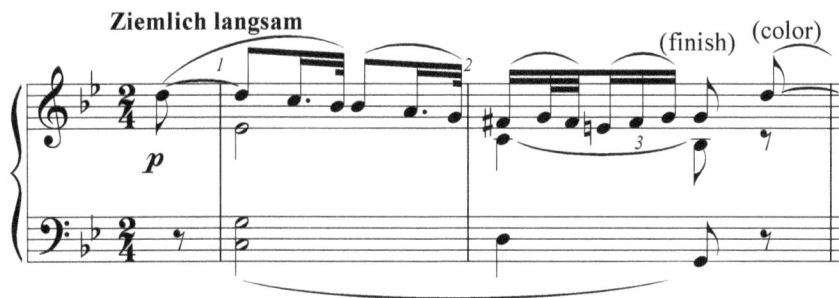

Example 16.11. *Faschingsschwank aus Wien*, Op. 26, mvt. 2, mm. 1–2.

M. 5. The E♭ colors, but it is not so loud. He gives the same word with a different intensity.

M. 6. That G is a different sound. That's what I mean by "listening." [Pressler plays measures 1–12]. When you have someone who says something very nice, he uses his words in such a way that you dream, yes? It has always a different color. [Pressler demonstrates the phrase played several ways.] I would like you to think about it.

M. 7. Give me a little bit more expressive sound.

M. 8. Move it a little.

M. 9. Here he has a *crescendo*, and you know why? Because here he doesn't have it running out; there is a second voice coming.

M. 11. Keep going so that you get there, but you died on your feet much earlier.

M. 12. No, *ritardando* and out. The C major is new. You have already been soft, so give a real sound.

M. 14. A cadence.

M. 18. If you do it the first time, don't do it the same the second time, certainly not the same way. It's more.

M. 19. And now the maximum. Play the chord with the fourth finger, and you have to have a nice voicing going in opposite directions. And you keep that G in there [the bass].

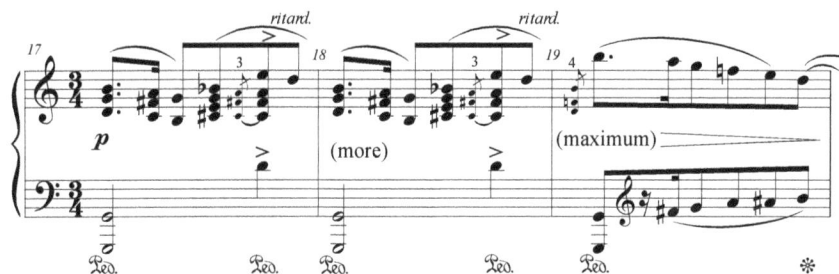

Example 16.12. *Faschingsschwank aus Wien*, Op. 26, mvt. 2, mm. 17–19.

M. 23. Surprise us with that deceptive cadence. That *crescendo* keeps the A♭ alive.

Mvt. 3. Scherzino

M. 1. Use 1-3, 1-2, 1-3 in the left hand so that it bounces.
M. 3. Hear the register change. Use 3-2-1 in the left hand.

Example 16.13. *Faschingsschwank aus Wien*, Op. 26, mvt. 3, mm. 1–4.

Mm. 9–12. The third phrase ends bigger.
M. 12. Finish.
Mm. 17–24. The slurs are not so much *diminuendo* as just shorter on the second note. And you must learn to connect the octaves. [Pressler has the student practice the two-note slurs in both hands, while the other part continues the dance from the beginning.]
M. 56. Make a nice *crescendo* so that you come down [m. 57].
M. 72. You can play the D in the right hand.
Mm. 95–97. Less, and less, and least.
Mm. 97–100. He actually stops the motion; he uses the same note with an harmonic shift. He stands still, and then he goes on with the Coda.
M. 101. Roll the chord, but don't hit, and don't lift your shoulders.

Example 16.14. *Faschingsschwank aus Wien*, Op. 26, mvt. 3, mm. 95–103.

Mm. 105–106. Group the two *staccato* notes together so that they say something; they're not just "short, short."

M. 109. That sounds so pedantic. It is not soft enough for my taste, and you do not hear the harmonic shape.

M. 112. *Diminuendo*, less on the second chord.

Mm. 116–121. You have the canon, the left hand following the right hand. But hear the accents [D-D, B♭-B♭].

M. 124. But not so fast; the *accelerando* just starts here.

Mvt. 4. *Intermezzo*

M. 1. This one needs a romanticism all over the place; it's "the cup runneth over." That's so gorgeous; there's no more beautiful melody than that. How rich that theme is; that alone makes it worthwhile. Quarter note equals 104 is a little slow for my taste. Play just the melody, and now accompany that. Now the relationship is good, but give us the tempo.

Example 16.15. *Faschingsschwank aus Wien*, Op. 26, mvt. 4, mm. 1–4.

M. 8. That would be less.

M. 9. Start less.

M. 10. A little more.

M. 11. And more. But you cannot play with a hit. If you enter the piano, if you caress the piano, if you hug the piano, if you love the piano, if you touch it like that [Pressler demonstrates the C], it will respond to you. It's like a person; it's the same.

M. 16. Start again.

M. 24. Start in *piano*.

M. 25. And more.

M. 26. And more.

M. 38. Now I want the ending. Can you imagine to write something like this and two hundred years later we respond like that to him? The passion that he had is wonderful, so young and so beautiful—two hundred years old and nothing like it. In principle, it's a duet, yes? First, just play the melodies; now play with the rest of the notes.

M. 41. And finish.

M. 43. It's running down.

M. 44. Go up to the second chord and down, or go down from the first one.

Mvt. 5. *Finale*

Mm. 1–4. That's Schumann; you play as fast as you can, then you play faster [*Presto*]. It begins with the signal of the trumpets, and I would like to hear the different registers. I play the first three sixteenths with the left hand and the next three sixteenths with the right hand. The pedal must come off before the G♭ because the F and the G♭ bite each other.

Example 16.16. *Faschingsschwank aus Wien*, Op. 26, mvt. 5, mm. 1–4.

M. 9. Less on the repeated note [B♭].

Mm. 10–11. You are slurring the *forte* chords; they are not connected.

Mm. 19–23. It comes down and gives measure 24 a reason for being.

Mm. 25–26. The accent can be more, but warm. The ear hears the B♭ going to the A.

M. 47. Raise the pedal a little bit so we can hear the line.

M. 59. When he has the quarter note in the left hand, it becomes a duet.

M. 67. When he has the rest, I would phrase.

Mm. 75–76. Since I know those *staccati* are coming [mm. 77–78], I would make these notes *legato*.

M. 79. More, and *legato* again.

Mm. 103–104. Not short.

Mm. 105–106. Those are short.

M. 115. [The second ending].

Mm. 134–135. A clear ending.

Mm. 135–137. Like a duet with echoes.

M. 148. Finish.

M. 149. Now turn it around; the lower one is first.

M. 150. It's all right in the beginning that the upper voice is more, but not here.

Mm. 191–192. Yes, it has a *crescendo*, but we know we are going to a *piano*.

M. 193. Can your top have a *vibrato*?

Mm. 255–257. It's the answer phrase; finish it.

Example 16.17. *Faschingsschwank aus Wien*, Op. 26, mvt. 5, mm. 253–257.

Mm. 277–284. Practice the right hand in blocked sixths so we can hear that. Now play it without the bottom left-hand notes so the triplet can be even.

Mm. 314–321. With maximum strength. Like a fanfare!

Mm. 317, 319. Lift the pedal for the rest.

Appendix A: Menahem Pressler's Musical Ancestry

Through his various teachers, Menahem Pressler's musical ancestry can be traced back to Bach, Beethoven, Mozart, Chopin, Liszt, and many other significant pianists and musicians. During his youth and early concert career, Pressler sought out the world's finest teachers—mentors who expanded his pedagogical training to include the German, French, and Russian heritages. His own teaching, therefore, is a blending of all his varied influences and traditions.

The following chart places Pressler in the center surrounded by each of his teachers, then traces their ancestry back through history.

Menahem Pressler's Musical Ancestry

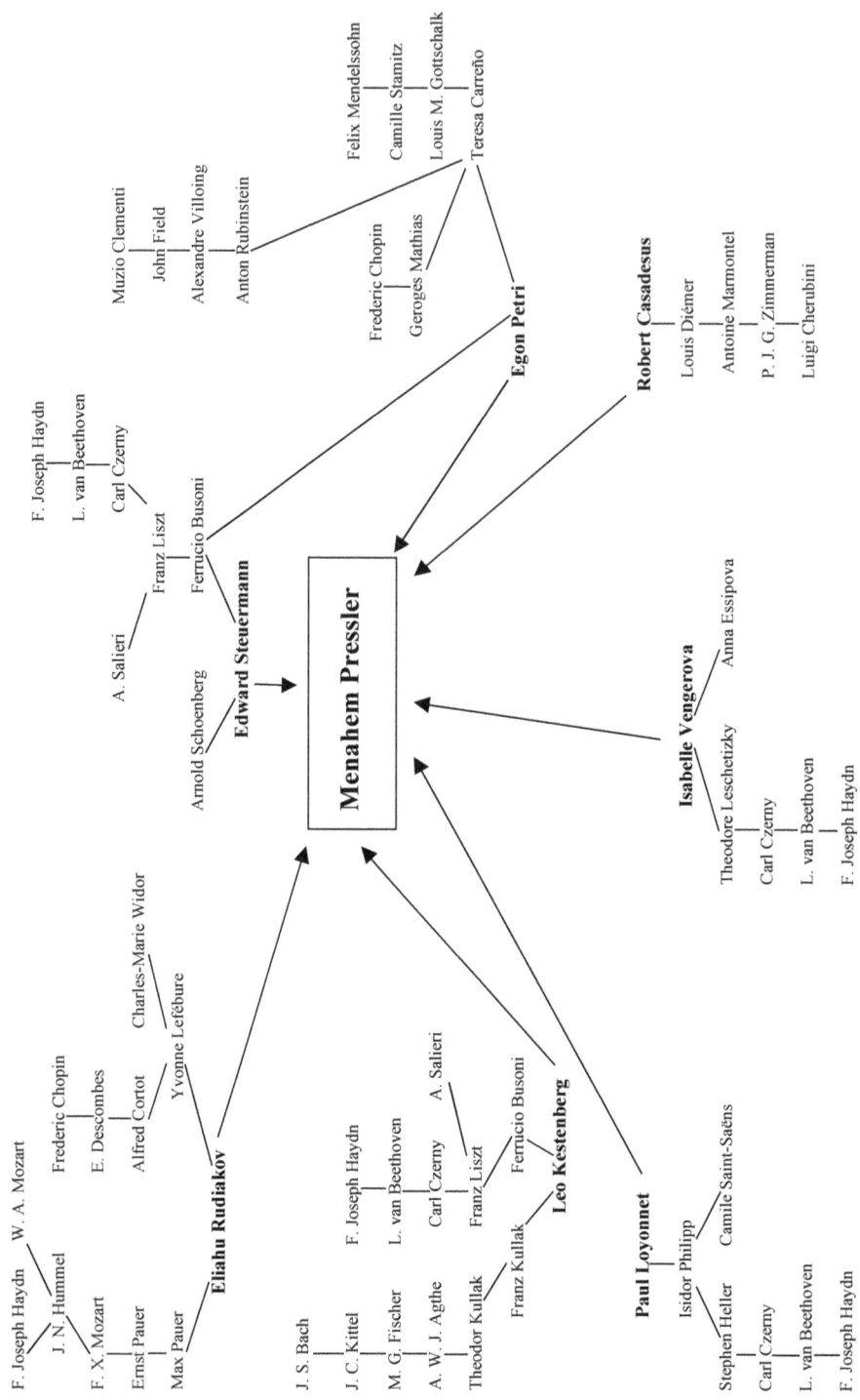

Menahem Pressler

Egon Petri

Felix Mendelssohn
Camille Stamitz
Louis M. Gottschalk
Teresa Carreño

Muzio Clementi
John Field
Alexandre Villoing
Anton Rubinstein

Frederic Chopin
Georges Mathias

Robert Casadesus

Louis Diémer
Antoine Marmontel
P. J. G. Zimmerman
Luigi Cherubini

F. Joseph Haydn
L. van Beethoven
Carl Czerny
Franz Liszt
Ferrucio Busoni

A. Salieri

Arnold Schoenberg

Edward Steuermann

Isabelle Vengerova

Anna Essipova
Theodore Leschetizky
Carl Czerny
L. van Beethoven
F. Joseph Haydn

F. Joseph Haydn   W. A. Mozart
J. N. Hummel
F. X. Mozart
Frederic Chopin
E. Descombes
Charles-Marie Widor
Ernst Pauer
Alfred Cortot
Max Pauer
Yvonne Lefébure

Eliahu Rudiakov

J. S. Bach
J. C. Kittel
M. G. Fischer
A. W. J. Agthe
Theodor Kullak
Franz Kullak

F. Joseph Haydn
L. van Beethoven
Carl Czerny
A. Salieri
Franz Liszt
Ferrucio Busoni

Leo Kestenberg

Paul Loyonnet

Isidor Philipp
Stephen Heller
Camile Saint-Saëns
Carl Czerny
L. van Beethoven
F. Joseph Haydn

Appendix B: Tributes from Former Students and Other Musicians

It's noteworthy to witness individuals in master classes or lessons attempting to thank Menahem Pressler for the impact he has had on their lives. Perhaps feeling a bit self-conscious, he brushes the comments aside and presses on to work on the music at hand. As Edna Pressler, his daughter, has expressed, "He doesn't want to take time for tributes. He values getting right to the instruction." Thankfully, on the occasion of important birthday celebrations, the Jacobs School of Music has gathered tributes and words of gratitude from students and colleagues. The following represent some of those tributes to this remarkable man, Menahem Pressler.

> Thank you for . . .
> *M*aking my years at IU some of the best in my life
> *E*xquisite beauty you bring to every musical phrase
> *N*ever speaking harshly toward me in my lessons
> *A*llowing me to play *Kreisleriana*
> *H*umor and laughter at each lesson and master class
> *E*ncouragement and support you gave me
> *M*otivating and inspiring me to do my best
>
> *P*erformer's Certificate I received which I've always believed says more about you as a teacher, than me as a student. . . . I owe it all to you!
> *R*isk you took in taking me on as your student
> *E*ndless patience with me and my shortcomings
> *S*ara's wisdom and interest in each of us
> *S*pectrum of color I never knew existed which you revealed to me
> *L*ooking out for my good, even outside of music
> *E*xample you've been as performer, teacher, and person
> *R*especting me as a musician

> May you know how very blessed you are by God
> and how very loved by us all!
>
> With best wishes,
> Lori Chew (Chiu)

"Color . . . bring out that inner line . . . use the weight of your arm . . ." In addition to all the ways you taught me to listen, to develop my ears, my hands, I was always in awe at your ceaseless quest to communicate the essence, the heart of the music. It is this conviction—this tireless and amazing gift of yours—that fed my imagination and allowed me to reach and reach as a musician!

—Liane Alitowski

Your influence is far reaching, your inspiration eternal. You have truly found what so many in this world have sought after: eternal life. You have found a way to go on living in the minds and hearts and souls of your students, who will never forget you.

—Melinda Baird

It is this remarkable combination of absolute love for the score married to an unrelenting pursuit of music excellence that has left such an indelible impression on me as a pianist and teacher. And, as a result, in my own years of college teaching, your influence has spread through my own students all over the country and beyond.

—Paul Barnes

When I teach, practice, or perform, I am very conscious of your example. One important lesson I learned from you is how much all these endeavors reflect upon one another. It's a paradoxical truth that we learn from teaching, and I can see so clearly why you derived so much satisfaction from teaching even though you could have chosen not to teach at all.

—Jonathan Bass

Setting personal challenges and goals, finding and respecting a unique musical voice, moving out into the musical world with something new, special, and different to offer—these abilities, desires, and ambitions you encourage in your students. It is amazing that despite your own sustained and phenomenal success, strong and impassioned opinions, and demanding schedule, you have the care and wisdom to allow your students this space.

—Alasdair Beatson

I would like to thank you for all those hours you shared with me working on great music, moments that inspired me and that will stay with me for the rest of my life. Also, I would like you to know that of all the beautiful qualities that make you such a great pianist, musician, and teacher, I will retain two above all: your amazing sense of hearing colors, phrases, and other musical characteristics, a quality that motivates me to do better; and finally, your work ethic and your absolutely fabulous energy in which I see not only an ideal for any young person who wants to embrace a career in music but also life lessons for any human being.

—Jimmy Brière

You gave me a gift that I never lost and that deepens over time. You were always pointing out sounds and colors, sharpening my awareness, and you also showed me, through your amazing hands, what sensitivity of touch is, what it looks like and feels like, and how to relate to the piano in an intimate, feeling way.

—Madeline Bruser

Your magnificent pianism and sublime artistry opened our hearts and ears. Because of you, our listening, understanding, and playing of this great music are completely transformed. Whatever good there is in our music-making, it is all because of you. We cherish the words you used to spark our imaginations, to make the music come alive inside of us. We also appreciate the lavish and undivided attention you brought to each of us week after week. It challenges us to do no less for our own students.

—Angela Cheng and Alvin Chow

You are a rare musician, one who values equally the art of teaching as well as the art of performing. In fact, in your work, these two aspects are completely interwoven and not to be separated. I benefited first from my studio lessons with you. I was immediately drawn to your particular and unique way of hearing the music, of understanding the music, of feeling the music, and of communicating the music. And when I hear you perform live in concert or in recordings, I still feel I am learning from you: that you are sharing with me what you have discovered about the piece and the composer and that you are communicating to me the depth and breadth of all the emotions inherent in the music—such subtlety of nuance. But not only do you share your knowledge and insights with me; most importantly you share your humanity with me. The beauty of your spirit flows generously from your performances and I feel this deep connection with the music because you lead the way for me.

—Alan Chow

Your complete dedication toward your art and the way you always give all of yourself in everything that you do remain a great life lesson for me.

—Jeffrey Cohen

Your teaching really inspires me, and I myself am trying to instill similar enthusiasm in my own pupils:
- to love the music they are playing and love performing
- to bring music alive and lift it off the page
- to enjoy filling the room with magical sounds all of which they are creating and in control of
- to really listen and care about the sound they are producing.

—Lynda Cochrane

You have the talent as a teacher to inspire each student, to open our minds, to develop our ears and imagination, and to challenge ourselves to strive for higher goals and achievements. Our own students benefit from the example you have set.

—Linda Ellison

Honesty, enthusiasm, warmth, energy, fairness, truth, humanity, love of work, love of music, love of beauty . . . so many qualities that make a real big Master. So many concerts and so many students . . . an example, a real driving force for them. I am aware of how lucky I am to have had a chance to study with you and at least get part of your message . . . only part of it as I know I would need a lifetime to learn everything from you!

—Anne-France Fosseur

Your playing is a model of eloquent, exquisite beauty. You are incapable of playing a meaningless note, and you make every passage come alive with sparkle and charm. Your vision of what music is, and the spiritual depth behind every note, reaches deeply into one's soul, and becomes a permanent part of everyone fortunate enough to experience it. . . . But this intensity is combined with a special warmth, tenderness, and humanity. Who cannot be touched by your gentleness and sincerity, uplifted by your ever-present youthful enthusiasm, and encouraged by your parental love? You turn the role of a pianist-teacher into one of an emissary of goodness.

—George and Susan Fee

I thank you for all you've given me: a sensitivity to sound, its color and broad palette, its nuances, its emotional depth; for being a paradigm of discipline and commitment, and for instilling an urge to "search for that moment of inspiration," sustenance of the artist.

—Rhoda Green

You cannot imagine the love, admiration, respect, and esteem in which you are held by the music lovers of this world. Thank you from the bottom of our hearts for sharing your enormous gifts for making music and teaching.

—Art and Nola (Marberger) Gustafson

You have been the greatest musical influence on my life, have given me a gift that blossoms ever more fully every day, literally. I can't thank you enough for the vision of joy and delight you imparted to me (all of us, those with ears to hear) in our years together.

—Christopher Harding

Your dedication to music is an inspiration to me. Your piano playing is art; you carefully shape every phrase and every note. You are always challenging yourself and your students to seek beauty in music and in life. Thank you for teaching me, for passing on the wonderful truths that you have discovered in music, and for challenging me to find it for myself. Your music and your investment in teaching is very special, and I cherish the treasures that you have shared with me.

—Grace Ho

The ways I approach sound, color, and shape have all been affected by your musicianship, and you did much to spur me onward to continue demanding the highest of myself. As much as your teaching and kindness to me found their mark, the example you set for me and so many others as a committed and ardent musician is a lasting inspiration.

—Daniel Paul Horn

Your incredible understanding of music, your unequaled knowledge of piano trio repertoire, and your love for your students and teaching has allowed us to receive a glimpse of the magic and beauty of music through ensemble playing.

—Valentina Wen-Ting Huang

Thank you for opening a completely new world of listening to music and for challenging me to stretch the borders of my limitations. Your devotion and passion for music, your unyielding strong will, and your work ethics have greatly inspired me and set the best example for me to be a musician!

—[name lost]

Your dedication to your students and to the art of music has been of the highest and noblest order. Thank you, a thousand times, for blessing the world with your playing. The music world has recognized your greatness with many awards. But those of us who have studied with you have an even greater gift— the gift of knowing you and your dear wife, Sara.

—Paul S. Jones

Your life as a musician set the example, your demands as a teacher challenged me to rise to this goal, and it has continued to be worth every effort decades later.

—Sherri Jones

In every class and lesson, you unlock the composer's intentions, showing us how to communicate the true meaning of the music. There is such deep satisfaction in rehearsing and performing great literature after you have given a lesson on it. I'm no longer stumbling in the dark, or fighting the piece, or just trying to conquer the notes, but there is direction, because you reveal the truth of the work.

—Barbara Kudirka

An artist larger than life, a teacher who reaches beyond times and miles, a man for all seasons. I remember your extraordinary performances that spoke of gold, not glitter, that always revealed the meaning and created magic moments that remain forever; your humanity; and your supportive friendship.

—Ludmila Lazar

Surely you are one of the great artists of our century. You have set a standard for chamber music that is unsurpassed. Your teaching is wonderful. You are so articulate in explaining the language of music and you are able to do it with grace, humor, and wit. I love to hear you play, but I also love to hear your thoughts on music. Thank you for sharing your insights with not only super-stars but anyone who has a passion for the piano and piano repertoire.

—Linda Lienhard

I want you to know that when I sit down and think of the things that I am most thankful for in my life, you are the first thing that comes to my mind because you help me to see a world of beauty and color. For me, you embody this beauty, and the fact that you take time to teach all of us students so that we may also partake of it is truly remarkable.

—Steven Mann

You led me to the magic in music and to the skills to share it. You recognized in my curiosity a teacher's heart, and gave me opportunities to strengthen it. You provided me with support, encouragement, challenge, and joy. I shall always be grateful.

—Robert Mayerovitch

I was often struck by what an extremely rare combination of artist-teacher you are: one who possessed innate, creative, musically correct instincts, and yet one who at the same time had that uncanny analytical awareness and self-knowledge of knowing just exactly how to communicate in the studio what you were doing musically.

—Dennis McGreer

You have made demands at every lesson, not necessarily in the same way, not always so obvious, not always so comfortable. Yet my work with you has always left me with a sense of reaching, searching, and with profound humbleness by your wisdom, your artistic discipline and insight, and more than anything your own humbleness before these great works and love. You have brought me closer to the spiritual life of music and guided me from wherever I was at the moment. For teaching me, for allowing me to be a part of your community, and for showing me your humanity I am deeply grateful.

—Janice Nimetz

Thank you for the gift of your extraordinary and inspiring artistry which you have so graciously and generously shared with the world and with us at Biola University. We are so privileged, honored, and humbled to be a part of your extended musical family, your musical children. You have opened our ears, eyes, and souls to unimagined beauty. You have challenged and inspired us to wonderful growth as performers, as teachers, as listeners, as citizens of this world. You have taught us how to live in and travel throughout this very challenging world, passionately seeking, sharing musical truth and beauty, and you have brought us closer to the hearts, minds, and souls of the greatest composers, the musicians who perform their works, the audience who listen, and to God who has gifted us with these miracles of creation. You have enriched our lives more than you'll ever know. We honor you, we love you, we cherish you.

—Marlin Owen

What I carry with me are your teachings of beauty and a quest for the divine. This changed me forever. The magic that I search for in music is what I have found in my life—joy and fulfillment beyond measure.

—Katherine Morgan Palmer

I am always inspired by your teaching and especially your attitude to music. You amaze me that you keep making endeavors for the essence of music even though you are the greatest pianist already.

—Eun-shik Park

Your teaching philosophy harmonically combines the absolute search for musical clarity and truthful expression with a strong distaste for sloppy phrasing and wrong notes. Your pedagogical methods are extremely varied: not only can you speak several languages but you also sing, yell, and display extraordinary imagination in describing one's faulty playing. Your work ethic has no limits: it ignores jetlag, holidays, busy performing schedules, snow, and power outages! You have provided lifelong doses of enthusiasm to hundreds of people, and your musical offspring are quickly spreading: octave scales and wrist exercises can be heard at 7:00 a.m. all over the globe.

—Vincent Planès

Your unparalleled teaching is given to each student with such love, respect, insight, and passion, and I am continually amazed at how quickly you grasp the unique problem of each student and in one short hour make such tremendous changes in our playing.

—Mark David Reiss

Whenever I am taught by you or talk with you, I am moved with your love of music and the devotion of you for music, from where the incomparable magnificent beauty of art is born and it gives me a happiest time. Taking your lessons, I am always brought by you to the height where I cannot reach by any means without your help. It is you who shows me the way of desire for ideals. For a long span of years, more than fifteen years, my music has been completely changed by your encouragement, and my love of music has been deepened. Thinking of these things, I cannot thank you too much.

—Michiko Sasaki

Your suggestions about tasting chords and hearing similar harmonies with new ears are things that stayed with me during my teaching career. I feel honored having had the benefit of your teaching.

—Joachim Segger

Being in your presence each day [at Adamant] allowed the essence of the music to seep into my heart, brain, and spirit. I shall never forget this experience and how it changed the way I approach playing the piano forever.

—Tiffany Seybert

You have always been an amazing inspiration to all of us through your tremendous work ethic and energy and through your brilliant teaching and playing. I feel so grateful to have worked with you and gained from your meticulous detail and love of every note, something I hope people find in my own playing.

—Nadine Shank

I truly believe there is not another living pianist so fully dedicated to a life which integrates both performing and teaching at such a high level. Your life stands as a testament to the beauty and inspiration that one gifted and dedicated individual can bring into the world.

—Mark Sullivan

Once in a while an institution is fortunate enough to become home to a handful of truly great artist teachers, whose presence and achievements lift it to unprecedented heights. Our Music School has been thus favored, thanks in large part to the inspiring example of your artistry, to the countless talents that gravitate to you, and to your lofty and uncompromising artistic standards.

—Karen Taylor

Through your shared insights and passion for music, you instill in us, your students, a desire to discover and probe more deeply the wonders of the music we study. It's been an inspiration to hear you perform, to teach and to share in your wisdom. Year after year you work hard to pull some artistic quality out of your students. These many years of lessons and master classes have given a special meaning and purpose to my life—indeed, a reason for living.

—Joyce Ucci

In eleven years you have changed me profoundly. I used to be a musical "Bohemian," making music with abandon, oblivious of how it sounded to others. You have encouraged me to develop greater self-discipline and higher musical standards. Thank you for always taking time to help me whenever I asked for it. I am proud to be your pupil!

—Ludolph van der Hoeven

I want to thank you for all the inspiration, knowledge, and memorable experiences that you have given me. Your master classes in Bloomington and Adamant have created a community of friends devoted to music, the piano, each other, and to you with love and gratitude. With each passing year, you have taught us with a sure sense of what must be done and how and when to do it. You have seen us grow and transform music making into a more vital and essential expression of ourselves. In Adamant, a place already blessed, you have created something miraculous. Thank you for furthering my horizons, for training my thinking, for sharpening my listening, for disciplining my practice, for teaching me to understand and play music better, for bringing me closer to wonderful friends, for embodying all that is best in art and in an artist.

—Victoria von Arx

It is only when you sit in the student's seat at the large Steinway in Menahem's studio that you can fully appreciate the meaning of those piercing eyes, the inevitable pleadings to "sing that phrase," his incredible ear that detects minute differences in pedaling, articulation, quality of sound, and direction of melodic line. Thank you, Menahem, for changing all of us, for helping us re-invent ourselves as musicians and artists, for inspiring us through brilliant performance and the most perceptive teaching, and for leading us truly to the "thresholds of our own minds."

—Charles Webb

Bibliography

Baird, Melinda. "The Eccentric Professor and the Learning Experience: A Look at the Teaching Techniques and Standards of Menahem Pressler." Unpublished paper, April 28, 2004.

Brown, William. *Menahem Pressler: Artistry in Piano Teaching.* Bloomington: Indiana University Press, 2009.

Buechler, Mark. "The Hunger Within." *Indiana Daily Student,* May 14, 2004.

DeBrunner, Mary. "Former/Current Students to Celebrate Prof's Birthday." *Indiana Daily Student,* December 15, 2003.

Delbanco, Nicholas. *The Beaux Arts Trio: A Portrait.* New York: William Morrow, 1985.

Duchen, Jessica. "Lucky Charm." *International Piano,* May/June 2005.

Duffie, Bruce. "A Conversation with Bruce Duffie." Accessed November 15, 2016. http://www.BruceDuffie.com/pressler.html.

Fine, Larry. "Irrepressible Pianist Pressler Going Strong at 80." Reuters, January 2, 2004.

Gelfand, Janelle. "A Master Class with Menahem Pressler." *Clavier,* July/August 1993.

Glazier, Harriet. "Menahem Pressler: *Belle Musique.*" *Arts Indiana,* October 1988.

Jacobi, Peter. "At 80, Pianist Menahem Pressler Looks Back—and Forward—at Life and Music." *Bloomington Herald-Times,* December 14, 2003.

Kageyama, Noa. "Menahem Pressler: On Following Your Heart." Accessed November 15, 2016. Audio interview, 29:08. http://www.bulletproofmusician.com/menahem-pressler-on-following-your-heart/.

Knudson, Erika. "Playing It Forward: Teaching, Performing, Are Senior Faculty Members' Gifts to Future Teachers, Performers." *IU Music* newsletter (Spring/Summer 2003): 4–6.

Logan, George M. *The Indiana University School of Music: A History.* Bloomington: Indiana University Press, 2000.

Monsaingeon, Bruno. *Sviatoslav Richter: Notebooks and Conversations.* Princeton, NJ: Princeton University Press, 2001.

Namer, Dina Michelson. "Pressler at Adamant." *Piano Quarterly,* no. 153 (Spring 1991): 32–34.

Oestreich, James R. "A Pianistic Quarterback Passes to a Younger Generation." *New York Times,* November 30, 2003.

Pressler, Menahem. Interview by Mark Sullivan. Los Angeles, CA, March 2, 1996.

———. Interview by William Brown. Bloomington, IN, January 6, 2004.

———. Interview by William Brown. Bloomington, IN, June 28, 2004.

———. Interview by William Brown. Adamant, VT, August 21, 2004.

———. Interview by William Brown. Bloomington, IN, May 26–27, 2006.

———. Interview by William Brown. Bloomington, IN, April 20–21, 2007.

———. Interview by William Brown. Bloomington, IN, February 11–12, 2010.

———. Interview by William Brown. Bloomington, IN, August 26–27, 2017.

———. Master Classes, Adamant Music School, Adamant, VT, August 17–21, 2004.

———. Master Class, Harvard University, Cambridge, MA, March 23, 2012.

———. Master Class, Music Teachers National Association Convention, New York City, NY, March 21, 2012.

———. "Preface." *Sonata No. 9, Op. 103 by Serge Prokofiev.* New York: Leeds Music, c. 1955.

———. "Suggestions for Performance." *Brahms, Fantasias, Op. 116.* Vienna: Schott/ Universal Edition, 1981.

Rezits, Joseph. *Beloved Tyranna: The Legend and Legacy of Isabelle Vengerova.* Bloomington, IN: David Daniel, 1995.

Schonberg, Harold C. *The Great Pianists.* New York: Simon and Schuster, 1963.

Slonomsky, Nicolas. *Baker's Dictionary of Musicians.* 8th ed. New York: Schirmer Books, 1992.

Sommer, Andy, dir. *In the Heart of Music.* Bel Air Media and the Van Cliburn Foundation, 2005. DVD.

Street, Eric. "Tracing Our Musical Ancestors." *Clavier,* December 2001.

Stryker, Mark. "Once More with Feeling: Pianist Shares Expertise." *Detroit Free Press,* October 20, 1995.

Sullivan, Mark. "The Beaux-Arts of Menahem Pressler." *Piano and Keyboard,* no. 182 (September/October 1996): 25–29.

Timbrell, Charles. *French Pianism: A Historical Perspective.* 2nd ed. Pompton Plains, NJ: Amadeus Press, 2003.

Wagner, Jeffrey. "Menahem Pressler: Multifaceted Musician." *Clavier,* May/June 1982.

Albers, Robert, dir. *Where Music Lives.* Originally aired on WTIU, Bloomington, IN, on May 18, 1987. DVD.

Wilson, Cynthia. *Always Something New to Discover: Menahem Pressler and the Beaux Arts Trio.* London: Paragon, 2011.

Wong, Jerry. "Always Give Your Maximum: A Conversation with Menahem Pressler." *Clavier Companion,* March/April 2016.

Index

Jerusalem Academy of Music and
   Dance, xvi
Jones, Paul S., 215
Jones, Sherri, xiii, 215
Juilliard School of Music, 3
Juilliard String Quartet, xv, 104

Kristallnacht, 154
Kudirka, Barbara, xiv, 215

La Figaro, xvii
Lazar, Ludmila, 215
Leeds International Piano Competition, xvii
Leipzig, Germany, xv, 122
Library of Congress, xv
Lienhard, Linda, xiv, 215
Liszt, Franz, 151: *Après une lecture de Dante*,
   S. 161/7c, 109; *Grande Étude de Paganini*
   in E-flat Major [*Andante capriccioso*],
   S. 141, No. 2, 109–11; *Grande Étude de*
   Paganini in G-sharp Minor [*Allegretto*] "*La*
   campanella," S. 141, No. 3, 111–13; *Mephisto*
   Waltz, S. 514, 109; Piano Concerto No. 1 in
   E-flat Major, S. 124, 109; Piano Sonata in B
   Minor, S. 178, 113–19
London, England, xv, xvii, 167, 192
Los Angeles Times, xvii

Madrid, Spain, 25
Magdeburg, Germany, xvi, 154
Manhattan School of Music, xvi
Mann, Steven, xiii, xiv, 215
Massachusetts General Hospital, 166
master classes, xvi, 3
Mayerovitch, Robert, xiii, xiv, 215
McGreer, Dennis, 216
memorization, 144
Menahem Pressler Archives, xiii
Mendelssohn, Felix, 54: *Études* for piano,
   Op. 104b; Piano Trio No. 1 in D Minor, Op.
   49, 104; Preludes and Fugues, Op. 35, 122;
   Rondo Capriccioso, Op. 14, 122–25; *Songs*
   without Words, 142
Menton, France, 142
Menuhin, Yehudi, xvi
Metropolitan Museum of Art, xv, 105
Michelangeli, Arturo Benedetti, 142
Mills College, 143
Mozart, Wolfgang Amadeus, 105, 156, 168:
   Piano Concerto in A Major, K. 488, 166;
   Piano Concerto in C Minor, K. 491, 130–
   37; Piano Concerto in G Major, K. 453, 104;
   Piano Sonata in B-flat Major, K. 281, 126–
   29; Piano Sonata in D Major, K. 576, 137–41

National Society of Arts and Letters, xvi
Naumburg International Piano Competition,
   xvii
Nazis, xv
New York City, xv, 96, 143
New York Philharmonic, 121
New York Times, xvii
Nimetz, Janice, xiv, 216
North Carolina School of the Arts, xvi

Oakland, California, 143
Orchestre de Paris, xv, xvii
Ormandy, Eugene, xv, 143
Owen, Marlin, 216
Oxford, England, 95

Palestine. *See* Israel
Palmer, Katherine Morgan, 216
Paloma O'Shea Santander International Piano
   Competition, xvii
Park, Eun-shik, 216
Patel, Virendra, 166
pedal, damper: before playing, 88, 96; changing,
   20, 62, 93, 97, 99, 100, 125, 147, 163, 180, 185;
   clearing, 18, 47, 48, 118, 145, 183; long pedals,
   54, 57, 59, 66, 79; touches of, 28, 31, 40, 55, 56,
   74, 103, 123, 126, 194; without pedal, 28, 101,
   110, 124, 200, 206, 207
pedal, *sostenuto*, 22, 145, 164, 202
pedal, *una corda*, 53, 57, 99, 145, 186
Petri, Egon, 143
Philadelphia Symphony Orchestra, xv, 143
Philips Records, xv, 120
Planès, Vincent, 216–17
Pollini, Maurizio, 142
practicing: blocked patterns, 36, 101, 106, 124,
   149, 207; separate elements, 53, 55, 67, 80,
   91, 98, 99, 100, 115, 199, 203, 206; separate
   hands, 8, 48, 57, 149, 180; skeleton, 107,
   127, 170; thumbs alone, 15, 23, 110. *See also*
   memorization
Pressler, Ami, xvii
Pressler, Edna, xii, xiii, xiv, xvii, 211
Pressler, Menahem: adjudication, xvii;
   appointed to IU faculty, xv; awards,
   xv–xvi; Beaux Arts Trio, *see* Beaux
   Arts Trio; biography, xv–xvii; Debussy
   Competition, *see* First International
   Debussy Competition; family, *see*
   names of individuals; master classes, *see*
   master classes; musical ancestry 209–
   10; performances xv–xvii; practicing, *see*
   practicing; recordings, xv, xvii; surgery,
   166–67. *See also* Menahem Pressler Archives

Pressler with William Brown, July 2009. Courtesy of Indiana University
Jacobs School of Music.

WILLIAM BROWN is Professor Emeritus of Music and Provost Emeritus at
Southwest Baptist University. He earned two graduate performance degrees
while studying with Menahem Pressler at Indiana University and is the author of
Menahem Pressler: Artistry in Piano Teaching.

www.ingramcontent.com/pod-product-compliance
Lightning Source LLC
Chambersburg PA
CBHW020410100426
42812CB00001B/271